CONVERSATIONS
WITH ECUMENICAL PATRIARCH
BARTHOLOMEW I

Conversations with Ecumenical Patriarch Bartholomew I

Olivier Clément

Translated from the French
by
Paul Meyendorff

ST VLADIMIR'S SEMINARY PRESS
CRESTWOOD, NY 10707
1997

Library of Congress Cataloging-in-Publication Data

Clément, Olivier,
    [Vérité vous rendre libre. English]
    Conversations with Ecumenical Patriarch Bartholomew I / by Olivier
Clément: translated by Paul Meyendorff.
        p.   cm.
    Includes bibliographical references.
    ISBN 0-88141-178-7
    1. Orthodox Eastern Church.   2. Orthodox Eastern Church—Relations.
3. Constantinople (Ecumenical patriarchate).   4. Bartholomew I, Ecumenical
Patriarch of Constantinople, 1940- .   I. Title.
BX320.2.C4313   1997
281.9—dc21   97-40111
                                                                            CIP

St Vladimir's Seminary Press
575 Scarsdale Road, Crestwood, NY 10707
800-204-2665

ISBN 0-88141-178-7

First published in 1996 by J.C. Lattès

PRINTED IN THE UNITED STATES OF AMERICA

Contents

"The truth will make you free."

(Jn 8:31)

"Out of compassion, God takes upon himself the sufferings of each person. In his love he suffers mysteriously, to the end of time, with the same suffering that is in each of us."

(Maximus the Confessor, *Mystagogy* 24)

Introduction

The aim of this book is to suggest a presence—that of a man, as well as of a high spiritual tradition which is too often abused or concealed. The Patriarch of Constantinople, or "Ecumenical Patriarch," is the primate of the Orthodox Church, and his task is to express, across all historical limits, its unity and universality. Yet little is known about this Church, about its immense patrimony, theological, liturgical, and particularly spiritual. Critics often denounce its weaknesses and compromises, yet they ignore the crushing weight of a history in which the West has not always played a positive role. Yet one also senses *something more* as one stands before an icon of the "Virgin of Tenderness," or of those three angels who symbolize the Divinity by their youth and beauty. In seeking better to understand—and here the abundant literature produced in the West by Orthodox emigrants is very helpful—one discovers a Christianity which is capable of uniting mystery and freedom, of perceiving beauty as a path to knowledge, of elaborating a mystical system which, while in many ways resembling that of the Far-East, ultimately leads to the fullest revelation of the person and of communion. An Orthodox missionary in outer Mongolia expressed his deep respect and admiration for the Buddhist sages. But their eyes are closed by the ineffable experience of introspection, and our task, he added, is to lead them to open their eyes to see the irreducible reality of the "other," even as they maintain their deep peace.

No one is better than Patriarch Bartholomew to open for us the gates of the iconostasis, this partition which, in an Orthodox church, affirms the transparency of the image even as it conceals the secret of the sanctuary. He can open the doors for us by negat-

the dead, by revealing the richness, for today and tomorrow, of a spirituality which aims at transfiguring all creation.

Bartholomew knows both Christian East and West "from the inside": the East of spiritual affirmations; the West of negations, but also of dialogue and research. Thus he is capable of explaining the wisdom of the former in the language of the latter, of expressing the approach of a form of Christianity hitherto unexpected (and until now almost never heard) to the great, global problems of our society, as well as to the many non-Christian religions which haunt our "new age"...

I have long known Patriarch Bartholomew. When I first met him, he was still a deacon, then a priest. I remember our conversations before the massive walls of Constantinople, a symbolic enclosure, the ramparts of civilization. I remember our dinners at a small restaurant on the European shore of the Bosphorus. I remember our common friendship with Metropolitan Meliton, this patriarch without a title. Meliton was a lion, I told Bartholomew, a lion who could neither roar nor leap into history because he was at that time prevented from leaving Turkish soil. And Bartholomew, his affection suffused with humor, presented Meliton with a New Year's gift—a small stuffed lion...

This book was composed in the following manner. I wrote the first three chapters as a kind of introduction, briefly summarizing Orthodoxy, the Patriarchate of Constantinople, and the historical details about Bartholomew. For the rest, I drew inspiration from the patriarch's own messages, and particularly from a number of long interviews with him. With his permission, I added two sections, the first on Orthodox spirituality, the second on the history of the Church in the first millennium.

In these troubling times, but also times of great spiritual thirst, these words of the patriarch, simultaneously ancient and modern, deserve to be heard.

O.C.

PART I

Discovery

1

The Orthodox Church

A Church Misunderstood

The Orthodox Church, with approximately 250 million baptized members, is one of the major expressions of Christianity. It is strongly conscious that the Church, "one, holy, catholic, and apostolic," subsists within itself. It does not deny, nevertheless—except among its ultra-conservative wing—the deeply ecclesial nature of other Christian confessions. This allows it to participate in the World Council of *Churches*—the Patriarch insists on this word—as well as to affirm its unity of faith with the ancient Oriental Churches[1] and to maintain a fraternal, though often difficult, dialogue with Rome.

In contrast with the communities which grew out of the 16th century Reformation, Orthodoxy does not define itself in relation to Roman Catholicism. It serenely refers to itself as "Orthodox Catholic" and, not long ago, easily spoke of the "western schism." It senses an absolute continuity with Christ, with Pentecost, with apostolic preaching, and includes numerous sees of apostolic foundation.

The Orthodox Church is certainly of eastern origin, in the sense that it developed in the eastern Mediterranean region, and later in eastern Europe, but also because of the symbolism of the East, where the sun rises (in the early centuries, Christians prayed facing East, and Orthodox churches remain "oriented" to the present day). Yet Orthodoxy can be found throughout the world: one finds Orthodox believers among Arabs, Americans, Austra-

---

1   The Armenian, Jacobite, Coptic, and Ethiopian Churches, long and erroneously called "monophysite."

3

lians, the French; an Orthodox cathedral, Nikolai-Do, dominates the skyline of Tokyo; Eskimos and Indians of the North-Pacific region are commonly Orthodox.

Orthodoxy has for centuries been squeezed between two great imperialistic forces: a chiefly Roman-Catholic West, and Islam to the South-East. To ensure its survival, it was often forced to contract itself into a merely ritual, popular expression, which to the casual observer often appears as little more than the preservation of folk customs. And it is often concealed under layers of nationalism which, reducing Orthodoxy to simple externals, use it to justify violence. At the same time, educated Christians in both Europe and America do not cease to wonder at its treasures; Catholic, and sometimes even Protestant, believers pray before Orthodox icons.

But it cannot be said that Orthodoxy is an ancient, passive treasure which others are to unearth and appropriate for themselves. It has never failed, when the vicissitudes of history have allowed, to manifest its creativity, witnessing to the Holy Spirit, who always renews and prophesies. Fourteenth-century Byzantine mystical theology, or the intuitions of Dostoevsky and the religious philosophers he inspired, represent a remarkable deepening of the Christian message—"We are all grandchildren of Dostoevsky," Christos Yannaras, a great contemporary Greek thinker, recently said. "Dostoevsky knew everything that Nietzsche knew, and something deeper."[2] The golden thread of those who are transfigured, such as St Seraphim of Sarov, and the red thread of martyrs provide continuity to a history which is often full of misery and discontinuity. The countless martyrs of the Communist era mysteriously expressed themselves in these words of Christ, heard by St Silouan of Mt Athos: "Keep your mind in hell and despair not!" Even today, these words help many of our contemporaries from falling into nihilism.

2   Nicolas Berdiaev, *The Spirit of Dostoevsky* (in French) (Paris, 1945, 1974), p. 70.

In these several examples, we can sense a way of being, an *ethos* enlivened by the power and the secret joy of the resurrection.

To acquaint the reader with this multi-faceted Church, I will try briefly to describe its history, its establishment, and its organizational principles.

The Church of the Councils and the Fathers

The great ideals of the primitive Church have persisted within Orthodoxy, and the work of 20th century theologians, particularly in the *diaspora*,[3] has led to their rediscovery. The Church is understood to be a spontaneously conciliar assembly of eucharistic communities, whose "normal" spirituality is that of the martyr: "Give your blood and receive the Spirit," says an ancient maxim. The tradition of martyrdom continues in Orthodoxy without interruption: martyrs in an empire that was at first pagan then frequently heretical; "neo-martyrs" in the Ottoman era; and the innumerable martyrs under the communists in our own century.

Certainly, after the "conversion" of the Roman emperors (we should not forget that the Byzantines have always considered themselves "Romans"), the temptation was strong to confuse the Kingdom of God and that of Caesar. The eschatological tension created by the existence of a time beyond history, which alone is capable of infusing eternity into time, was maintained by the monks, who exercised a strong influence on Orthodox culture. Fraternal communities, based in the very heart of the city, conducted an active social ministry. Hermits, or small groups gathered around a spiritual father, practiced "the art of arts and the science of sciences" which open the inner heart to divine light. These are called "hesychasts," from the Greek *hesychia*, which expresses the silence and peace that come from union with God.

3   The "dispersion," born from a large emigration of Orthodox to the West.

Among them appeared "spiritual fathers" (*gerontes* in Greek, *startsy* in Russian, meaning "elders"), who were endowed with an authentic "discernment of the spirits." The monastic experience was communicated to the Christian faithful through example and counsel, but most particularly through the development of an all-encompassing work of art, the so-called "Byzantine" liturgy, which in fact owes much to Syro-Palestinian hymnographers.

This experience, as well, allowed Greek philosophy—that great expression of the Indo-European genius—to incorporate biblical revelation, the transfigured expression of the Semitic genius, resulting in a theology of the person and of communion. Étienne Gilson has said that, for western medieval theology, the proper name for God is "Being." For the Fathers of the Greek Church, the proper name for God is "Love." These important witnesses were often bishops, men of thought, inspired commentators on Scripture, active in social life in order to bear witness to the "sacrament of the brother." Their theology of celebration, in which faith illumines thought, was inscribed in the dogmas of the seven ecumenical councils, in which East and West collaborated. These dogmas do not constitute a system but preserve a way of life. They lead to contemplation through negation, symbol, and antinomy. The Orthodox Church later held numerous other councils, right up until 1872—and there is a renewal of conciliarity today—but none were called "ecumenical," both out of respect for the separated West and out of reverence for the great cycle of Trinitarian and Christological proclamations of the first millennium. Orthodoxy likens the seven councils to the seven pillars of Wisdom.

In the fourth century, the councils of I Nicea (325) and I Constantinople (381), through the antinomy between the absolute unity and the equally absolute distinction within God, pointed to the mystery of Divine Communion, the source of all communion. The Council of Ephesus (431) condemned those who re-

fused to call Mary *Theotokos*, Mother of God: because the subject
of Christ's humanity is the divine person of the Word. The Council of Chalcedon (451) affirmed that the union of divine and human in Christ takes place without confusion or separation, thus
clearly defining the original perspective of Christianity. Just as
Christ is totally one with his Father, who makes his Spirit to dwell
in him, so he is also one with humanity. This is why everything
about Christ concerns us, as is expressed in the adage, "God became man so that man might become god," not in emptying his
humanity, but in fulfilling it. Thus II Constantinople (553)
taught that the humanity of Christ onto which we are grafted is
both deified and deifying, while also stressing the proper consistency of created nature and the unity of the human being, who
bears the image of God in both soul and body. III Constantinople
(680) affirmed, against a tendency to fuse the two natures in
Christ, that the human will of Christ had to adhere freely to his
divine will, thus fully establishing human freedom. II Nicea (787)
justified the veneration of icons. The incarnation has sanctified
matter, God has made himself an image, the image of a man, and
through grace humanity discovers its true image. The icon allows
a sanctified personal presence to radiate, leading to the praise of
God. Thus the veneration of an image is directed to its prototype.

From I Nicea, which affirmed the "consubstantiality" of Christ
with his divine Father, to II Nicea, which spelled out the ultimate
consequences of the incarnation, a cycle is completed, proclaiming
the victory over separation and death—already won, but yet to be
manifested. Significantly, "Nicea" means "city of victory."

The Rise of the "New Rome"

The period from the seventh century to 1453, the year Constantinople was captured by the Turks, marks the properly
"Byzantine" era. Three basic tendencies are characteristic: the
gradual separation between Christian East and West; mission-

ary vigor; and remarkable theological development. Two dates are signposts in the "estrangement" (a word Fr Yves Congar liked to use) between East and West: in 1054, an attempt to heal the breach failed and led to an exchange of anathemas between a papal legate and a patriarch of Constantinople; in 1204, armies of the Fourth Crusade, arriving after a century of growing hatred, attacked Constantinople and sacked it in a frenzy of profanation.

In addition to political, economic, and cultural factors which are no longer relevant, the schism, from an Orthodox perspective, also had properly spiritual causes that touched upon the criterion of truth in the Church: the status and role of primacy, as well as the theology of the Holy Spirit.

While the East remained faithful to the communion ecclesiology and the conciliarity of the first millennium, in the West Roman monarchy tended towards absolutism. This notion, which provoked the Schism of the Reformation, was fully realized only in 1870, when Vatican I simultaneously proclaimed both papal infallibility and the "immediate and absolute episcopal jurisdiction" of the pope over bishops and the faithful alike.

The controversy about the Holy Spirit centered on the *Filioque* formula. Despite the fact that no properly ecumenical council had discussed the question and that the people of God had not given their assent, the West added the expression "And from the Son" (in Latin, *Filioque*) to the words of Christ in John's Gospel about "the Holy Spirit, who proceeds from the Father." When the *Filioque* expression appeared among the Latin Fathers, there was no apparent opposition to the Greek formulation, but simply a different, and legitimate, approach. Nevertheless, later western scholasticism seemed to compromise the "monarchy" of the Father (that the Father is the "sole principle" of the Trinity), as well as the relation of reciprocal dependence and mutual service between the Son and the Spirit, the "two hands of the Father," as St

Irenaeus of Lyons described them in the second century. This development was a sign, rather than the cause, of an overall evolution in which the liberating and prophetic roles of the Spirit were subjugated to the hierarchy and quasi-monopolized, or at least restricted, by the "sovereign pontiff."

As the second millennium was dawning, Byzantine missions, turned away from Bohemia and Moravia by Germanic feudal authorities, converted all of Southwest and East Europe, as far as the Arctic Sea. In keeping with the multi-lingual tradition of the Christian East, Scripture and the liturgy were translated into the native languages. Often, missionaries provided these languages with alphabets and grammatical structures. In the ninth century, Cyril and Methodius, Greeks from Thessalonika, created in Bulgaria a powerful center of Slavic Christianity with a new alphabet, the "Cyrillic," which to this day is used by Russians, Belorussians, Ukrainians, Bulgarians, and Serbs. The latter nations were evangelized during the subsequent century, and Christianity was also reawakened in the Romanian lands, which had already been christianized in Antiquity. Orthodoxy also spread to the Caucasus. In 988, Kievan Rus' (as well as the people of Novgorod) were baptized. Constantinople organized these young Churches into autonomous metropolitan districts. Constantinople also supported and guided the monastic reform of St Sergius in the 14th century—a reform which penetrated throughout Russia and deeply affected the entire nation.

Third, the theological richness of this era is becoming better known today, particularly the Palamite synthesis of the 14th century, which was confirmed by a council held in Constantinople in 1351. According to St Gregory Palamas, the Living God, totally inaccessible in his "superessence," allows us, out of pure love, to participate in his "energies," which come from the Father, through the Son, in the Holy Spirit. These "energies" are the light of Mt Tabor and of the Parousia.[4] They call humanity to transfigure itself and the entire universe. Whether we speak of God or about humanity in his image, we are placed in a dialectic of Mystery and of Love, of a knowing-unknowing, which is precisely the movement of communion itself.

This theological development—closely linked to the experience of "deification"—is the leaven of a powerful cultural development leading to a transfigured Renaissance. Whether one thinks of the Christian humanism of St Nicholas Cabasilas, of the art in Mistra in the Peloponnesus, or of Chora in Constantinople, the human person is manifested as divino-human, not by separation, as would soon happen in the West, but by exaltation.

A Time of Retreat, Theology in Images

From the fall of Constantinople (1453) to the close of the 18th century, Orthodoxy, caught between the weight of Islam and the aggressiveness of western "missionaries," underwent a long period of retreat. The Church was preserved by liturgical and monastic prayer, as well as by the unifying service of the Patriarchate of Constantinople, whose direct jurisdiction extended from the Baltic to Cappadocia until the end of the 17th century. The Ottoman Empire made of the patriarch an "ethnarch," responsible, civilly and spiritually, for the Orthodox nation, or *millet*, second in size and importance to the Sunni *millet*. Faced with Uniatism—in other words, the attachment to Rome of vast Orthodox regions, allowed to preserve their "rites," but not their theology—the patriarchate organized an effective defense by supporting powerful lay brotherhoods in Poland-Lithuania. Intellectually weakened—even if the memory of the Palamite synthesis was not entirely lost—Orthodoxy developed a "school theology" influenced at times by Catholicism, at times by Protestantism. Nevertheless, numerous 17th

4 The word "Parousia" means both expectation and presence—the hidden presence today of Christ, whom we expect to return in glory.

century councils succeeded in maintaining the essentials of Orthodoxy in the midst of Reformation and Counter-Reformation. At the same time, the gradual development of "ritualism" and of "radical conservatism" led to the exaggerated growth of the iconostasis, to a decline—out of fear of the sacred—in the frequency of communion, and, in Russia, to the schism of the "Old Believers," fanatically attached to a national messianism, as well as to an almost magical approach to the rite and to the customs which control daily life.

The authentic theological creativity of this period is to be found in its art: on Mt Athos, in Crete, in Epirus, in Syria, and particularly in Romanian frescos and the Novgorod icons of Holy Wisdom (despite the overall decadence of Russian iconography of that era). An original, often prophetic, approach is apparent: the accent falls on ascesis, on the voluntary humiliation of the God-man, as well as on the paradoxical victory of the immolated Lamb, on a "kenosis" which at times (as, for example, in Hurez, in Little Wallachia) assumes and surpasses the melancholy of the pre-Romantic West, and finally on the cosmic mystery of divine Wisdom...

Death and Resurrection

The 18th century represents a moment of agony for the Orthodox Church. The decay of the Ottoman Empire contaminated Orthodoxy in Greece and the Balkans. In Russia, Peter the Great abolished the patriarchate, which, despite its weaknesses, remained a powerful symbol of the independence of the church. Now the church was submitted to a civil functionary through a synod of bishops. The new Russian elite, rationalist or occultist, seemed alienated from the traditional faith.

Signs of renewal did appear, however, through contacts with a Europe in which the "Enlightenment" led not simply to a critique of religion, but also to a sense of personal responsibility and the development of education. In Greece, St Cosmas the Aetolian aimed his evangelistic efforts at the spread of schools and social justice. St Tikhon of Zadonsk, inspired by Anglican and Lutheran mysticism, did much the same in Russia.

The renewal burst forth at the turn of the 18th and 19th centuries with the efforts of St Nicodemus the Hagiorite, assisted by Macarius, the aged Metropolitan of Corinth. Following similar, though partial, attempts in Romania, Nicodemus composed a monumental anthology of mystical theology, the *Philokalia* (literally, "love of beauty"), which was published in Venice in 1782. His work, soon translated into Slavonic, underwent two somewhat revised editions in Russia during the 19th century. In our own day, an even ampler *Philokalia* has been compiled in Romania by Father Dumitru Staniloe.

The *Philokalia* elaborates a method, that of the "prayer of the heart," as well as the very highest form of theology, which is accomplished and transcended in adoration. It is the guide for the spiritual father, it was the traveling companion of the "Russian pilgrim"[5] on his charismatic apostolate. In the 19th century, the renewal inspired by the *Philokalia* led to an increase, throughout the Orthodox world, in the number of such "elders." These were men of prayer, but also of great culture; they attracted not only the simple faithful, but also artists, writers, and philosophers. The two greatest Greek Romantic authors of the end of the last century, the "two Alexanders," Papadiamantis and Moraitidis, counted "elders" among their friends. Dostoevsky found the answer to the modern dialectic between master and slave in the sacrificial fatherhood of these "elders," and it is because of them that he was able to discover Christianity as a religion of the person and of freedom. In modern times, the *Philokalia*, translated into countless languages, has become surprisingly popular in the West.

5   The "Accounts of the Russian Pilgrim to His Spiritual Father" were published in Kazan ca. 1870. They describe the method of the "prayer of the heart" or "Jesus Prayer."

In 1848, in response to an appeal from the papacy, which was preparing the dogma of infallibility, a major encyclical by the eastern patriarchs, issued by their own synods together with that of Constantinople, recalled that, for the Orthodox, the truth "is preserved by the entire body of the Church." New national churches were created in the Balkans, but the 1872 Council of Constantinople condemned "ethno-phyletism," or religious nationalism.

In late 19th and early 20th-century Russia there developed a highly influential religious philosophy which, far from rejecting modernity, embraced and surpassed it from the inside. We could mention the innovative re-reading of the Fathers by Epifanovitch and Nesmelov, the existentialist and personalist approach of Berdiaev and Shestov, the daring reflections on the religious sense of *eros* by Rozanov, the bold speculation about the religious dimensions of the cosmos among the "sophiologists" such as Solov'ev, Bulgakov, and Florensky. In conjunction with this prophetic lay movement, the Russian episcopate was emboldened and prepared for a council, which finally gathered in Moscow in 1917-18. This council restored the patriarchate and reestablished the tradition of the election of bishops by both clergy and laity, but it was dissolved by the new regime just as it was preparing a widespread reform of the Church. Already in 1920, Constantinople appealed for ecumenical collaboration among the Churches, and Patriarch Meletios considered the convocation of a pan-Orthodox assembly to discuss a genuine *aggiornamento* of the Church.

History dealt these promises a fateful blow: Russian totalitarianism hardened; Greeks fled Asia Minor; a new Turkey arose; and in Constantinople, Meletios was forced to resign.

Yet Another Death and Resurrection

It is indeed peculiar how the history of Orthodoxy follows the rhythm of the cross and resurrection.

The Russian Church in the 1920s, the Balkan Churches after World War II (except for Greece, although Greece experienced a frightful civil war)—all were ravaged by one of the worst persecutions in Christian history. Martyrs and confessors of the faith number in the tens of thousands. The Russian Church, annihilated in 1940, partially rebuilt as a result of more liberal policies made necessary by the war, was again crushed beginning in 1959. All religious, cultural and social activity was forbidden. Only religious worship endured, magnificent and beyond time. But the Church was marginalized, and, as one of her defenders has observed, it risks becoming a "liturgical ghetto."

The fall of Communism has freed these Churches. But they were far from ready for this change. The number of adult baptisms has greatly increased, but the problem lies in the absence of a catechesis suitable for our time, as well as with a Slavonic liturgical language which few can understand. Innovators and conservatives confront each other on this issue. Western modernity, spreading in its most superficial forms, generates fear and anxiety, as does the proselytism of American sects or the often violent awakening of the Uniate Churches which were liquidated on Stalin's orders in the aftermath of World War II. Many Orthodox are torn between an aggressive traditionalism born of anguish and a tendency toward greater openness and renewal. The awakening of nationalism also leads to schism, notably in Ukraine.

In the course of this tragic history, at times because of it, Orthodox thought in our century has been purified and deepened. Particularly in Paris, Russian religious philosophy has borne its last fruits. From 1940 to 1960, due especially to the efforts of Vladimir Lossky, one of the greatest Orthodox theologians of our time, the neo-patristic and neo-Palamite synthesis was achieved.

In Greece, this creative thrust has been continued in the writings of Nikos Nissiotis, Panayiotis Nellas, Christos Yannaras, and John Zizioulas, whom the Patriarchate of Constantinople has appointed Metropolitan of Pergamum. Voluminous "dogmatics" have been composed in Serbia by Father Justin Popovich and in Romania by the expert on the *Philokalia*, Father Dumitru Staniloe. In the Middle East, a profound dialogue has been launched between Orthodoxy and Islam, inspired by Metropolitan Georges Khodr.

An Overview of Orthodox Geography

The Orthodox presence across the entire globe is arranged along three or four major axes, whose origins can be traced in the history we have just described.

The North-South axis, in fact "oriental," traces its origins to the area where biblical revelation occurred and where Christianity first took root. Here one finds Orthodox, primarily Arabic-speaking, who belong to the "apostolic patriarchates" of Alexandria, Antioch, and Jerusalem, as well as to the Church of Sinai. Here one also finds a vigorous Greek Orthodoxy: the semi-autonomous Church of Crete (attached to Constantinople), the autocephalous Churches of Greece and Cyprus, each headed by archbishops. Then comes the Patriarchate of Constantinople, *primus inter pares*, and the Churches it has spawned or taken under its wing: first, three Churches which are neither Greek nor Slavic, in Albania (restored by Constantinople in 1991), in the Caucasus (the Patriarchate of Georgia), and particularly the "Latin" Orthodox of Romania (the Patriarchate of Bucharest). The axis continues to the North, with its cluster of Slavic churches: the Patriarchates of Serbia and Bulgaria; the Patriarchate of Moscow, which, without fully resolving all the difficulties, has granted a kind of internal autonomy to the Churches of Ukraine, Belarus, and some Baltic countries. In Ukraine and Macedonia, there are also schismatic communities, which are not recognized by the rest of the Orthodox. The autocephalous Church of Poland is headed by a metropolitan. The autonomous Churches of the Czech and Slovak Republics, as well as of Finland, are dependent on Constantinople.

A far-eastern axis across northern Asia and the North Pacific corresponds to the historical trail of the Russian missions, spreading as far as the Churches in China, Japan, the Aleutians and Alaska. A Greek mission is developing in Korea.

The western axis was created out of the massive migrations of the late 19th and 20th centuries, caused by both economic and political factors, following the Communist revolutions, the collapse of Greek Asia Minor, as well as various conflicts in the former Yugoslavia and the Middle East. Thus one finds significant Orthodox minorities in Western Europe, in North and South America, and in Australia. This *diaspora*, very fragmented, is, nation by nation, organizing itself into "assemblies of bishops," each presided over by the representative of the Patriarchate of Constantinople.

An African missionary axis is developing today, with clusters of Orthodox communities in Kenya, Uganda, Zaire, and Cameroon.

Principles of Organization

Orthodox ecclesiology is essentially an ecclesiology of communion, seeking to express the fundamental mysteries of Christ, of the Holy Spirit, of the Trinity.

The Church, first of all, defines itself as the Body of Christ, insofar as it is composed of eucharistic communities. Surrounding its bishop, the local church is the full manifestation of the universal Church, as long as it remains in communion with all other local churches in the unity of faith and the eucharistic cup, attested to by "apostolic succession" and the conciliarity of bishops.

The Body of Christ, constituted in the Holy Spirit, is the locus of a permanent Pentecost, either manifest or hidden. All the baptized, anointed with the Spirit, are "kings, priests, and prophets." Thus, as the 1848 Encyclical stressed, they are all "guardians" responsible for the truth, of which the bishops are "judges": a truth whose essence is love, and which is therefore expressed in their communion—this time communion among individuals, and not only between eucharistic communities.

Thus the Church, in its multiplicity, is revealed to be a profound unanimity in the image of the Trinity. The magisterium functions in conciliar fashion. All decisions, even if they are made by a council assembled with all canonical guarantees of ecumenicity, must be "received" by the entirety of the People of God. This reception may be immediate or quite difficult, a process which may well require efforts at clarification, or even the convocation of another council. The "Robber Council" of Ephesus in the fourth century, the iconoclast Council of Hieria in the eighth, and the Council of Florence in the 15th were all rejected by the conscience of the Church. On the other hand, a regional council held in Constantinople in 381 was proclaimed as "ecumenical" long after the fact, and a pan-Orthodox significance has been ascribed to the 1848 Encyclical of the eastern patriarchs. In essence, the Church is permanently conciliar.

The communion of local churches has been concretely organized around a hierarchy of centers, whose primates have received the prerogative of meeting with local communities to prevent their isolation. Very early on, the churches of each province organized themselves into metropolitan districts, each with a metropolitan bishop. Later, larger autocephalous bodies were formed, as communities were shaped culturally and historically: the Latin world around Rome; the Greek around Constantinople, the semitic and "oriental" around Antioch; the African around Alexandria. In modern times, since the emergence of Russia and the rise of nationalism in the Balkans, most autocephalous churches have become national. The primate of an autocephalous church, usually entitled "patriarch," is elected by his own church, in other words by the synod, sometimes with the participation of the entire assembly of bishops and, although rather rarely today, also the clergy and the faithful. A new patriarch must be recognized by the other primates, and particularly by the first among them.

By tradition, one of the primates has exercised a universal primacy. In the undivided Church, this position was held by the Bishop of Rome—today, it is held by the Archbishop of Constantinople-New Rome. This primacy does not imply domination, but neither is it simply honorific. Being in communion with the first bishop, as well as having the right of appeal before him, are signs of belonging to the Universal Church. He also has prerogatives to initiate actions and to preside, issues to which we shall return.

From these perspectives, Petrine succession is to be found at all levels: in the communion-in-faith ("communion of saints" and communion of "the holy gifts") of each believer; in the privileged witness of bishops, each of whom presides at the eucharist, and all of whom, in the words of Cyprian of Carthage, sit *in solidum* upon the *cathedra Petri*; and finally in the responsibility of the "first bishop," who must express the unity of the Church by "analogy" with the role of Peter in the Apostolic College, as Byzantine theologians would say.

It must be admitted that the vicissitudes of history have led to something of a deformation in the application of these principles. In some autocephalous churches, dioceses are too large, and the real eucharistic community is in fact the parish. National churches have adopted administrative structures based on secular models, ignoring intermediate primacies, such as those held by metropolitans, and eliminating the independence of bishops. In those countries which have so long ignored the laity, the freedom of the Church is very recent and cannot be taken for granted. Autocephaly all too often becomes a sort of absolute independence: taken to the extreme, this results in the transformation of Orthodoxy into a federation, a confederation of independent churches. Here lies the indispensable and difficult role of the Ecumenical Patriarchate.

2

The "Ecumenical" Patriarchate of Constantinople

Origins

Eusebius of Caesarea, the great historian of the ancient church, notes that the Apostle Andrew, brother of Peter and "first-called" of the apostles, evangelized the European shores of the Euxeinos Bridge (i.e., of the Black Sea). According to a symbolic tradition, he also founded the church of Byzantium. St John Chrysostom, Archbishop of Constantinople early in the fifth century, celebrated the capital as "the city of the apostles," adding: "Behold the accomplishments of her who has such a founder."[1] The prestige of the city, however, came with the transformation of Byzantium into Constantinople, the city of the Emperor Constantine, who made this "New Rome" the capital of the empire. The official inauguration took place on May 11, 330. One of Constantine's successors, Theodosius, who ensured the victory of the faith of Nicea and who allowed the convening of the Second Ecumenical Council, definitively transferred his residence to Constantinople, which by now had all the civil institutions of the ancient Rome. The bishop of the capital city in fact held exceptional authority. Canon 3 of the Council of 381 affirmed that this bishop "shall have the prerogative of honor after the Bishop of Rome, because Constantinople is New Rome." This was a moral authority without geographical limits, as was the case with the old Rome. In the words of Gregory of Nazianzus, who

---

1 *PG* 56:264.

went there to preach about the Trinitarian mystery against the Arians[2] and who was for a brief time its archbishop, was not Constantinople "the first city after the first [city] of all"?[3]

In 451, the Council of Chalcedon spelled out the parallelism between the imperial structures and those of the Church. It set the foundation for the great Byzantine edifice, the "symphony" between Church and State, with the former represented by what would later be called the "Pentarchy," with the five great patriarchates (Rome, Constantinople, Alexandria, Antioch, and Jerusalem) considered as the "five senses" of the Church. The "prerogative of honor" of Constantinople is transformed into the right to consider appeals (Canons 9 and 17). Canon 28 rephrases the definition of 381:

> The city, honored by the presence of the emperor and of the senate, and enjoying the same privileges as the old imperial Rome, should also be magnified in ecclesiastical affairs, and rank next after her.

This time, the jurisdiction of the future patriarchate was clearly spelled out: it encompassed the metropolitan districts of northwest Asia Minor and the southeast portion of the Balkans. Metropolitans of these areas "shall be consecrated" by the Archbishop of Constantinople, as well as the "bishops in these dioceses who are among the barbarians."

Rome at first refused to accept this 28th canon, basing itself strictly on the decisions of Nicea, which awarded "prerogative of honor" to only three Sees, Rome, Alexandria, and Antioch. All three, in the words of Pope Leo, were of "Petrine" origin. He also argued that it was not possible to replace the "apostolic" criterion with a "political" one. But this ignored the fact that, for the East-

---

2   Arius considered that the Logos, the principle of creation, was himself created, and made his dwelling in the man, Jesus.

3   *Oration* 36:2. He is referring, of course, to Rome.

erners, the capital of the empire was not primarily a political center, but a sacred one, an image of the New Jerusalem: "I have surpassed you, Solomon," said Emperor Justinian a century later as he entered Hagia Sophia. The emperor, to some extent, also stood for the "royal priesthood" of the laity. Moreover, Constantinople little by little responded to the Roman argument by appealing to the apostolic origin of Byzantium.

Due to opposition from the pope, Canon 28 was omitted from lists of canons appearing immediately after the council. But the situation canonized by the council endured. The canon was included in the sixth century *Syntagma*, as well as in later Byzantine collections. From the sixth century onward, the canon also appeared in the *Prisca*, the most ancient Latin collection of canons.

At the end of the sixth century, as the "ecumenical" empire had disappeared in the West (though it continued in the East), the Patriarch of Constantinople assumed the title of "Ecumenical Patriarch." It is not possible to describe here the immense role played by the patriarchs of this See, often in a very trying "symphony" with the emperors—but the "bipolar" nature of the system was always reestablished by the monks, from among whom patriarchs were recruited. We should at least name Gregory of Nazianzus, John Chrysostom, Flavian, Tarasius, Photius, as well as the great 14th century "hesychast" patriarchs, particularly Athanasius I. We should likewise remember the ecumenical councils held in Constantinople or its environs, the Second in 381, the Fourth in 451, the Fifth in 553, the Sixth in 680. The only successful union councils with Rome were the one held in that city in 880, and the Palamite councils of the 14th century.

As the empire contracted toward the end of the Middle Ages, ultimately encompassing only the European suburbs of the capital and a portion of the Peloponnesus, the patriarchate prepared for life without a Byzantine emperor, as it administered vast territories under Islamic control or belonging to the Polish-Lithuanian Kingdom (and, until 1448, to the Principality of Moscow). In 1354, Patriarch Philotheos wrote that the Church of Constantinople "manifests its solicitude and care for all the holy Churches of the universe." In 1370, he described himself to Grand-Duke Dimitri of Moscow as the "common father of Christians." And in 14th century patriarchal decrees, Constantinople presented itself as the primary witness of the true faith.

The Ethnarch

The collapse of the Byzantine Empire left a historical and juridical void, since it was the emperor, for example, who convened councils. This void was filled by the Patriarch of Constantinople, whom the Sultan appointed "ethnarch," responsible for the Orthodox *millet*. The "ethnarch" was the head of the Christian "nation," since for Muslims the civil and religious realms could not be separated. To be sure, Moscow proclaimed itself autocephalous in 1448, on the pretext that Constantinople had "betrayed" the faith at the union Council of Florence. The easterly expansion of Poland-Lithuania, however, allowed the patriarchate to restore, under its own jurisdiction, the Ukrainian Metropolitanate of Kiev (until Ukraine was absorbed by Muscovy at the end of the 17th century).

Under these different circumstances, the primacy of Constantinople continued to function until the 19th century. With some regularity, the patriarchate was able to assemble the eastern patriarchs and their synods, and often other bishops as well, whenever serious problems arose. Only with the agreement of the primate and what remains of the Pentarchy can a local Church be elevated to the level of a patriarchate. In the case of Russia, this elevation, granted in 1589 by Patriarch Jeremiah II, was affirmed by councils held in Constantinople in 1590 and 1593. The Church of Russia, awarded the fifth place in a reconstituted Pentarchy, was subsequently always consulted, even after the introduction of the synodal system in 1721 under Peter the Great. In 1848, for example, Constantinople was very careful to reach agreement with the Russian Holy Synod in the preparation of the conciliar encyclical on the problem of papal infallibility.

Numerous councils were therefore held in Constantinople: in 1454 and 1484 (to reject the Union of Florence); in 1590 (to establish the Russian Patriarchate); in 1638 (to clarify the Orthodox position *vis à vis* both the Reformation and the Counter-Reformation); in 1663 (to deal with internal troubles in the Russian Church); in 1735 (to resist the Uniate offensive and to challenge the rebaptism of the Orthodox, imposed by Rome after centuries of sporadic *communio in sacris*); in 1848 and 1872 (to deal with difficult ecclesiological problems). The establishment of the Moscow Patriarchate and the role of arbitrator played during the 17th century crisis in the Russian Church served to define the primacy of Constantinople in terms which demonstrate that, in a "divided" Church, Constantinople plays the same role Rome played during the first millennium:

> Can every decision of other Churches be appealed before the throne of Constantinople, and can it resolve all ecclesiastical matters?

> Answer: This privilege was held by the pope before the Church was torn apart by presumption and ill will. Henceforth, the Church being torn, all affairs are brought before the throne of Constantinople, which pronounces judgment because, according to the canons, it has the same primacy as the old Rome. (Patriarchal and Synodal Tome of 1663)

The Battle Against Religious Nationalism

In the 19th century, the retreat of the Ottoman Empire and the rise of nationalism led to a multiplication of nation states in southwest Europe. Each nation simply claimed and unilaterally declared its ecclesiastical independence, except for Serbia, which first obtained Constantinople's assent. Politics and nationalism turned the traditional hierarchy of values on its head. No longer was the State protected and defended by the Church—the Church became one dimension of the nation, a sign of national identity, and it therefore had to serve the State.

Thus the traditional form of autocephaly was gradually transformed into an autocephalism that was both absolute and homogeneous: no longer interdependence but independence. Ecclesiastical administrative structures were now modeled on those of the State, and the bishops were transformed into quasi-functionaries.

Little by little, a new theory of autocephaly developed, affirming that the basis for ecclesiology is not the eucharistic principle, but the ethnic and national. The "local" Church was transformed into the "national" Church, with an absurd application of the Trinitarian analogy: "primacy of honor" became "equality of honor."

The last council at which the entire Pentarchy was present was held in 1872 in Constantinople. This council issued a strong condemnation of *phyletism*, i.e., ecclesiastical nationalism (the Church of Bulgaria, which had just declared its autocephaly without the agreement of Constantinople, was demanding the creation, in Constantinople itself, of a diocese for the Bulgarian minority—a diocese subject to the Bulgarian Church, and therefore removed from the jurisdiction of the local bishop):

> Phyletism, in other words, a distinction founded on differences of ethnic origin and language, as well as demands and the exercise of exclusive rights by individuals or groups from one country and of the same race, may have some basis in secular states, but it is foreign to our own order... In the Christian Church, which is a spiritual communion, intended by its Head and Founder to encompass all nations in

the unique brotherhood of Christ, phyletism is something foreign and totally incomprehensible. The formation, in one place, of distinct churches based on race, accepting believers of only one ethnic origin...and led by pastors of the same ethnic background, as the supporters of phyletism desire, is an event without precedent.

...As each ethnic Church seeks to preserve its own particular identity, the dogma of "one, holy, catholic, and apostolic Church" is dealt a mortal blow. If the situation is such—or if the Churches hold this view—then phyletism is in direct contradiction with the spirit and teaching of Christ, and opposes it...

A Radically New Situation

From the beginning of the 20th century, Constantinople has come to the realization that a new form of organization is needed, one in which the national Churches, both those it recognizes and those it will recognize in the future, participate fully in a restored unity. The condemnation issued in 1872 has had no effect. The Ecumenical Patriarchate admits that the Pentarchy is defunct. In 1902, Patriarch Joachim II proposed that the Orthodox churches consult together every two years. But to no avail.

Political developments, however, were to change the situation of the patriarchate even more radically. The Balkan wars in 1912-13, the First World War, the emigration of Christians from Asia Minor, the end of the Ottoman Empire and the emergence of a Turkish nation not only drastically reduced the patriarchate's jurisdiction but totally transformed its circumstances.

The system of an Orthodox *millet* is finished. The Lausanne Treaty in 1923 defined and guaranteed the status of the patriarchate as a religious establishment based in Constantinople and su-

pervising exclusively the spiritual affairs of a minority of Turkish
nationals of "Greek-Orthodox religion." A decree of the city government of Constantinople, dated December 6, 1923, ordered
that, "When spiritual and religious elections are held in Turkey,
the electors must be Turkish nationals and holders of religious positions within Turkey at the time of the election, and the elected
candidate must meet the same requirements." Thus lay persons,
who had previously participated in large numbers in patriarchal
elections, were now excluded, as were all metropolitans and bishops residing outside Turkey. Only one clause from the previous
statute remained: the right of the government, when a patriarchal
election is being prepared, to remove whomever it wants from the
list of eligible candidates.

The "population exchange," foreseen in 1923, initiated the departure of a large portion of the Greek-Orthodox population, and
this flight reached massive proportions during the Cypriot crisis
in the 1950s and 60s. Thus the direct jurisdiction of the patriarchate is now reduced to a few small communities remaining in
Turkey (in Istanbul, and on the islands of Imbros and Tenedos),
Athos, the Dodecanesian islands, Crete (which is semi-
autonomous), the Greek *diaspora* throughout the world (which is
particularly large and influential in the United States), and to a
portion of the Russian and Ukrainian *diaspora* (particularly in
France and Western Europe, where one finds an archdiocese of
Russian origin, though today *de facto* pan-Orthodox, based in
Paris. This archdiocese came under the protection of Constantinople at a time when the Patriarchate of Moscow was totally enslaved by the Communist regime). The Orthodox Churches of
the Czech Republic, of Slovakia, and of Finland are autonomous.
Dioceses in the "New Territories," in other words, the regions of
Thrace and Macedonia annexed by Greece in 1912-13, remain
dependent on Constantinople, but their administration has for
the most part been handed over to the Church of Greece.

The patriarchate's theological school, on the small island of Halki, in the Sea of Marmara, was closed by the Turkish government in 1971. Several schools or centers of study have since been established outside Turkey, which creates some problems. These include: the Patriarchal Institute of Patristic Studies in Thessalonika; the Orthodox Center of the Ecumenical Patriarchate in Chambésy, near Geneva; the Patriarchal Monastery of St Anastasia Pharmakolytria in Chalkidike; The Orthodox Academy of Crete; and the Holy Cross School of Theology, located in Brookline, MA, in the United States.

The Renewal of Orthodox Ecclesiology

The 20th-century renewal of Orthodox ecclesiology, which began in the Russian *diaspora* with Georges Florovsky, Nicholas Afanasiev, and John Meyendorff, and later carried on in Greek theology with Nikos Nissiotis and John Zizioulas, has led to a new interpretation of primacy. We can summarize it as follows:

• Each local church (in the proper sense of "local") is a eucharistic community in communion with all other local churches. This communion, as we have said, is organized around "centers of agreement." This permanent conciliarity of the Churches is expressed in the phenomenon of "reception." Certain churches have greater moral authority, and hence a more prestigious capacity of "reception." These include either sees of apostolic foundation, or cities whose political, cultural, or even symbolic role is, or has been, more significant. In the ancient Church, these "centers of agreement" formed a living and complex hierarchy, spreading from the local level to that of the universal Church, serving as compasses for civilization. Autocephaly is one factor in this complex fabric of multiple interdependencies. The national church, therefore, is only a contingent development which, far from hardening into an absolute autocephalism, should be relativized.

• Universal primacy or "priority" fundamentally consists of service on behalf of the communion of Churches. It is, if we wish, a primacy of honor, as long as we agree that honor brings with it real responsibilities and prerogatives. In the Orthodox Church, primacy belongs to the Church of Constantinople, based on the canons and on long historical experience. When the unity of faith is restored, primacy will again revert to the Church of Rome, according to the model, only now clearly elucidated, of the first millennium.

Together with the Byzantine theologians and the virtually unanimous eastern witness of the first millennium, we must accept a Petrine ministry in the universal Church. The primate functions among the bishops as Peter did among the apostles. But we must also underscore the *interdependence* of the primate and of all the bishops, as well as the importance of the *sensus ecclesiae* of the people of God, inspired by the "apostolic men," the elders (*startsy,* or *gerontes*) who manifest a strictly personal charism and whom Paul Evdokimov considered to be the "Johannine" dimension of the Church.

Even though he disagreed with the Ecumenical Patriarchate on the question of American autocephaly (which was unilaterally granted by Moscow in 1970 to Orthodox of Russian and Carpatho-Russian origin in the United States), Father John Meyendorff, from a chiefly pragmatic point of view, wrote the following in 1978 in an article entitled "NEEDED: The Ecumenical Patriarchate":[4]

> It is unquestionable that the Orthodox conception of the Church recognizes the need for a leadership of the world episcopate, for a certain spokesmanship by the first patri-

4   *The Orthodox Church* 14, No. 4 (1978) 4.

arch, for a ministry of coordination without which conciliarity is impossible. Because Constantinople, also called
"New Rome," was the capital of the Empire, the ecumenical
council designated its bishop—in accordance with the prac-
tical realities of that day—for this position of leadership,
which he has kept until this day, even if the Empire does not
exist anymore...[and the Patriarchate of Constantinople]
was not deprived of its "ecumenicity," being always answer-
able to the conciliar consciousness of the Church.

In the present chaotic years, the Orthodox Church could indeed use wise, objective and authoritative leadership from
the ecumenical patriarchate.

Towards a New Definition of Primacy

This great theological work culminated with the prophetic attitude of Patriarch Athenagoras who, already in 1953, pledged
to reunite Orthodoxy. This effort has been faithfully continued by his successors, Dimitrios and Bartholomew. Using the
statements of these patriarchs, I will attempt to show how the
primacy of Constantinople is being redefined. I will also draw
on the works of Metropolitan Maximus of Sardis, *The Ecumenical Patriarchate in the Orthodox Church*, as well as a collection of his articles, *The Local Church and the Universal Church*
(both in French), published by the patriarchate's Ecumenical
Center in Chambésy.

Primacy is not merely honorific, but neither is it an eastern papacy. Constantinople's weakness on the material plane, its poverty, ensures its impartiality and, paradoxically, increases its
prestige. The ecumenical patriarch has no pretensions to being a
"universal bishop." He claims no dogmatic infallibility, no direct
jurisdiction over all the faithful. He has no temporal powers. As a
center of appeal whose aim is to preserve the faith and the unity of
all, his primacy consists not in power, but in a sacrificial offering

of service, in imitation of the One who came not to be served but to serve. He is ready, within a fraternal, synodal context, to place himself at the service of the sister Churches in order to strengthen their unity and to further the mission of Orthodoxy. His service is one of initiative, of coordination and presidency, always with the accord of the sister Churches. An ever-changing form of creative self-offering, which, dare we say, must be earned, primacy derives from the very structures of the Church and is indispensable to ensure the unity and universality of Orthodoxy. It places the sister Churches in relationship, brings them to work and to witness together, and advances their common responsibility. Since the disappearance of the empire, Constantinople assumes the role of the Church which "convenes." After consulting with and obtaining the consent of the sister Churches, it can become their spokesperson. Finally, it offers recourse for communities in exceptional or dangerous circumstances.

This service carries with it two presuppositions: the principle of conciliarity must be maintained, as well as the principle of non-intervention in the interior affairs of the other Churches.

Patriarch Athenagoras (1948-1972) was the first to apply this notion of primacy. Beginning in 1961, he succeeded in gathering a series of pan-Orthodox conferences, at which, to the surprise of many, the "miracle of unity" blazed forth. In Chambésy, near Geneva, he created a "hearing post," where he also established a preconciliar secretariat. His two successors visited all the Orthodox Churches, convened several preconciliar conferences, and also held two "synaxes" of all the Orthodox primates—the first in 1992, held in Constantinople itself, the second in 1995, on the island of Patmos. In 1993 and 1995, as a result of this preconciliar work, progress was made on the difficult problem of the *diaspora*: the creation, in each country, of "episcopal assemblies," which we have already mentioned.

3

Bartholomew I

An Orthodox Childhood in Turkey

His name, before he was ordained to the diaconate, was Dimitrios Archondonis. He was born on February 29, 1940, in Turkey, on the island of Imbros, then populated by a Greek Orthodox majority. It is a mountainous island, with steep slopes and wild hilltops clear of trees, a rocky terrain covered with rough thorns, green in the winter, reddish-brown in summer. The sparkling sea offers an immense panorama as one ascends. But there are also three large valleys, cool and fertile, filled with large orchards of olive trees. Chapels are everywhere, white chapels uniting earth to heaven.

The village was called The Holy Theodores, in the plural because two Theodores are venerated: St Theodore Teron and St Theodore Stratelates, both holy warriors represented on icons on horseback. Dimitrios' father owned the village café, in which the villagers gathered to rest and to chat, drinking a little, chatting a great deal, calmly clicking their worry beads, whose slow rhythm calms the soul and reminds one of prayer. In one corner of the café stood a chair in front of a mirror: on occasion, his father also served as barber.

There were four children: the eldest was a girl, then three boys, the second of whom was Dimitrios. The father was hard, strict, and he transmitted that characteristic severity to his son. The mother, an extremely gentle woman, was the children's refuge. She refused to inflict punishment and left that task to her husband! The parents were both able to attend the patriarchal enthronement of Dimitrios, now called Bartholomew. Both are now deceased.

The island was then populated by Greeks, and solidly Orthodox. Its small capital was named Panagia, the "All-Holy," one of the
names given by Orthodoxy to the Virgin Mary. When the patriarch was a child, 8,000 Orthodox lived here. Today, no more than
300 remain. Around 1964, at the height of the Cypriot crisis, the
government in Ankara, doubtless afraid that Greece would try to
claim the island, decided to replace the Greeks with people of pure
Turkish origin. The process was indirect, because the status of Imbros and the neighboring island of Tenedos had been guaranteed
by the Lausanne accords. Much land was confiscated for the needs
of the state. Greek schools were closed. A prison was built, and its
prisoners cultivated the land; left unsupervised, they terrorized the
Greek women. The result was a massive emigration. The Archondonis family village lost its too-obviously Christian name: it is now
called the "Village of Olive Trees." Such is the path of history,
down to the present day, in southeast Europe and the Middle East.

The elder sister lives now in Athens. The older brother emigrated to Australia, where he has prospered—perhaps he will re-
tire back to Imbros, where life has become more peaceful. The
youngest brother, settled in France, lives and works in the Savoie
region. This is close to Geneva, and the patriarch visits him each
time he comes to this city, which provides a home for the World
Council of Churches, and near which the Patriarchate of Constantinople has established an Orthodox Center.

But let us return to the patriarch's childhood. When he was
not in school, Dimitrios willingly worked at the café. He continued to do so in his student days during vacations. Sometimes, to
earn a little pocket money, he would recite poetry, which the cus-
tomers greatly appreciated. Ouzo, oriental coffee, slow conversations to the rhythm of clicking worry beads, poems: all this was
part of the old Greek-Ottoman world! Hence the patriarch's
long-standing taste for poetry, and for art in general. His maternal
uncle, John Skarlatos, was a well-known painter.

The Attraction of Orthodoxy. Another Father

Very early in life, Dimitrios felt strongly attracted to Orthodoxy, to its sober and familiar beauty which, imperceptibly, fills one's entire existence.

The village priest, Father Asterios, was an old man without the slightest trace of intellectual formation (he had at most completed primary school). But he was nourished, appeased, and illumined by the words and gestures of the liturgy, by the immense poetical river of Byzantine hymnography, a theology which sings and is sung... Each day, he had to celebrate in one of the numerous chapels dotting the countryside—and the mountains—at the request of the families who cared for them and who wanted a service performed for an anniversary, a memorial, a feast, for a friend, a relative, living or deceased. Dimitrios volunteered to accompany him. There he was, crisscrossing the countryside with the old priest, lighting candles and the censer, singing alone in place of the choir, as he still loves to do today, and often does at the hermitage of St Spyridon, on the island of Halki. All this did not prevent him from highly successful study at the village school. But it was only an elementary school: what was he to do next, except work with his father?

It was at this point that the man intervened who would become his spiritual father and who would ensure his future, Metropolitan Meliton.

Meliton was then Archbishop of Imbros and Tenedos. He was an extraordinary man. He became the friend and closest collaborator of Patriarch Athenagoras, whom he would naturally have succeeded had he not been removed from the list of eligible candidates by the Turkish authorities. Becoming Metropolitan of Chalcedon and senior member of the Holy Synod, he brought new life to the patriarchate, until his death during the tenure of Dimitrios. He was short, of leonine features, endowed with a deep and quick intelligence. He was a brilliant improviser, able to discern the deeper trends in history. He played the role of prince of the Church with a simple majesty, ready to abandon it all at a moment's notice, asking forgiveness from simple believers.

On Imbros, Meliton was close to the simple faithful and knew them by name, a closeness for which he doubtless later grew nostalgic. He showed interest in the Archondonis family and took note of Dimitrios for his precocious intelligence. Having convinced the family to allow him to continue his studies, Meliton, at his own expense, sent Dimitrios to Istanbul. Soon, however, he opened schools on Imbros which taught the first three secondary years. Dimitrios returned to the island, where for three years he attended the school in Panagia. Each morning and each evening, he had to walk five kilometers. His inexpensive shoes wore out. Seeing this, the metropolitan gave him the present of a solid pair of boots. After Dimitrios had completed this first cycle, Meliton sent him to the patriarchal school of Halki, where a high school stood next to the faculty of theology.

Halki was a prestigious school located on a small island in the Sea of Marmara. In fact it comprised a whole flock of islands, which were once called the "islands of the princes" because, in the Byzantine era, disgraced princes were exiled here. Halki is an island about ten kilometers in length, with two pine-covered hills. A valley between them opens onto a small port, around which rises a village then dominated by corbelled wooden houses. Wealthy families from Istanbul spend their vacations here. With their shaded cafés, the docks are peaceful and carefree. Rapid boats provide ferry service to Istanbul, barely an hour and a half away. On the eastern hill, an old Greek school of commerce has become a naval school. On weekends, handsome midshipmen in spotless white uniforms come to make the crossing to the capital. On this hill overlooking the sea, one also finds the hermitage of St Spyridon, a saint from Corfu whom Patriarch Athenagoras, who was at one time metropolitan of this island, particularly loved.

On the western hill, just at the summit, sits the school of Halki. One reaches it on foot or by carriage (there are no cars on the island), following a trail which winds between the pines. Entirely white, the building which houses the school rises in the middle of a beautiful garden dominated by a bust of Ataturk, on which are inscribed the vigorous words he pronounced affirming the secular nature of the new Turkey and the value of knowledge. A school of theology, a high school, and a monastery surround a small church, which is reached by passing through an arbor. The iconostasis is made of carved wood, in a baroque style, highly elaborate, but framing sober icons.

For Dimitrios, Halki represents knowledge and friendship. To this day he cherishes a notebook into which he and his best friends copied out their favorite poems: Severis, Kabafy, Kostis Palamas, all the great poets of modern Greece. It is a small monument to beauty and friendship.

In 1961, Dimitrios Archondonis received, with honors, his licentiate in theology. On August 13 of the same year, he was ordained deacon by Metropolitan Meliton and given the name of Bartholomew, one of the Twelve Apostles.

From 1961 to 1963, he fulfilled his military obligation in the Turkish army at Gallipoli, completing his tour as an officer in the reserves.

Apprenticeship in Europe

From 1963 to 1968, Deacon Bartholomew, whose intellectual and moral qualities had so struck Metropolitan Meliton and Patriarch Athenagoras, received a scholarship from the patriarch to pursue his studies in Europe. He enrolled first at the Oriental Institute of the Gregorian University in Rome, then at the Bossey Institute in Switzerland, a school run by the World Council of Churches, and finally at the University of Munich, in Germany. Strongly inspired by the necessity of uniting Ortho-

doxy, he dreamt of systematizing eastern canon law. Back in
Greece, the best scholars had told him: To study canon law, go
to Rome and Munich!

Delayed until early December because of difficulties in obtaining a visa, he took up residence in the French seminary. With an
ear for languages, he effortlessly achieved a mastery of French.
Discreet and efficient, he gained numerous friends. The present
bishops of Aix-en-Provence, of Digne, of Saint-Claude, as well as
the rector of the Catholic University of Lyons, were among his
companions.

Pope Paul VI and Patriarch Athenagoras had just met in Jerusalem. Vatican II was in full swing, and the seminary welcomed
French bishops and theologians: Bartholomew Archondonis
crossed paths with Daniélou, Congar, and De Lubac!

With other students, he performed volunteer construction
work in the vicinity of Rome, notably at the residence of Father
De Foucauld's Little Sisters of Jesus, in Trefontana. It was difficult
work: their task was to level a hill on which the Little Sisters were
erecting small wooden houses. Bartholomew was touched by
their spirituality, which consisted of poverty, hospitality, discreet
assistance for those in great deprivation, making their witness by
their way of life rather than by their words. Later, in Istanbul, he
was to help their little community in that city.

At the Gregorian University, Bartholomew discovered, to his
great surprise, that courses were taught in Latin. He knew not a
word of the language. It was early December, and the first examinations were coming in February! It was a difficult moment. Near
despair, he tackled Latin on his own, learned it a word at a time
until he was able to follow the lectures, and successfully passed his
examinations two months later.

At the Bossey Institute, at that time directed by the late Nikos
Nissiotis, an important Greek theologian, he discovered an entirely different method of thought, an approach influenced by

trends in contemporary philosophy, particularly existentialism and personalism, open particularly to the mystery of the Holy Spirit. Finally, he went to Munich to finish off his formation in the discipline of canon law, but particularly, as the patriarch says today, to learn German.

He completed his doctorate at the Oriental Institute of the Gregorian University, writing a dissertation on "The Codification of the Holy Canons and Canonical Institutions in the Orthodox Church." His thesis was later published in 1970 by the Patriarchal Institute for Patristic Studies in Thessalonica. Two traits characterize his work: a sense of history and a concern for Orthodox unity. Bartholomew refuses to consider the canons as purely static. The literal sense of the canons can often no longer be applied. Rather, one must discern their spirit and the larger theological issues which they sought to apply to concrete, historical situations – situations which no longer exist. This is all the more the case because their content, applied at different times and places, is occasionally contradictory. New canons, applying the same principles in a modern context, are therefore necessary.

The essential goal would be to establish a single code of canon law for the Orthodox Church, systematizing whatever is common to all the autocephalous churches. Those elements belonging only to a single, local church, or to a group of such churches, would be placed in appendices.

At the Service of the "Great Church"

Upon his return to Istanbul, Bartholomew was named assistant to the dean of Halki. On October 19, 1969, he was ordained to the priesthood; and, soon after, Patriarch Athenagoras elevated him to the rank of archimandrite.

After the death of Athenagoras, Meliton and the other leading members of the Synod were removed at a distance from the patriarchal throne. Dimitrios, a simple bishop, was asked to accept the daunting task of Patriarch. Shedding tears, he refused, accepting only after numerous entreaties. But he needed assistance. He created a private patriarchal office, and Fr Bartholomew was placed at its head. From this moment, Bartholomew never left the patriarch's side. He accompanied the patriarch on his trips and composed his messages. He knew the world and spoke six languages (seven, if one counts Latin): Greek, Turkish, French, Italian, English, and German. He worked very closely with Metropolitan Meliton, who reinforced in him the sense of Constantinople's universal mission. On Christmas day in 1973, Bartholomew was consecrated bishop and made metropolitan of the ancient see of Philadelphia, in Asia Minor. On January 14, 1990, after Meliton's death, he was elected Metropolitan of Chalcedon, thus becoming the senior member of the Holy Synod.

At the same time, his ecumenical role took shape. He became a member, then, for eight years, the vice-president of the Faith and Order Commission of the World Council of Churches, the only commission in which Roman Catholics participate fully. It is undoubtedly in the Faith and Order movement that substantial ecumenical reflection has made the greatest real progress over the last twenty years. Bartholomew was vice-president during the development of the BEM ("Baptism, Eucharist, and Ministry") document, whose chief points are derived not only from Scripture, but also from the tradition of the undivided Church, while difficulties and divergences are clearly and faithfully exposed, in order to invite further reflection.

Bartholomew participated in the Council's General Assemblies. At Canberra in 1991, he was elected to the Central Committee.

A year earlier, in 1990, he chaired a meeting of the Inter-Orthodox Commission preparing for the Pan-Orthodox Council. At this meeting, he initiated discussions aimed at resolving the difficult problem of the *diaspora*, in which, for ethnic and political reasons, "jurisdictions" had multiplied.

Patriarch

After the death of Dimitrios in October 1991, Bartholomew, as *locum tenens*, presided over the Synod. In the name of the Synod, he informed Ankara about the death of the patriarch and presented a list of eligible candidates. Then came a period of uncertainty. One morning three weeks later, as the Synod sat in session, the answer came: we object to no one, do whatever you wish. There was great excitement. Bartholomew restored order and requested a review of the current situation. Only that afternoon did the Synod gather in the patriarchal church to conduct the election. Bartholomew was elected unanimously. He was 51.

Enthroned in the same church on Saturday, November 2, 1991, he pronounced a speech in which he took the measure of his destiny. All is centered on the mystery of the Cross. From the hands of Dimitrios, he said, he takes up "the cross of Andrew, 'the first-called,' to continue the ascent toward Golgotha in order to be crucified in our Lord and in his crucified Church, to perpetuate the light of the resurrection." We have no refuge other than "the mercy of the Lord, whose grace we implore so that he may permit us to manifest his strength in our weakness."[1]

He also affirmed the historical mission of the patriarchate: "The service and the witness of Orthodoxy and the building up of Christian unity." It is a ministry which, fully respecting "the conciliarity through which the Spirit speaks to the Church,"[2] concerns "the totality of the Orthodox Church in the entire world."

"A loyal citizen subject to the law of our country," the new patriarch stressed that the institution for which he was now responsible "remains purely spiritual, a symbol of reconciliation, a force

1   Cf. 2 Cor 12:9.
2   Cf. Rev 2:7, taken up again in vv. 17 and 29, and in 3:6, 13, 22.

without weapons," which "rejects all political goals and maintains its distance from the deceiving arrogance of secular power."[3]

Turning "in a spirit of communion" to "his brother primates," Bartholomew promised "to take up with them a collegial responsibility," because it is vital that a solidly unified Orthodoxy be able to bring its effective witness "to a world which is torn apart, and yet aspires to unity and reconciliation as, perhaps, never before in history." For this world, the example of a Church which is at the same time one and diverse could be essential. Humanity has suffered so much in this century: it aspires to a word of truth—not only about God, but about "man as the image of God," about "the universe as God's creation." The constant theme: "Orthodoxy can offer much, much more" to contemporary humanity.

And Bartholomew offered "his kiss of peace and love" to the primates of the non-Chalcedonian churches, whose faith "is so close to our own," as well as to the pope, to the primates of the Anglican and Old-Catholic Churches, to the heads of all other Christian churches, and particularly to the World Council of Churches.

The new patriarch stated his intention to forge good relations with "the principal non-Christian religions" in order to preserve the values of authentic civilization.

Turning finally to those of the atheistic world, whether hostile or indifferent to Christianity, he proposed dialogue, because it is "precisely to them" that he wishes to transmit "the witness of the love of Christ, who left the ninety-nine sheep to seek the one that was lost." "It is precisely for them," he specified, "that Christ was crucified."

In order to evangelize—and how can one not do so?—one must oneself accept "to be constantly re-evangelized." In this way, one is able not to repeat, but to "interpret the Orthodox tradition in the context of our own era."

3   Mt 7:15.

At both the beginning and end of his speech, Bartholomew repeated the saying of St John Chrysostom: "Glory to God for everything." He concluded with the affirmation of St John the Evangelist: "God is love."[4]

On All Fronts

Since that time, the Patriarch has taken initiatives in all of the above directions. He has maintained good relations with the Turkish authorities, even as he has tirelessly campaigned for the reopening of the theological school on Halki.

He has multiplied efforts to strengthen and express Orthodox unity. On March 22, 1992, on the "Sunday of Orthodoxy" (the day on which the Church celebrates the restoration of the veneration of icons in 843—the icon which depicts humanity transfigured), the patriarch convened the primates of the autocephalous Churches at the Phanar for a "Synaxis." All concelebrated at the eucharist, "meeting one another face to face, exchanging the kiss of peace and love, sharing in the Cup of life [...], thus receiving from God the gift of Orthodox unity." All expressed the desire to confront contemporary problems "as one body," and "to account for the hope that is in us"[5] with humility, love, and courage.

Facing the ruins of ideologies which enclosed humanity in on itself, Orthodoxy must witness to humanity as consisting of spiritually free persons, created in the image and likeness of God. In the relations between Churches, faced with certain unfortunate initiatives on the part of Rome and the frantic proselytism of fundamentalist Protestants, a distinction needs to be made between proselytism, which ignores the "other," and genuine evangelization, which collaborates with him.

Europe, presently in the process of unification, must not forget or underestimate its Orthodox component. The Synaxis condemned

4   1 Jn 4:16.
5   1 Pet 3:15.

"the fratricidal confrontations between Serbs and Croats in Yugo-slavia," and particularly the use of religious sentiments to further political or national passions. It called for peace in the Middle East.

A new Synaxis, unfortunately not fully representative, gath-ered on Patmos in late September 1995, to commemorate the 1900th anniversary of the writing of the Book of Revelation.

Between the two assemblies, Bartholomew exchanged numer-ous visits with primates of the autocephalous and autonomous churches. The Patriarchs of Serbia and Georgia, Archbishop John of Finland, and official delegations from the Churches of Russia, Romania, and Greece came to the Phanar. In July 1995, the patri-arch received Archbishop Anastasios, an exceptional figure who is primate of the Orthodox Church in Albania. Anastasios is pro-foundly evangelical, a man of great culture, with a significant knowledge of Buddhism. He played a major role in the Patriar-chate of Alexandria, organizing the young Church of Kenya, and the Phanar recently sent him to Albania to rebuild a church which was nearly destroyed during the Communist era.

Bartholomew, in turn, tirelessly visited the various Orthodox churches: in 1993, Alexandria, Sinai, Antioch, Russia, Serbia, Ro-mania, Bulgaria; in 1994, Georgia; in 1995, Jerusalem. But the newly independent countries born out of the disintegration of the Soviet Union created severe tensions between Constantinople and Moscow (hence the absence of Patriarch Alexis II from the Synaxis convened on Patmos in September 1995). Bartholomew was able to allay the Estonian crisis for the moment by the application of "economic" means that violated ecclesiological principles.[6] And

6   Eastern Estonia, largely Russian-speaking, was evangelized in the 12th century by missionaries from Novgorod and Pskov. Western, coastal Estonia, however, where Orthodoxy also developed but which today uses the local language, belonged for much of its history to the Baltic sphere, from which the Russian Empire removed it late in history, thus allowing its integration into the Church of Russia. In 1923, when Estonia became independent, its church asked for and received the protection of Con-

sooner or later, the question of Ukrainian autocephaly will arise again.

At the same time, the patriarch visited the churches under his own jurisdiction: Imbros, and his native village, in June 1992; Mount Athos and the Church of Crete in the same year; the Archdioceses of Scandinavia and Germany in 1993; those of Dodecanesus and Belgium in 1994; the Church of Finland in 1995, and the French Metropolia at the end of that same year.

A second front involves ecumenical dialogues. At the Phanar, Bartholomew received the Archbishop of Canterbury, Patriarch Paul of Ethiopia, Konrad Raiser, the new Secretary General of the World Council of Churches, as well as official delegations from the World Lutheran Federation and, with regularity, from the Church of Rome. In 1993, he visited the Lutheran Church of Sweden and the Catholic and Evangelical Churches of Germany. In January 1995, he paid a return visit to the Patriarch of Ethiopia. In May of the same year, he traveled to Norway for the millennium of its conversion to Christianity. In July, rejecting as always any "anti-Catholic hysteria" and keeping open the dialogue with the great sister-Church, he visited Pope John-Paul II. At St Peter's, he pronounced, in Italian, a stern and austere homily about humility and service and, in a joint communiqué, defined the ways and means for real rapprochement.

stantinople, becoming an autonomous church under the Ecumenical Patriarchate. This situation lasted until 1944, when Estonia was forcibly integrated into the Soviet Union and its church to the Patriarchate of Moscow. An Estonian Church in exile was subsequently created in Sweden by Estonian refugees, while the Soviet authorities supported Russian immigration and the russification of the land. With the restoration of Estonian independence, the problem of the status of the Church of Estonia arose once more. On February 20, 1996, Constantinople restored the autonomous status that prevailed between the two World Wars. Moscow responded by breaking off communion. On May 16, 1996, after difficult negotiations, Constantinople and Moscow agreed "to allow the Orthodox in Estonia freely to choose their ecclesiastical jurisdiction." This was "by extraordinary dispensation," because Orthodox ecclesiology requires local unity of all in the eucharist and the bishop.

A third front, where the spiritual must enlighten the temporal, is that of European restructuring. Bartholomew has never ceased to affirm that Europe cannot be reduced to Western Europe alone, born out of Rome and the Reformation. There is, he insists, another Europe, which is no less indispensable for the harmony of the continent. This is the Europe born out of Christian Hellenism, spawned by Orthodoxy, but which at first Communism, and then a paranoiac nationalism, have deformed and continue to mask. Here, he affirms, is to be found a culture incessantly crushed by history, but whose embers, never extinguished, can burn again if fanned by the wind of the Spirit. Far from being the enemy of the West, this East-European culture can perfect the West by means of a Christianity that successfully combines the sense of mystery with that of freedom, the sense of personhood with that of communion, and can decipher the "vertical" dimension of creation in the radiance of the divine energies. Three times Bartholomew has met with Jacques Delors, in May 1993 and twice in 1994 (in Strasbourg and Brussels); in November 1994, he also met with Jacques Santer, Delors' successor as head of the Commission for European Union. In addition, the patriarch, even though he is not, like the pope, a head of state, was invited to address the European Parliament on April 19, 1994. Alluding at the beginning of his speech to the Bosnian drama, Bartholomew condemned all fanaticism and violence, reminding his audience that, just a few weeks earlier, he had convened in Istanbul a group of Christian, Jewish, and Moslem leaders from the Balkans and the Middle East for a conference on "Peace and Tolerance." This conference prepared the "Bosphorus Declaration," which stated that any war waged in the name of religion was in fact a war against religion!

The building of European unity—of the "cathedral of Europe," said the patriarch—involves more than just economy and defense. It requires also a search for a "new cultural order," a "new consciousness." Serious problems such as unemployment and ecology require fundamental cultural and spiritual choices, and not simply political or economic ones. To overcome a frenzy of consumption and blind obedience to the rules of productivity, a new model of civilization is needed, a civilization of being and faces, of being as communion: the rediscovery, by a humanity that has become overly technological, of the divine and cosmic depths of existence. This was the speech of a visionary, and it concluded with an invocation to the Holy Spirit.

The patriarch is constantly preoccupied with the need for a new Christian ecology. While his predecessor, Dimitrios, had made September 1, the opening of the liturgical year, the "feast of creation," Bartholomew initiated a collaboration with Prince Philip, Duke of Edinburgh, who created the World Fund for the Preservation of Nature. The Prince came to the Phanar in 1992, and the Patriarch visited him in Buckingham Palace in November of 1993.

The last front concerns interfaith dialogue. In November 1994, the Patriarch addressed the world conference of the "Religion and Peace" Association, assembled in Riva del Garda, Italy. Amidst the ruins of our tragic century, he said, the heart of humanity still beats, the spirit (should this word be capitalized?) emerges. But we must be watchful. The world is tired of the fanaticism which, here and there, rears its head. The hunger for spiritual life is great, and we must respond. Witnesses to what is essential must abandon their cloisters to bear their witness and to act among humanity. They must again take up Jesus' injunction in the lengthy teaching reported by Matthew at the beginning of his Gospel: "Beware of false prophets, who come to you in sheep's clothing but inwardly are ravenous wolves."[7] Today's false prophets are the drug dealers, the leaders of sects who entice the unaware, the folly of nationalism, religious extremism leading to terrorism, wars without end, hunger—and here Bartholomew develops a reflec-

7   Mt 7:15.

tion by Berdiaev that "bread, for me, is a material problem, while for others, it is a spiritual one." The "developed" world administers and distributes material wealth in an unjust and often criminal manner. It is therefore imperative that we denounce and discredit the false prophets and heal the ills of our peoples. In the words of Rabbi Hillel: "If not us, then who? If not now, then when?"

In April 1995, the patriarch set the tone at the International Colloquium on "Religions and the Preservation of Nature," assembled in Atami, Japan. He manifested an excellent knowledge of Judaism and Islam, twice citing the Koran at some length.

In May of the same year, while visiting the Patriarch of Jerusalem, he was received by leaders of state, among them Ezer Weizman and Itzhak Rabin, as well as Yasser Arafat. Bartholomew had the sensitivity to evoke both the destiny to martyrdom of the Jewish people and the suffering of the Palestinians. He made himself the messenger of mutual understanding and peace between "the children of Abraham, the faithful of the three monotheistic religions, who confront each other here in a fratricidal conflict which breaks our heart." And he knew as well the importance of promoting Mediterranean unity, the need to develop the southern shore of the Mediterranean and to rediscover the common values of the various cultures along the shores of this sea.

Between Glory and the Abyss

As a person, the Patriarch is full of contrasts, complementary facets of a strong personality. He is frail, willful, kind and discreet on the one hand, active and enterprising on the other. Unassuming, almost timid, yet, when necessary, he can be domineering. He reveals a sharp sense of humor, but with a sober and determined sense of his mission. He is rigorous, attentive to detail, yet wisely visionary.

He is of medium height, with a clear face remarkable for its fine features, and particularly for the piercing blue eyes behind large glasses. Simultaneously young and old, he unites the modern culture which glorifies youth with a traditional culture whose ideal was the "noble old man." As patriarch, he grew a convincing, almost white beard. His hair has turned white—he must have been blond, or auburn, one cannot now say. His face is now crowned with white. What is striking is an extreme refinement—physical, as well as moral—such that, despite the kindness of the eyes and of the smile, one feels rather dull and awkward in his presence.

He loves art, poetry and nature. Whenever possible, he takes refuge on Halki, in refreshing solitude, to reflect and to work in peace. He detests ritualism, preferring brief and meaningful celebrations. He appreciates the virile sobriety of Byzantine music, and takes care to see that the doors of the iconostasis always remain open.

He loves children and knows how to speak with them, to amuse them, to offer them sweets or small change. "They preserve something of paradise," he says.

He has the gift of friendship. He remains faithful to friends made at school, during his military service, at Halki and in Western Europe, and to those he has met on his trips. He maintains a regular correspondence with them. At a time when the Phanar appeared to Muslim Turks to be a mysterious and hostile place, a source of plots against the country, he was able to strengthen ties of friendship with Muslims in positions of responsibility in business, politics, culture, and journalism. He has opened the doors of the Phanar to them, invited them in, brought some of them along on his journeys. He dreams of reconciling Greece and Turkey, but the difficulties are great and a fundamentalist press often denounces his amicable gestures. Yet he does not become discouraged.

He works hard—in fact he is an indefatigable worker. He has an exceedingly strong sense of responsibility for Orthodoxy in the world of today and tomorrow. The unwieldiness and divisions of the Orthodox Church weigh heavily in his heart. He longs to see "an ecclesial consciousness freed from all ideological structures and from a passive retreat into institutional formalism." He knows that human beings are inseparable from one another, "without respect to race, gender, religion, ideology, because it is for us all that the God who created us has become incarnate, even to the Cross," and who, in himself, raised everyone and everything. He knows also that it is necessary to respect the entire human being, and therefore also the earth which humanity represents and to which it can communicate God's grace. These, he affirms, are the criteria for evaluating life and Christian conduct in the world, both for individuals and for churches.

Orthodoxy is a witness soiled by history, but nevertheless a witness of the undivided Church, a call to the undivided Church, both one and diverse, in the image of the Trinity.

The task is immense and, as he well knows, it is not without risk. Bartholomew stands "between glory and the abyss," a friend who admires him whispers to me. More exactly, he stands between the Cross and the Resurrection.

Serving in Communion

When Bartholomew reflects on his role, he defines it as follows (I summarize here his writings and his words):

The Ecumenical Patriarch has the task of watching over the universal character of Orthodoxy, to manifest its unity and, when necessary, to provide the necessary impetus in this direction. In the words of St Ignatius of Antioch, the primate must "preside in love," or rather, "toward love." It is for this reason that the patriarch has tirelessly visited and consulted with all the Orthodox churches, that he has assembled, and hopes again to assemble, all their primates. The Patriarch of Constantinople is *primus inter pares* in the episcopate of the Church. He is responsible for coordinating the sister-churches. The great collection of canon law in Greek, the *Pedalion*—a word meaning "rudder"—has the following definition: "The task of the patriarch is to oversee teaching and, without hesitation, to consider himself the equal of all, both great and small." At his enthronement as Ecumenical Patriarch, Bartholomew declared that, in truth, "the immense task assumed by the Patriarch of New Rome, as well as the many temptations and opposing tendencies he must combat, require that he be experienced in steering this great ship." He is the equal of all, or rather, the servant of all. And this is not simply a rhetorical expression, as so many formulas in Christianity have become! As the patriarch recalled in his homily at St Peter's in Rome, pastors must live in humility and repent of the temptation to power because, as Christ has said, "This type of demon can be cast out only through prayer and fasting." Primacy is a ministry of service, a ministry of crucifixion: one must seek not to be admired by men, but to please God. If the primate's words do not bring life, they become mere talk that betrays the Gospel. Orthodoxy must be "orthopraxy"; if it is not, it becomes merely a proud Pharisaism. If we understand something of what the monks say, that is, the ability boldly to take responsibility, we discover that sins, errors, and the sufferings of the brother weigh upon each of us, and that each is responsible for all. Such is the task of the primate, in the double sense of both duty and burden: to be responsible for one's brother. For one cannot be saved alone; one is saved with all humanity and with the whole universe. Referring to his disciples, Christ said to his Father: "As you have sent me into the world, so I have sent them into the world. And for their sake I consecrate myself, that they also may be consecrated in truth" (Jn 17:18-19). "Yes, he, the Lord who is without sin, said this! How much more must the primate—sinner that he is—purify and consecrate himself in his humble service!" In the Epistle to the Philippians, we read that

Christ "did not count equality with God a thing to be grasped, but emptied [*ekenosen*] himself…" (2:6-7). This is what theologians call "kenosis." When he reveals himself, our God does not appear in the fullness of his glory, which would crush us, but as an overture of love in which the "other," the human person finds his or her vocation and freedom. In this way we too, who are in the image of Christ, are called to act, so that the "other" might be saved, *so that the "other" might truly be.* Primacy therefore does not consist of power, but of a "kenosis" which seeks only to bring life to others. His predecessor, the gentle Patriarch Dimitrios, says Bartholomew, was a true incarnation of Christ's humility, that humility which the Church must put on if it wishes to be among men what it is in its eucharistic essence: the community of the *anawim*, the poor people of Christ.

This is why the patriarch must try to consecrate himself to the Lord and to his Altar. He is to serve the Lord and the people who belong to the Lord. The patriarch must be crucified in a crucified Church, so as to be resurrected with all in the resurrected Church. As St John has shown, the Cross and the Glory are one and the same; Holy Friday and Pascha are inseparable. As Jesus says,

> The kings of the Gentiles, exercise lordship over them; and those in authority over them are called benefactors. But it is not so with you; rather, let the greatest among you become as the youngest, and the leader as one who serves. For which is the greater, one who sits at table, or one who serves? Is it not the one who sits at table? But I am among you as one who serves! (Lk 22:25-27)

The primate must ceaselessly earn an authority which consists not of power, but of the capacity, in the original sense of the word "authority" (which comes from the Latin verb *augere*, to "cause to grow"). He must submit himself to all life, to make it grow to its fullness. The Ecumenical Patriarch always acts in communion, be-

cause it is communion that he must promote. He can do nothing
without the agreement of all the churches; he cherishes as invalu-
able the conciliarity through which the Holy Spirit speaks to the
Church.

Already in his enthronement speech, Bartholomew declared:

> United by a common faith, around the same chalice and in
> the love which inspires faith, we face our venerable brother
> primates and promise to assume a collegial responsibility
> with them in order to bear witness in the midst of a divided
> world which aspires to unity and to reconciliation, perhaps
> as never before in history.

This manifestation of communion knows no limits. The patriarch must be an "ecumenical watchman," who prays and works
tirelessly for the unity of Christians. Beyond that, he witnesses to
and fights for peace among all men—among all cultures, all faiths.

For, the Patriarch affirms, we all belong to one single human
family and have the same celestial Father. Christ bears all humanity within himself. We should remember the Parable of the Last
Judgment in Matthew's Gospel. The symbolic "King" calls those
on his right hand "blessed of the Father," because "I was hungry
and you gave me food, I was thirsty and you gave me drink, I was
a stranger and you welcomed me, I was naked and you clothed
me, I was sick and you visited me, I was in prison and you came to
me." And in response to their wonderment, he explains: "Truly I
say to you, as you did it to one of the least of these my brethren,
you did it to me" (Mt 25:34-40).

✳ ✳ ✳

The patriarchate is located in Turkey. Bartholomew affirms
that he is a loyal citizen of this country which, he says, is his
own and is dear to him. It is a modern, secular state in which
Jews and Christians of all confessions coexist with a Moslem
majority. The Greek-Orthodox minority consists of citizens

who are well-integrated in the Turkish democratic state. Moreover, Turkish hospitality is traditionally generous. In the patriarchal residence, one sees a mosaic representing Mohammed II, the Conqueror, with Patriarch Gennadios Scholarios concluding an alliance guaranteeing the religious rights of the Orthodox. The patriarchate is an institution whose nature is purely spiritual. In Turkey itself, its usefulness in promoting spiritual values common to both Christians and Moslems is incontestable. It does not meddle in politics. But this does not at all prevent it from sharing the pain of individuals and peoples who have been victimized by history.

The patriarchate is itself a victim of history. It suffers the consequences of the poor relations between two countries, Greece and Turkey—countries which, nonetheless, are condemned to live together, whose peoples resemble one another, having been forged together in the crucible of the eastern Mediterranean. Certain Greek words have been adopted into Turkish, and vice versa. The domes of the great mosques of Istanbul imitate those of Hagia Sophia. In music, one finds the same mellismatic patterns. Not to mention the cuisine! Good relations were in part destroyed during the Cypriot crisis. The Orthodox population of Turkey served as hostages. Now those relations are further threatened by the Bosnian drama and disputes over the Aegean Sea. As a result, the Greek-Orthodox population of Istanbul has been vastly reduced. Fifty years ago, it consisted of more than 100,000; today, no more than 5,000 remain. The theological school on Halki remains closed (although attempts are being made to reopen it). Who will keep the patriarchate alive? The rise of fundamentalist Islam worries all the democratic forces in the land. In 1993, the Orthodox cemetery of Neochorion, as well as other cemeteries, were desecrated. Ironically, the Turkish press accuses the patriarch of harboring sympathy for Greece, while the Greek press accuses him of favoring Turkey. Yet he desires nothing but reconciliation and peace… Move out of Istanbul? That, he says, is out of the question. The patriarchate has never left this city, save for a 57-year period in the 13th century, when the city was occupied by the Latins and the patriarch took refuge in Nicea. To move to Thessalonika or to Patmos today would be to identify the patriarchate with Greece, whereas it stands above any nation. In this sense, Bartholomew considers it a blessing to be located in a country with a secular constitution and a Moslem majority. Istanbul is at the crossroads of the world, a bridge between Europe and Asia, between East and West, Christianity and Islam. And the patriarchate considers it also as a bridge between peoples, rejecting all walls of division.

Certainly, the Patriarch does not wish to conceal his obviously precarious situation, which seems to him to coincide with the spirit of the Gospel. It is wrong to think that spiritual witness needs wealth and power. Just look at the monks, he says: the more they live in poverty, the more they fast—not only from food, but from our illusions and follies—the more room they make for the power of the Spirit, the more they shine, in the invisible world as in the visible, within the hidden depths of history.

PART II

Aspects of a Message

4

Understanding the Faith

Crucifixion, Resurrection

If there is one point on which the patriarch insists, it is that Orthodoxy cherishes and venerates the humanity of Christ, but never separates it from his divinity. In Christ, God himself comes to us in order to vanquish death and to open for us the way to divinization. The incomprehensible mystery of the incarnation of God, which inspires both awe and love, brings meaning, hope, and the possibility to overcome passions to a humanity obsessed with anguish and emptiness. The mystery of the incarnation determines our theology, for Christianity is not a system but *Someone*. In particular, the incarnation passes judgment on our behavior, our behavior as Christians. We are always so quick to condemn others, while we are in fact the ones truly responsible for everything that has happened in the world since the coming of Christ. The meaning and goal of the incarnation is nothing other than the life-giving Cross, which, the Fathers affirmed, is the only "theologian." On the Cross, the God-made-man descends fully into our broken state, into our hopelessness, to our daily experience of hell and death. He offers something vital of himself, the humanity which he bears, and for this reason we are affected. He offers it to the Father, the First Principle, the unfathomable source of divinity, who is that abyss into which the religions of Asia never cease to delve. But he, the Christ, reveals it to us as a *paternal* abyss from whom, through Christ, we obtain love and freedom. "*Abba*, Father," he says—a word of incredible, childlike boldness. He makes his offering at the very moment when he assumes our most terrible agony—the agony of Job, and perhaps even Job's revolt—as he cries out: "My God, my God, why have you forsaken me?" Then everything is transformed. For even the agony, even the revolt, becomes an offering: in Christ, human freedom finally adheres to the will of God. On Gethsemane, it is "Not what I will, but what you will,"[1] and on Golgotha, "Father, into your hands I commit my spirit."[2] The psalm of despair which Jesus cries out—for such is the first verse of Psalm 22, *Eli, Eli, lama sabachthani?*—becomes a psalm of praise. Then the abyss of death and hell is destroyed, like a minuscule drop of hatred in the infinite depths of love. The Spirit pours forth with the water and the blood from the pierced side of Jesus—the water of baptism, the blood of the eucharist, say the Fathers and as the Gospel of John already suggests. For this reason, as the patriarch stressed in reference to his episcopal service, St Paul dared to apply the notion of "kenosis," of "self-emptying," to the God-made-man, and even to God himself. "God is love," St John declared: "kenosis" transposes into history this eternal movement of love which Jesus reveals at the very heart of divinity. "In the beginning was the Word, and the Word was with [toward] the God [the use of the article before God indicates the Father], and the Word was God."[3] This is an attraction in love of the "Other" for the One, assuming all of humanity through the Cross, which the *Didache*, one of the most ancient Christian documents, calls "the sign of the ecstatic attraction [*epektasos*]."[4]

This is why, Bartholomew notes, the word of the Cross is, for most people, scandal and folly. But for us who are weak and so

1   Mk 14:36.
2   Lk 23:46.
3   Jn 1:1.
4   16:6.

few, it is the power of life—and not only for us, but through us, through the Church, for all humanity.

On Easter morning, after the victorious descent of Christ into Hades, the uncreated light poured forth from the tomb in the form of a Bridegroom, radiant with the beauty of the Resurrection.

As in the early Church, Pascha, or Easter remains at the center of the faith and the worship of Orthodox Christianity. All our liturgy, our entire theology, is centered on this victory which Christ has won, and never ceases to win, over death and hell—a victory which *is* Christ himself, and which we are all called to share with him.

Yes, the resurrected Christ raises us, for he carries all humanity within himself: Christ who is not broken, who is pure "existence in communion." As we sing at paschal matins:

> Yesterday, I was crucified with Christ,
> today I am glorified with him.
> Yesterday, I was dead with him,
> today I unite myself to his resurrection.
> Yesterday, I was buried with him,
> today, I awake with him from the slumber of death.

Biological death—with all the partial deaths which precede it and tragically mark our existence—is from then on merely a *passage*, a "pascha" in the proper sense of the word. It is a passage in which we are filled with the resurrection to the measure of our faith, because the spiritual death which surrounds it and which it symbolizes has been abolished. Everything has a meaning, an eternal meaning. Gregory of Nyssa explains that "all humanity had to be recalled from death to life. God approaches our corpse, extends his hand to us who lie there... He gives our nature the impetus to rise from the dead."[5] Or again, "After snatching our being from death, he joined himself to it in order to deify it by his

5   *Great Catechesis* 32 (*PG* 45:80).

touch...Because his resurrection becomes for our mortal race the principle of our return to immortal life."[6]

The resurrection, therefore, does not consist in reanimating a corpse according to the categories of a fallen world. It consists rather in the radical transformation of those categories, the transfiguration of humanity and of the entire cosmos. Ever since Pascha—and it is always Pascha—it is no longer nothingness, but rather Spirit, a life of meaning, indeed, life itself, which is more powerful than death and which overturns its effects—all this comes to us through death and through the life-threatening conditions of our daily existence—if only, in humble confidence, we unite our life to the life-giving wounds of the Resurrected One.

For this reason, the only sin, according to St Isaac of Syria, is to pay insufficient attention to the resurrection. Humanity no longer needs to fear judgment or to "merit" salvation. It must only faithfully accept the love that brings resurrection. The decisive word here has been spoken by St Maximus the Confessor: "The death of Christ on the Cross is the judgment of judgment, the condemnation of condemnation."[7]

The Resurrection Is Already Present

Such is the originality of Christianity: it teaches not just the immortality of the soul, as did the great Greek philosophers, nor the resurrection of the dead at the end of time, as both Jews and Moslems correctly hope, but our resurrection in Christ, already here and now. Eternal life begins here on earth: "I know that I will not die," said St Symeon the New Theologian at the beginning of the ninth century, "because I feel the fullness of life surging within myself."[8]

6   *Ibid.*, 25 (PG45:68).
7   *Quaestiones ad Thalassium* 43 (PG 90:408).
8   *Sermon* 57.

Humanity and the world often experience the bitter taste of death, the patriarch observes. Our present century has seen this bitterness intensify to an unbearable extent. The slaughter of two World Wars and of revolutions, genocide, the Holocaust in particular, Nazi and Communist concentration camps, wars and famines have all left in us memories of horror, barbarity and absurdity. The isolated man, turned in on himself and on his precarious destiny, despite his obsession with security, seems doomed to follow either totalitarian ideologies or the preachers of self-idolatry. In so doing, he allows a perverse emptiness to invade the world, to disfigure nature, to compromise creation.

Yet man at all times, of all races and ages, has rejected death with all his being. Through love and beauty, but also through eroticism and drugs, he seeks life. Searching for it but not knowing where, seeking life but not finding it, he hates the very fact of existence, in himself and in others. Then comes the temptation to kill others and the self—suicide, the ultimate and absurd form of self-adoration! Yet it is precisely in the bitter heart of our nihilistic civilization that we must witness to the Resurrected One. To witness is to believe in life touched by eternity. Nicholas Fedorov, a 19th century Russian religious philosopher whom Bartholomew likes to cite, said that there is only one crime: consenting to die. In the resurrected Christ, we no longer agree to die, we no longer agree to kill others and ourselves. We walk, hand in hand, into "non-death," toward the day without end in the Kingdom. Tenderness, boldness, and the power of the resurrection are the hidden aspect of history, the hidden aspect of the world. Tears, blood, shame and heartbreak prevent us from seeing this. Yet it appears in the tranquil beauty of our liturgical worship. And, wherever we may be, a simple act of trust or kindness makes it perceptible.

The resurrection is the message of freedom, because death is the root of our enslavement which prevents us from loving, which turns our loves into something ephemeral and derisive. The hidden anguish of death, according to Maximus the Confessor, leads to the two "mother-passions": greed and pride. This is why all Christian life is rooted in the resurrection. Our confidence, our humility, our surrender to Christ have no other goal than to replace, deep within ourselves (in what the Bible calls the heart), the agony of death with the joy of the resurrection.

Despite its often miserable conditions, Orthodoxy lives and breathes an uninterrupted paschal faith; and this faith leads to communion, because the God whom the Resurrected One reveals to us is himself Communion.

Communion in God

God is communion and the source of all communion. This is the mystery which Tradition—in the third century in the West, the fourth in the East—has called Trinity, or rather, "Tri-unity."

In the Gospels, Jesus constantly affirms his unity with the First Principle, the Source of divinity, whom he calls his "Father." "No one knows the Son except the Father, and no one knows the Father except the Son and any one to whom the Son chooses to reveal him."[9] Jesus seems to exist only in this relation and, through the name *Abba*, he expresses his filial being.

The one God, therefore, is not a solitary God. So great is his unity—his "super-unity," according to Dionysius the Areopagite—that it carries within itself the very impulse of love.

At the same time, Jesus' own existence is existence in the Spirit, the Spirit of the Father, who rests on Jesus and is imparted by him. Luke's Gospel ascribes the conception of Jesus to the Holy Spirit, as well as the manifestations and words announcing or celebrating his birth. "The Spirit of the Lord is upon me,"[10] declares Jesus when he speaks for the first time in the synagogue. The Synoptic Gospels specify that he "leaps for joy" in the Spirit.

9   Mt 11:27; Lk 10:22.
10   Lk 4;18.

It is in the Spirit that Jesus prays, speaks, and acts, confronts the Devil, accomplishes the "signs" announcing and anticipating the Kingdom. "Being therefore exalted [i.e., raised and glorified] at the right hand of God, and having received from the Father the promise of the Holy Spirit, he has poured out this which you see and hear," says Peter in the Book of Acts.[11] The "Last Discourse," recounted by St John, contains a lengthy teaching about the Spirit. Jesus promises him as "another Paraclete" (advocate, defender, comforter) in whom he will remain present after his departure. "The Counselor, the Holy Spirit, whom the Father will send in my name, he will teach you all things, and bring to your remembrance all that I have said to you."[12] "He will bear witness to me."[13] On the evening of his resurrection, Jesus breathes the Holy Spirit upon the apostles. "Seated at the right hand of the Father" (spatial metaphors, of course, connote degrees of proximity), he intercedes before the Father so that Pentecost might arrive—or, rather, that the Spirit might blow freely in the unity of his Body. And in the Acts of the Apostles, the names of Jesus and of the Holy Spirit are interchangeable.

Each divine Person is not a part of the divinity, but a unique, incomparable way of being God, of receiving and giving unity. "Each Person contains unity through his relation to the others no less than through his relation to himself," says St John of Damascus.[14] Three is a "meta-mathematical" number which, while remaining identical to the One, signifies the infinite overcoming of opposition, not by being reabsorbed into the impersonal, but in the fullness of communion, where each, far from opposing, posits the others. The Trinitarian mode of life, in achieving plenitude, surpasses both the isolation of the one and the opposition or fusion of two. The fact that the Father is the inexhaustible source of

11 2:33.
12 Jn 14:26.
13 Jn 15:26; 16:13-15.
14 *On the Orthodox Faith* 2:8.

divinity and the principle of the Son and the Spirit does not in the least imply superiority. To his Word, his *alter ego*, the Father gives everything that he is, and he makes his Spirit to dwell upon him—this is the eternal anointing of the Son and also the Kingdom of the Father. "I am in the Father and the Father in me,"[15] said Jesus, and, addressing the Father: "All mine are yours, and yours are mine,"[16] and he in whom they love one another is the Holy Spirit, the breath that sustains creation.

"Come, let us worship the divinity in three persons, the Father, in the Son, with the Holy Spirit," we sing at a service on Pentecost,

> For the Father before all time engenders a Word who reigns eternally with him, and the Holy Spirit is in the Father, glorified with the Son—one single action, one single essence, one single divinity. This divinity we worship when we say: "Holy God," who has created everything through the Son with the cooperation of the Spirit; "Holy Mighty," through whom we have known the Father and through whom the Holy Spirit has come into the world; "Holy Immortal," the comforting Spirit who proceeds from the Father and dwells in the Son—O holy Trinity, glory to you!

God is thus a reciprocity of love, the love of the Three turned toward one another, each dwelling fully in the other two through the immobile movement of love called "perichoresis." It is possible to say that God is not just personal, but interpersonal, the patriarch affirms. He is not merely unity, but union in paternal Super-Unity. In him there are three "I-you" relationships. As Metropolitan John (Zizioulas) of Pergamum has pointed out, "The being of God is a relational being." It is striking that in their efforts to describe the tri-unity of God, the fourth-century Cappa-

15 Jn 14:11.
16 Jn 17:10.

docian Fathers, Basil the Great in particular, preferred the word *koinonia*, which means communion.

To say that God is Trinity is to say that he is love, that there is in him a life which is poured out on the world as a whole. The Spirit is the hidden, interior, immanent God, who almost identifies himself with our most personal existence, gives it its impetus, its ability to respond to the divine call. He leads us toward Christ, reveals him to us, allows us to say that "Jesus is Lord." If the Spirit is our breath, Christ is our brother, our secret companion and the fullness of transfigured humanity. In him all human potential blossoms before the bright rays of the Father, and therefore also in us, because we become brothers of Christ by adoption and are thus grafted members of his Body – "one single shoot with him," says St Paul. In him, in his image, as we face him, we little by little become what we truly are: persons in communion. To be in the image of God is to be in the image of Christ. In the Spirit, we can see in every human being the image of God, the Person who requires unconditional respect. And he leads us toward the Father, makes us adopted sons in the eternal Son. Standing before the mystery of the Father—at the same time unfathomable depth and perfect tenderness, absolute power and therefore absolute weakness in love—we can only stand in silence and pray without words. Certainly, the Bible tells us, the Father has a dimension of maternal mercy as well, but the paternal symbolism must ultimately be maintained, without forgetting the maternal, because our relationship with God consists not in fusion, but in communion.

A Trinitarian Anthropology and Ecclesiology

The Trinity is *at once* the source of all unity and of all distinction, whereas Asian religions place the accent on unity, and the modern West on distinction. It is because of the Trinity, wrote Dionysius the Areopagite, that "all things are both united and

distinct, identical and opposed, similar and dissimilar, that op-
posites can be in communion and that united elements escape
confusion."[17] Our understanding of humanity, as well as of the
Church, flows from the mystery of the Trinity.

In Christ, through the Holy Spirit, Trinitarian communion is
bestowed on humanity. "That they may all be one; *even as* you,
Father, are in me, and I in you, that they *also* may be in us," Jesus
prays.[18] The expressions *even as* and *also* are essential for our salvation, Bartholomew emphasizes. In Christ, we are all one body, all
"members of one another." And Christ favors each one, welcomes
each as a unique "you." The Spirit guarantees our communion—Paul's expression, "the communion of the Holy Spirit," is
found in nearly all Christian liturgies—but, at the same time, the
flames of Pentecost separate, and one tongue descends on each
person, as if to consecrate his unique character and to unfold the
infinite scope of his liberated freedom. Thus the person, created
but growing in a process of deification, only appears to be a part
of the universe and of humanity, a biological individual, socio-
logically conditioned in various ways. In the "divine light" which
illumines his inner being, the person transcends the world and society, not in order to abandon them but to liberate, enlighten, and
offer them up. Because the person is, in the image of God, both
Mystery and Love.

The patriarch continues: To be myself, I need you. If we do
not look one another in the eye, we are not truly human.

"Blessed is the Kingdom of the Father, and of the Son, and of
the Holy Spirit." The eucharistic liturgy begins with this Trinitarian proclamation. In the Church, man is called to understand
what he is, and therefore what he must be, through participation
in Trinitarian communion. Consider the symbolic representation
of the Trinity in the form of Abraham's hospitality, as we can see

17 *Divine Names 4:7.*
18 Jn 17:21.

particularly in the famous icon by Andrei Rublev. At the oak of Mamre, Abraham welcomes three "men," or three "angels." Genesis indicates that they are sometimes three, but also sometimes one, and that it is the Lord.[19] At the center of the composition, on the table, which has the appearance of the altar around which the Three are seated, lies a cup containing the food Abraham offers his guests and which, in stylized form, seems to represent the eucharist. Thus this icon evokes not just the Trinity, but also the Church. Each Person, or Angel, inclines with sacrificial tenderness toward the other two, thus emphasizing their equality and consubstantiality. In the Holy Spirit, the Trinitarian "unity in diversity" is inscribed in the "unity in diversity" of human persons. The Three, in Trinitarian communion, are one single God: in the Church, each person finds his unique, incomparable character in this "Unique Man," who is the Christ. In God, each of the Three is completely free in unity, i.e., in love. It is the same in the Church. There can be no contradiction—except inosfar as we betray the Church—between freedom and authority, between self-fulfillment and communion. It is not totalitarian collectivism, nor a divisive individualism, but a fundamental unity which is offered and always to be discovered, in the freedom of love. Such is the model we should offer to the world.

To become what we are sacramentally in Christ, led by the Spirit, to answer the call which defines us, is to be united with the self and with others by going beyond the self. The individual is ultimately a biological category subject to death. Personhood, on the other hand, even if it cannot clearly be discerned, is a spiritual category inseparable from God and from the neighbor. Love is part of the very structure of the person. This union of the particular with the universal constitutes the very mystery of the Church.

19 Gen 18:1-9.

The Church as Life in Christ

The Church is baptismal and eucharistic. Christ "gave himself up for her, that he might sanctify her, having cleansed her by the washing of water with the word."[20] "Go therefore and make disciples of all nations, baptizing them in the name of the Father and of the Son and of the Holy Spirit," Jesus enjoins his disciples at the end of Matthew's Gospel.[21] The Church has developed this Trinitarian formula in her confession of faith and given us baptism by triple immersion, with the water symbolizing both death and resurrection. The baptizand descends into death with Christ and rises with him, anointed with the Spirit, adopted by the Father. In a great "Paschal leap," he "puts on Christ." This is why, after emerging from the water, he is clothed with a white garment, the robe of light. "For as many of you as were baptized into Christ have put on Christ. There is neither Jew nor Greek, there is neither slave nor free; for you are all one in Christ Jesus."[22] The unity of humanity is restored, while at the same time a boundless personal dignity abolishes ethnic differences, social and gender-based inequality. And so we too must abolish them, because, in the New Testament, the indicative is nearly always an imperative as well. How can we fail see in this passage by St Paul the most positive goals of our civilization? Nothing impressed the society of Late Antiquity more than the sight of the coexistence, in perfect equality, of slaves and free, men and women of all ethnic backgrounds, within the Christian communities. Such was the seed which, little by little, grew and continues to grow in history.

Together with baptism, the eucharist makes the Church to be the Body of Christ in the most real sense. "The mystery of myster-

20 Eph 5:25-26.
21 Jn 17:21.
22 Acts 2:46.

ies," the eucharist properly constitutes the Church. Paul's expression, "the Body of Christ," is clearly eucharistic. Each eucharistic assembly sums up our faith and our hope, fully expresses the catholicity of the Church. Each eucharistic assembly—"at the awesome sacrificial altar," in the Patriarch's words—is the realization of the cave in Bethlehem, of the theophany at the Jordan, of the transfiguration on Mt Tabor, of the redemption of Golgotha, of the tomb from which emerges our common resurrection in anticipation of the Second and Glorious Coming.

When Jesus explains the meaning of the Last Supper, he identifies the bread with his Body, the cup with his Blood. Through them he offers himself "for many," thus fulfilling the biblical traditions of the Suffering Servant and the Son of Man, of whom Daniel speaks—each of these, as Metropolitan John (Zizioulas) of Pergamum has stressed, is a collective being, individual and multiple at the same time.

Communion with Christ and communion in Christ, therefore, also unite men and women, all humanity, among themselves. Those who know this, i.e., faithful Christians, offer thanks, serve, and witness "for the life of the world," so that all may, through the Holy Spirit, receive the resurrected life. Christ has put on not just an individual human nature, but *the* human nature; and the word "nature" here stands less for a concept than for mystical experience. Persons exist because, in their inexhaustible essence, they are founded on and enlightened by the divine-human person of Christ. It is in the eucharist that his "priestly prayer"—"That they may be one as we are"—is fulfilled. What is required of us is that we concretely realize, in our life and our death, something of that immense unity which creates us, which is offered to us, which calls us...

Orthodox ecclesiology in its entirety, therefore, flows from the mystery of Tri-unity. All the local churches, as eucharistic communities, are identified with the One Church. Episcopal conciliarity witnesses to this identity. And this identity is situated in the personal communion of all the faithful.

If one sees the Church from this Trinitarian perspective, then, as Bartholomew notes, the division among Christians becomes tragic indeed. For it contradicts the very nature of the Church. In searching for unity, the ecumenical movement does nothing else than reaffirm the consequences of our faith in the Trinity.

There is an evident connection—"...so that the world may believe," says Jesus[23]—between the unity of Christians in the image of the Trinity and the missionary vocation of the Church. The Church does not exist for itself, but for the salvation of the world. It truly expresses the mystery of the Trinity only when the bounds of its communion are ceaselessly being expanded. Faith in the Trinity calls us equally to social efforts in all areas, in interpersonal as in cultural relations, affecting both the neighbor and societal structures. For us, the social is sacramental, as St John Chrysostom pointed out when he showed that the "sacrament of the brother" was the indispensable extension of the "sacrament of the altar." As an old monastic saying, dear to the patriarch, puts it: "My brother is my life."

The Trinity is therefore the source that inspires all the cultural and social activity of Christians, all our fight against suffering, injustice, disease, and every form of death that ravages our civilization. Our battle for human rights, for the dignity of each human person, is waged in the name of the Trinity. "Our social program is the Trinity," says Nicholas Fedorov, quoted once more by Bartholomew.

Today as never before, in our age of both suffering and promise, we perceive Christ coming in all the creative power of the Spirit. This is expressed in what Nietzsche (though from a totally different perspective) called "joyful knowledge": inspiration, freedom, beauty, the transfiguration of the body and of the world.

23 Jn 17:21.

The Spirit who gives us the Father reveals him as a Liberator. The Spirit, of whom the Body of Christ is the repository, overflowing "for the life of the world," reveals to us a God crucified on behalf of all human suffering, in order to open for humanity the unexpected way of resurrection. One often has the sense that the drama of contemporary Christianity, weighed down by pietism, moralism, and, especially within Orthodoxy, by ritualism and a paganizing nationalism, is the "stifling of the Spirit." As a result, prophecy and efforts to achieve justice and beauty, which are the poetry of the cosmos, are called anti-Christian. As a result, they risk being either exhausted or perverted. The time is coming when Christianity, or Orthodoxy, will have to recover its prophetic power, and prophecy its sacramental roots.

Orthodox Ethos, Christian Ethos

The mode of being which makes Orthodoxy—i.e., Christianity, rooted in the undivided Church—not a "religion" like all others, but the very depth of life, is summarized in the Beatitudes.

> Blessed are the poor in spirit, for theirs is the Kingdom of Heaven.

The "poor in spirit" are those who have "simplicity of heart,"[24] because, in the Bible, the spirit is identified with the heart. They have been "converted," they have allowed grace to unite their hearts, to overcome that division, that ambivalence, which characterize fallen humanity. They have discovered the "other" as having an existence just as interior as their own. To be poor in oneself is to know that others exist.

Spiritual poverty is an awakening. It accepts the world as gift, rather than seeking to possess it as something it is due.

24 Acts 2:46.

Jesus does not tell the "poor in spirit" that the Kingdom of Heaven *will be* theirs, but that it *is* theirs. The word "heaven" is used as a title of respect to name the One who cannot be named, i.e., God. His Kingdom is his presence, the blazing forth of his "energies." In Christ, the Kingdom is opened for us: it is "among you," or "in you," Jesus tells us.[25]

> Blessed are the meek, for they shall inherit the earth.
> Blessed are those who hunger and thirst after righteousness,
> for they shall be filled.
> Blessed are those who are persecuted for righteousness' sake,
> for theirs is the Kingdom of Heaven.

Meekness, the meekness of the powerful, opposes destructive violence. It hungers and thirsts for justice and, if necessary, suffers for it, knowing that it is better to be persecuted than to persecute.

In the great biblical prophecies with which Jesus was raised, justice consists primarily of respect and service for the poor, the free sharing of riches with them. Today, this is a global need. Justice demands the voluntary reduction of personal wealth. It is sufficient to recall that 20 percent of the planet's population consume 80 percent of its resources and spend most of their time feeding their dogs and fighting obesity!

In the Gospel, justice consists of the resurrection communicated to others. While continuing to combat social and cultural inequity, it contagiously spreads respect and friendship in the ongoing life of the communion of saints. Christians, together with all persons of good will, must develop a new way. This is not the path of communism, which denies the freedom of the spirit, nor of liberalism, which scoffs at the suffering of souls and bodies. It is the path to communion. The patriarch cites Henri Bergson, the 19th century French philosopher, who affirmed that liberty and equality are contradictory, and that this contradiction can be

25 Lk 17:21.

overcome only through a large infusion of fraternity, which can come only from Christianity![26]

The Greek word for meekness also means humility. The word "humility" derives from "humus," that which makes the earth life-giving, fertile, allowing it to absorb air and water, to breathe. Humility therefore means not humiliation but fertility. Meekness purifies our greedy inclination, and therefore our scientific and technical efforts. It allows us to perceive the truth of this earth, which is both the Wisdom of God and creation's call for help, because "it suffers from the pangs of childbirth" and "impatiently awaits the revelation of the sons of God."[27] "Possession of the world" does not mean control, but efficacious contemplation. It means not just discerning the spiritual essence of things, their *logoi*, in the words of Maximus the Confessor, which is what monks and poets do, but also respecting, from a technical perspective, the rhythm and equilibrium of nature, working to embellish and spiritualize it. (It is well known that the patriarch is particularly interested in ecology.)

> Blessed are those who mourn, for they shall be comforted.
> Blessed are the pure in heart, for they shall see God.

Mourning means first of all an awareness that our heart is stone and that we need to break it. Our fears, our cares, our constant condemnation of our enemies upon whom we project our own dark side—all this conceals a fundamental anguish which, as the monks say, is laid bare by the tears of the "remembrance of death." Then, in the light of faith, at a yet deeper level, we discover the incarnate and crucified God who places himself for ever between ourselves and nothingness. Finally come tears of thanksgiving, tears of joy.

26 Translator's note: This is a direct allusion to the French national motto, "Liberty, Equality, Fraternity."
27 Rom 8:10.

Washed by these tears, the depth of the heart wakens and becomes that bright eye which sees all things in God and is finally filled with the unfading light that comes from the Father, the light which illumines the face of Christ on the mountain, and is virtually identical to the life-giving Spirit.

> Blessed are the merciful, for they shall obtain mercy.
> Blessed are the peacemakers, for they shall be called the sons
> of God.

God is the one who gives beyond measure and who also forgives beyond measure. He continues to give even when we think that everything is lost, and that no more solutions are possible. As miserable as we might be, we can nevertheless continue to live by his mercy. So how could we not show mercy in return? Mercy is like an overflowing river. The Gospel condemns the merciless servant whose master forgives him an enormous debt, but who then demands repayment and seeks to imprison his fellow servant, who owes him a mere pittance.

These words are well-worn: "pity" and "mercy" today connote a degree of condescension. In actuality, they imply a sort of empathy—this is the exact meaning of the word "compassion"—a sharing in the other's suffering, healing it if that is within our power, leading the "other" on the path of redeemed, renewed life. For I am responsible for the "other."

And because we live only in relation to others, we are called to become "peacemakers." Peacemakers establish connections between people. They enable people to listen to each other with respect. They bring peace by redirecting violence into ascesis, creativity and beauty, even into forms of play, as in ancient Greece where everything became peaceful competition. When the resurrection replaces death deep within me, then I can attempt to "love my enemies," in accordance with the apparently paradoxical demand of the Gospel. "As you wish that men would do to you, do so to them... Love your ene-

mies, and do good, and lend, expecting nothing in return; and
your reward will be great, and you will be sons of the Most High;
for he is kind to the ungrateful and the selfish."[28]

> Blessed are you when men revile you and persecute you and
> utter all kinds of evil against you falsely on my account. Re-
> joice and be glad, for your reward is great in heaven...

Jesus adds: "For so men persecuted the prophets." It is the entire Church which is, or should be, prophetic, as Peter stressed on
Pentecost. The prophets anticipate the "upside down world" of
the Beatitudes. Persecutions, insults, calumny are like the shards
of broken glass that fly as the domain of death is smashed by the
onslaught of the Kingdom, or like the bark of trees pushed aside
by springtime buds. We shall have to fight against foolishness and
hatred, against the powers of nothingness, until the end of the
world. But for those who keep their courage—who know that the
glory and honor of the nations will enter the new Jerusalem—the
"heavens" will never cease to enter into the deepest recesses of
their being, into that "heart" which is called to "see God."

Orthodoxy lives by the joy of the resurrection much more
than by the agony of the Cross. Nevertheless, in the course of history, it has not escaped this agony. But it has been able to produce
persons of prayer who are able, in secret, to transform the suffering of history into the joy of the resurrection.

Icons

Perhaps it is the veneration of icons which, more than anything
else, best expresses this understanding of the human person
and the universe.

As was affirmed during the iconoclastic crisis, the incarnation
not only justifies, but demands the icon *par excellence*, the icon of

28 Lk 6: 31, 35.

Christ. This union without separation or confusion of the divine and the human is also expressed, with great tenderness, in the icon of the Mother of God. The icon of the Vladimir Mother of God, in particular, a Greek icon which has become the "defender" of Christian Russia, radiates with a sense of kindness which is at once sober and light This icon characterizes what one important Balkan novelist has called "tender Orthodoxy."

"When Christ who is our life appears, then you also will appear with him in glory."[29] The icon attempts to anticipate this appearance, toward which the entire life of the Church leads. It suggests what the world truly is beneath the ashes of our sins: the Body of Christ, the true "burning bush" on fire with the Spirit, in the words of St Maximus the Confessor.

Employing a soberly "transfigurative" art form, the icon places before our eyes a personal presence in the image of Christ that expresses the sacrament of divine beauty. This presence invites us to communion.

The icon reminds us that Christianity is a "religion of faces," in the words of a contemporary theologian. To be a Christian is to discover a face which always lives and loves, a face which comes to us in our greatest distress: the face of Christ. And in Christ, the face of the Mother of God, together with all those sinners who accept forgiveness: their faces do not judge, they welcome.

The icon teaches us to sense the "inner being" of the "other," his infinite depth, his secret being "hidden with Christ in God."[30] This secret appears on the face of a sleeping child, in the flash of a smile or in the gaze of friendship, in the peaceful look of some deceased persons—perhaps the sign of a true "dormition." The face thus becomes the luminous manifestation of a heart at peace.

The icon, and the entire Orthodox ethos, are linked to the momentous event of the Transfiguration, to those divine "ener-

29 Col 3:4.
30 Col 3:3.

gies" blazing from Christ and illuminating not only his face, but also his clothing—the work of human hands—and all surrounding nature. Ever since the Cross and Pascha, this light is no longer exterior to us, as it was for the three apostles on Mount Tabor. It now comes to us in infinite gentleness from the very depth of our being, which is grafted onto the glorified Body of Christ. We discover that all creatures and things are woven with this light. There is no more sacred or profane, but only that which is profaned and that which is sanctified: profaned by the opaque shadow of our hardened selves; sanctified by the omnipresent light of the transfigured Christ. The "religious" is no longer just an aspect of culture alongside others—economic, esthetic, or athletic!—but the very depth of existence.

✱ ✱ ✱

Excursus I

A Mystical Approach

One of the tasks of contemporary Orthodoxy seems to be to unveil its immense patristic tradition, both ascetical and mystical. This should be done not simply with an archeological or repetitive approach, but to reveal entirely new, and possibly salvific, perspectives.

Monks are the guardians and privileged witnesses of this heritage. But this treasure is of value to all of us.

This is a life-giving heritage, and we must attempt to express it in words that will resonate with the life experience of modern humanity. Only then will we come to understand the strikingly concrete character of Orthodox theology. We will learn also that liturgical beauty and peace are not simply fleeting emotions, but can open up paths of interior life for us.

Asceticism

The point of departure for the ascetic life is the passage from suffering to desire, or, to put it differently, from desire as a lack of something to desire as impetus.

Man is created in the image of God, an image whose goal is to attain the likeness of God. One is truly human only if one freely accepts this condition. But this fullness is constantly concealed from us. There develops a kind of mutually possessive link between man and the world. I constantly become my own idol, as St Andrew of Crete puts it. In this way, existence "according to nature" (nature is here inseparable from grace) falls into an existence "against nature," although it is preserved by the mercy of God. Human nature is divided: the image, with its flavor of paradise, is not eliminated. And it is precisely its deviated dynamism which engenders what the ascetical tradition calls the "passions." Passions are a form of idolatry, an obscure desire for God, but ignoring him, breaking itself against a wall of emptiness and getting up again by ascribing an absolute character to realities that are only relative.

There are two chief passions: the first, more irrational, concerns desire and power; the second affects the rational senses.

The first, irrational passion expresses itself in avidity, while the second, rational one, manifests itself as pride. Avidity and pride define a kind of metaphysical captivity which tends to twist reality around the *ego*, in order to control it but, inevitably, ends up being controlled by it.

Avidity leads to the perversion of desire, the objectifying of Eros, to debauchery, in which the other becomes simply an object. Avidity and debauchery engender avarice: one desires to possess everything. Avidity, debauchery and avarice engender sadness and envy: sadness that one does not possess everything and resentment toward those who have more than we do. Hence the desire for destruction, hatred and anger directed at the self and others.

Pride—the other enslavement which parallels the first—leads to vainglory, that narcissistic parade of enticements, and consequently to anger and hatred when one fails to obtain the adoration of others, as well as sadness, "a sadness for death," says Paul, that immense weariness, the taste of ashes left by passion when it is gone, and when one realizes that it did not exalt the self, but left only emptiness.

Finally comes forgetfulness, in the sense of spiritual insensibility. We lose our sense of awe, wonder and gratitude. Our hearts harden. Covered with dirt and filth they cease to be infinitely sensitive antennae.

Behind all this, Maximus the Confessor sees an anguish, "the hidden fear of death." We should write Death using the upper case, and our biological disappearance is but its expression, and perhaps even its remedy.

But this anguish—just like the nostalgia for paradise, so close to us in love and beauty, yet always lost—this anguish and nostalgia serve to awaken us, not yet to the light of faith, but to its shadow, where we dimly perceive the presence of Christ. The anguish then becomes the perception that we risk being swallowed up by "this world" in a web of illusions, platitudes, and emptiness. The anguish becomes a fear of God, preserving us from identification with the deadly game of "this world." And we discover, at a still deeper level, the presence of Christ. Despair no longer leads to nothingness; someone stands between us and the abyss. Then asceticism comes to liberate the dynamic quality of our true nature. Christ—if we turn toward him, if we make room for him—allows us, in his humanity united to his divinity, to pass from a condition which is against nature to one according to nature, one permeated by grace. This ascesis is a Christian ascesis, because it is the personal adhesion to a God who is both hidden and revealed. This ascesis opens the way to both confidence and humility. We must first adhere to Christ in all of our anguish, in all of our nostalgia, and even in all our inability to repent, to purify ourselves, or to pray: for he is our repentance, our purification, and our prayer.

St Isaac of Syria writes:

> O Lord, Jesus Christ, our God, by your sufferings heal my sufferings, by your wounds heal my wounds...Let your body stretched out on the wood of the Cross raise to yourself my spirit, which is crushed by demons...Let your holy hands, pierced by nails, snatch me from the abyss of perdition...Let your face which endured blows and spitting enlighten my face, which is soiled by unjust deeds...My heart is not broken enough to seek for you, I have no repentance, no mercy...I have no tears to pray to you. My spirit is in darkness, my heart is cold, I am unable to warm it with tears of love for you...I have abandoned you. Do not abandon me. I have alienated myself, come look for me. Lead me into your pasture, among the sheep of your fold...[31]

Humility, confidence, the attitude of the stammering child, interior poverty, deprivation—these are the true desert. Now comes the tremendous grace of the "remembrance of death"—always Death with the upper case. It is something resembling Sartre's "nausea," or Ionesco's "derision," turned not toward emptiness, but toward Christ. "Can a woman forget her sucking child, that she should have no compassion on the son of her womb? Even these may forget, yet I will not forget you. Behold, I have graven you on the palms of my hands" (Is 48:15-16). Then, through the Christ who has defeated death and hell—which is the absence of God ("My God, my God, why have you forsaken

---

31 *Oeuvres spirituelles* (Paris, 1981), pp. 67-68.

me?")—the remembrance of death become the remembrance of God. The anguish itself becomes confidence.

The remembrance of death and the remembrance of God develop in us that spiritual sensibility which expresses itself in sober emotion, ultimately in the gift of tears. These are at first tears of despair, but then, as we discover how greatly we are loved, tears of thankfulness and joy. Tears turn despair into hope. They prophesy. They signify the moment at which the soul and the body together, refusing the inevitable, exchange heart-rending words: "No," says Hagar, "I will not see this child die," when her little boy is about to die of thirst in the desert. Hagar weeps: a spring opens in her heart, a spring surges from the ground. And God comes to weep all our tears, to fill them with his light in order one day to dry all the tears from our eyes, as the Book of Revelation says. Jesus weeps before the dead Lazarus. He, the Living One, stands somehow on the outside. Lazarus represents the stench of rot. You have turned the image of God into rotting meat. Jesus saw the separation, the hatred, the lie—sin—of which these are the shadow. "Jesus wept." This is the shortest verse in the Bible. In Gethsemane, Jesus' entire body sweated blood. One could say that his entire body wept, wept tears of blood. Then follow the paschal Cross and the resurrection, of which the raising of Lazarus was a sign.

For this reason the heart can "repent" through tears. "Blessed are those who mourn, for they shall be comforted." Spiritual tears are linked with the coming of the Holy Spirit, the Spirit of resurrection, the Comforter. "God secretly consoles the broken heart."[32] The heart of stone is softened by tears, becomes a heart of flesh, infinitely vulnerable, infinitely consoled. a child who was lost and is now found, man smiles through his tears.

Metanoia means a change of heart, the transformation of our entire approach to reality. The resurrection, the grace of baptism

---

32 St John Climacus, *The Ladder*, step 7, 54.

can then develop in us, and we must remove all the obstacles which hinder this growth. True ascesis, an ascesis of humility and faith, consists of our *active surrender* to grace, which little by little strips us of our dead skin, our outward appearance and the roles we play, allowing us to breathe more deeply of the Breath of life.

Fasting and Wakefulness

According to the Fathers—and this is a theme which has become a part of the liturgy since the time of Romanos the Melode—Adam received the command to fast already in paradise. This was a voluntary abstention, out of total confidence in God, in order to overcome the temptations of avidity and pride, and to enable him to see the sensible world not as prey, but as eucharist. By fasting in the desert, Christ taught us not to nourish ourselves "by bread alone, but by every word that comes out of the mouth of God." Voluntary abstention allows us, in the words of contemporary psychology, to liberate, at least partially, the desire for need, so that it can be transformed into a desire for God, a hunger for a God who gives himself to us as food. Thus fasting is more or less the direct opposite of contemporary advertising, which sees the fundamental human desire as the multiplication of needs. And voluntary abstention further allows for a fairer distribution of resources, favoring the justice that love demands.

Fasting from food is of necessity linked to spiritual fasting, and vice versa: fasting from the desire for power, from vain rationalizations and vain words; in other words, from all patterns of thought which suppress the unifying power of love. One must fast particularly from slander, for, as one of Desert Fathers has said, the only sin is the desire to destroy the other, even if only in word, if only through scorn.

As for vigilance or wakefulness, it is first of all a sense of wonder before existence, before the sacrament of being. Art can be very helpful here. A child asks a painter: "Why are you painting this tree, since it is right here?" And the painter replies: "So that you can see it." As Jacob said after his vision, "God is holy, this place is holy, and I did not know it." According to Sergius Bulgakov, ever since the incarnation the whole earth becomes the holy grail which receives the blood pouring from the pierced side of Christ. Thus the Bridegroom comes to us, through the darkness of all that exists. Time is now pervious to eternity. The separation is not between the profane and the sacred, but between the old and the new, as Fr Schmemann liked to say: there is, as one who is watchful can see, only that which is profaned and that which is sanctified. The Kingdom is coming now, and in its light, a person who is awake and vigilant is able to perceive the neighbor as an icon. They can already perceive that Day on which, in the words of the prophet Zechariah, "there shall be inscribed on the bells of the horses, 'Holy to the Lord.' And the pots in the house of the Lord shall be as the bowls before the altar" (Zech 14:20).

From this perspective, the virtues are signs of a person restored and reestablished in its harmony and unity. The impulse of distorted nature, which leads to separation, causes the passions. The same impulse of a nature restored calls forth the virtues. All the Fathers insist on the fact that we are not asked to reject and eliminate our natural activities, but to purify them. "For nothing exists," says the Areopagite, "which cannot participate in the Good."[33] This is the transformation so aptly described by Maximus the Confessor:

> In a man whose entire spirit is turned to God, even lust gives strength to the burning love for God; even the violence of anger moves directly toward divine love. This is because the participation in the divine light, uniting all the force of the

33 *Divine Names*, in *Oeuvres complètes*, French trans. By M. de Gandillac (Paris, 1943), p. 111.

elementary powers, ultimately transforms them into a burning, insatiable love.[34]

This transformation is achieved through the integration of
man with the crucified and glorified humanity of Jesus. For this
reason, Maximus can also write: "*Christ is the essence of all the virtues.*"[35] The virtues are therefore both *divine and human*. Each of
them participates in a certain way in the presence of God, in a divine Name, in a divine energy which, through the mediation of
Christ's humanity, evokes a corresponding energy within
ourselves.

Little by little, therefore, man acquires the detachment and the
freedom which are the very conditions for love. In Christ,
crowned with the Spirit's tongue of fire, he becomes a king, a
prophet of the Kingdom, a priest of universal existence.

> Be like a king in your heart, on the throne of humility. You
> command the laughter to go, and it goes. You command the
> sweet tears to depart, and they leave. You command the body,
> now a servant and no longer a tyrant: do this, and it obeys.[36]

The Knowing Heart

The heart or, more precisely, the spirit-heart, is the organ that
knows both God and the "glory of God hidden in all beings
and all things."

In the Bible, the heart is the locus not only of affectivity, but of
intelligence and knowledge; it is the battlefield of spiritual warfare
and the site where the decision is made for or against God. In
ascetical literature, the word "heart" appears to carry two meanings.

On the one hand, the heart is the absolute center of man, his
deepest interior, in which man in his totality is called to collect

34 *Centuries on Charity* II, 48 (SC 9, pp. 108-9).
35 *Ambigua* (PG 91:1081).
36 St John Climacus, *The Ladder*, step 7, 40.

and to surpass himself, before a light which is pure transparency. Except at brief moments, this heart remains closed and ignored. One could call it the "super-conscious," or the "trans-conscious," in the language of existential psychoanalysts. For theorists such as Viktor Frankl and Igor Caruso, it is not religion that causes neurosis, but precisely the refusal to accept religion. There exists a spiritual subconscious dominated not by the principle of pleasure, but by the desire for meaning, in which man finds himself linked to God, in whom resides his irreducible freedom. It is the involuntary but radical ascesis of concentration camps—Nazi camps for Frankl, Soviet camps for Solzhenitsyn—that has revealed what the latter called the "kernel of kernels," "the image of the eternal within ourselves." In *The Cancer Ward*, a wise old physician, when questioned about the uncanny accuracy of his diagnoses, answers that at certain moments he allows his heart to become peaceful, to empty itself, until, he says, "the heart becomes like a peaceful lake which can reflect the moon and the stars."[37] Then he is able to see deep within the personal interiors of his patients, beyond mere social or biological appearances. This heart, says Mark the Monk, is the inner sanctuary illuminated by baptismal grace, from where "the intelligence receives good and beautiful intuitions."[38]

On the other hand, the heart in ascetical tradition also represents a subconscious haunted by the powers of darkness. This is an individual, but also a collective subconscious, doubtless also cosmic. The ascetical tradition places so much value on our true nature that, in order to explain the actual state of humanity and the world, it needs the intervention of alien powers, with their dark enchantments. The Devil (*diabolos*, the one who divides, is the opposite of *symbolon*, that which unites) is at once ourselves and outside of ourselves, our double who decomposes us—he is

37 *Le Pavillon des cancéreux* (Paris, 1968), p. 635.
38 *On Baptism* (PG 65:985-1028).

"legion," as he admits to Christ when being expelled from the possessed Gadarene. The Devil is, if one wishes, a person, but a split person, because personal existence is a relation to God, while he is the refusal of this relationship. And it is precisely this diabolical tearing asunder, the expression of our own complicity, of our narcissism and our split personality, that also shatters our own destiny, as well as that of humanity, and even that of the entire cosmos, which is wrapped in a kind of "nocturnal magic."

One could use the image of an hourglass. The top half represents the subconscious, endowed with the light of God, filled with baptismal grace; the bottom half is the immensity of cosmic life, a dark ocean in which frolics the Leviathan. The entire problem is to become aware of the heart of light, so that this light can penetrate the vastness of the human and cosmic subconscious, allowing Christ to triumph over the powers of death.

This is the guardian role of the heart. We must first learn to distance ourselves from the flow of thoughts and images, that whole psychic web that plays itself out within us. "It" thinks and "it" speaks ceaselessly within us, and we must separate ourselves from this constant flux by attaching ourselves to the rock of Jesus' Name. Then we must lay bare the psychic core of each "thought" and clothe it with the same Name, incorporate it into the immense sacrifice of reintegration fulfilled by Christ. Mark the Monk, for example, explains that we must immediately offer to Christ, at the altar of the depth of the heart, the luminous heart, each new "thought," even if it is only the most humble sensation; for it is important, says another writer, to "circumscribe the incorporeal into the corporeal," to mingle the savor of faith with the simple fact of existing, breathing, walking, smelling the ground after rain, touching the bark of a tree, or greeting someone by offering a smile. If a given thought somehow escapes our control, or if it becomes obsessive, we can bombard it with rays of prayer, for example by quickly repeating the Jesus Prayer, until the thought is either integrated or disintegrated.

In this way the unity between the intelligence and the heart is gradually restored, for the essence of intelligence is the heart. It would even be better to speak of the unification in the heart of intelligence and of the vital force, of what St Gregory Palamas calls desire "restored to its original purpose." To achieve this "descent of the intelligence into the heart," the invocation of the name of Jesus and the rhythm of breathing are most often used. "The Lord God formed man of dust from the ground, and breathed into his nostrils the breath of life; and man became a living being" (Gen 2:7). There is an analogy between the Holy Spirit as the life-giving Breath of God and respiration as the vital breath of man. Man is called to mingle his breath with the divine Breath, to "breathe the Spirit," says Gregory of Sinai. This is what man does when he "attaches the Name of Jesus to his respiration," for the Spirit, in both God and man, is the "proclaimer of the Word" (St John of Damascus).

All this leads to the notion that intelligence is not purely cerebral. (And the more artificial intelligence is perfected, the more this contemplative intelligence will be shown to be unique. Machines present us with a kind of negative anthropology.) This leads also to the notion of a "feeling," a "sentiment" which arises not only from the gut. It leads finally to the concept of the intelligence of the spiritual heart, an intelligence with the immediate and total character of sensation, which Diadochus of Photice calls the "sensation of God."

The "Contemplation of Nature"

In Orthodox tradition, contemplation consists of two stages: direct communion with God, of course, but first a "knowledge of beings," the "contemplation of nature." "Seeing the spiritual sense of beings through their visible form," says Maximus the

Confessor,[39] is a true cosmic eucharist: visible things appear as the "body" of the Lord, and their heavenly roots as his "blood." Man appropriates the interiority of things—"The world is interior," says the poet—he shares in their praise, he hears it in them, and in himself he makes it conscious and expressive. Thus the world becomes an immense dialogue between God and humanity. The world reveals itself to be an "ocean of symbols," in the oft-repeated expression of St Ephrem of Syria. The symbol anticipates, or manifests sacramentally, the incarnation of the Word. It is the sprouting of the Inaccessible, an absence filled with presence through the Nativity, the Cross, and the Resurrection. "Both anonymity and every name of every being are appropriate for the Cause of everything who is beyond everything…"[40]

Originally, the word "symbol" designated a ring. In many cultures, it was a broken ring, of which two relatives or two friends would each take half when they parted from one another. Years later, the two halves would serve as signs of recognition. The symbol is a sign of recognition between God and man. Ever since the incarnation, Christ sacramentally fulfills the truth of symbols. Christ is the primary symbol of the great interpenetration of divine and human energies. From the spiritual world, from the divine will and ideas, creation receives its existence, an existence whose proper consistency cannot be separated from a secret transparency, for the natural is itself supernatural. It is through these subsisting words, which are created things, that the Word expresses and symbolizes himself.

The man who is *logikos*, in the image of the Logos, discovers meaning everywhere. *Logikos* means much more than "reasonable." One could, paraphrasing Heidegger, translate it as "shepherd of meaning." Even in the density of things, in their appearance

39 *Mystagogy* 2 (PG 91:669).
40 Dionysius the Areopagite, *Divine Names, op .cit.*, p. 75.

which is revealed to be apparition, he can perceive divine Wisdom. "Nothing is closed," writes Nicholas Berdiaev, "the world is transparent, it does not know opacity."[41] Nietzsche's faithfulness to the earth becomes Alyosha Karamazov's faithfulness to the earth: in the light of the "wedding at Cana," Alyosha embraces the earth, but the earth, united to the invisible by symbolic stars, is itself sacrament... "Symbolic knowledge," proper to the deep and knowing heart, sees in things the glory of God which by definition cannot be grasped, but is revealed through sensation. Symbolic knowledge affects one's entire being. We should remember the importance placed in the Old Testament on the word *eloah* (to admire), and that the biblical aesthetic is not an aesthetic of colors, but of light: colors are symbols of light! The symbol cannot be separated from beauty, that amazement before the "ah! of things" so important to Japanese spirituality. The symbol provokes a "philocalic" cognition, based both on the brilliance of its own evidence and inseparable from what might be called an all-encompassing "emotion": here we find the coincidence of knowledge with sensation.

For the Fathers, this is not the rejection, but the affirmation and transfiguration of rationality. In the light of the "glory of God concealed in all things,"[42] reason forms part of a knowledge which is both integral and partial, freed from all desire for power and therefore always rigorous and respectful. The rational capacities are both fulfilled and overshadowed by the superabundance of light.

In the "contemplation of nature," the knowing heart becomes an "eye of fire," an "abode of light." It is able to connect with the concealed light in all things, "that ineffable and prodigious fire hidden in the essence of things as in the [burning] bush," says Maximus.[43] The separation between subject and object is over-

41 *Esprit et liberté* (Paris, 1984), p. 91.
42 St Isaac of Syria, *Oeuvres spirituelles*, (Paris, 1981), p. 365.
43 *Ambigua* (PG91:1148).

come without the two becoming confused, any more than the persons of the Trinity become confused, or human beings with Christ, despite their consubstantiality. The subject enters into communion with the object or, more precisely, enters into communion with the Word of whom the object is an expression. One enters into communion with Christ, whose deified human intelligence is communicated to our own intelligence.

The man who is aware of the *logoi* of things and their unity in Wisdom is able, in the expression of the *Russian Pilgrim*, to achieve "the knowledge of the language of creation." "Everything around me appeared to be filled with beauty: ...everything prayed, everything sang the praises of God."[44] And Maximus writes:

> Thus the soul takes refuge in the spiritual contemplation of nature as in a church and a place of peace. It enters there with the Word, and with him, our High Priest, and under his direction, it spiritually offers the universe to God as on an altar.[45]

The things that can give our lives a mystical flavor are so simple. Through the grace of the Cross and the resurrection, they can enable us to enter a world where everything is sacrament. God always asks Adam to name the living creatures—and living creatures now live by the resurrection, and their name is "Christ."

The Apophatic Approach

The knowledge of God through his *logoi*, through nature, history, Scripture, constitutes a "positive" way. Little by little, however, the intellect senses that the affirmations that it develops about God, reached through analogy with the created world, are far from expressing the divine mystery. Here the apophatic way becomes necessary.

44 *Récits d'un pèlerin russe* (Paris, 1966), p. 57.
45 *Mystagogy* 2 (PG 91:669).

The first step in the apophatic approach is *negative theology*. This comprises the ultimate work of the intellect, but it includes also an element of intuitive shock. St John Chrysostom, in his *Homilies on the Inaccessibility of God*, compares the spiritual dimension to a hiker who suddenly reaches the edge of a cliff: the fog breaks and he glimpses the abyss, he hears the song of immensity. Thus the intellect, in an existential effort affecting the entire person, must move beyond all the positive attributes ascribed to God. The intellect compares the abyss that it glimpses to every image, every concept of God, and becomes aware of their radical inadequacy, their limitation before the One who is not only absolute, but Totally Other. Such an approach does not consider positive notions of God as useless. These notions always need to be refined—and surpassed: God is such and such, but he is also other. Negative theology leads neither to skepticism nor to laziness. It requires a constant deepening of positive theology, in the process of which negative theology constantly intervenes by emphasizing the symbol, by challenging the sufficiency of concepts through negation and antinomy. Nevertheless, writes Dionysius, "if we name the super-essential Mystery either God, or Life, or even Essence, Light, or Reason, our intelligence is able to grasp only those powers which descend from him to us, to deify us, to give us being, life, Wisdom."[46] The Mystery remains beyond, beyond being (particularly when we speak of the supreme Being, beyond even the notion of God: *hyper-Theos*. For Dionysius, the absolute transcendence of God is expressed in the metaphor of mystical darkness, which provokes in the one who contemplates it the symmetrical attitude of unknowing and silence, that of "the heart of a child plunged into ecstasy by a mere trifle."[47] "It is in silence that one learns the secrets of this darkness..."[48]

---

46 *Divine Names, op. cit.*, p. 84.
47 Stan Rougier, *Aime et tu vivras* (Paris, 1985), p. 245.
48 Dionysius the Areopagite, *Mystical Theology*, in *Oeuvres complètes*, p. 177.

Nevertheless, both Dionysius and Maximus, who interprets him, indicate that the apophatic approach leads to a kind of qualitative transmutation of both meaning and structure: "As regards God... neither of the two properties... can properly be contemplated—I mean being and non-being... For God is beyond all affirmation and all negation."[49]

Why? Negative theology, which is also the approach of Plotinus and the *Vedanta*, here becomes fully Christian and is transformed into *apophatic antinomy*. The abyss which is beyond everything is now revealed as a paternal abyss, an abyss of love, and it is precisely because it is personal that it cannot be conceptualized. If the living God, the God of the Bible, is super-essence, super-unity, it is not simply because of his divinity without limit, but because he is the fullness of personal existence, and because he carries, deeply hid within himself, the secret of the Other and of reciprocity. God is beyond being not because he is absorbed into nothingness (one can use this expression only when one wishes to compare him to other "beings'), but because he is love: the being is the vessel of love. Thus the Inaccessible One transcends his own transcendence not in order to become some impersonal deity, but to come to us, to become incarnate, to take on our suffering, to die all our deaths—and to raise us up. The apophatic antinomy—which alone radically crucifies the intellect, because simple negative theology can easily remain a refined intellectual game—is engraved in the properly incomprehensible identity of the Inaccessible One and of the Crucified One, of God beyond God and of this man covered in blood and spittle, who has no more "comeliness or beauty."

At this stage of shock before the unthinkable comes the second level in the apophatic approach, that of "pure prayer." "Pure prayer" can be achieved when the intellect is able to repel every thought, even if it is infinitely good or positive, all imagination, all vision. The intellect is then stripped completely bare, empty

---

49 *Mystagogy*, introduction (PG 91:664).

and exposed, concentrated deep inside the heart; it becomes "simple" and "without form." "Prayer," writes Maximus the Confessor, "dissolves every intellectual concept and places it empty before God."[50] The intelligent heart in which man concentrates himself is pure expectation, pure prayer, a silence which is prayer, a prayer which is no more than the pulsation of silence; the intellect "without form" has no form but the Name of Jesus which instills itself in the silence and reveals its mystery. The purified intellect, Maximus repeats, becomes "the place of the abyss,"[51] and the abyss calls the abyss.

Then the intellect—and this could be the ultimate temptation, or at least a stumbling block—sees itself as light. As Evagrius notes, "During prayer, it [the intellect] sees itself as similar to a sapphire, or having the color of the firmament."[52] And Diadochus adds, "One cannot doubt that the intellect... becomes fully transparent, to the point that it can to a great extent perceive its own light..."[53] This may perhaps be the Indian experience of the identity of the self with the absolute. The Christian approach, however, is very clear: the intellect, in its luminous fullness, must be offered up, must pass through death in order to know, in Christ, the resurrection, to be recreated, to be raised on the basis of his ultimate humility. To cite Maximus once more, "Just as the body dies and is removed from all the things of life, so too the intellect dies at the heights of prayer... For if it does not die this death, it will not be able to live with God."[54] Standing before the face of God, man feels insignificant. He implores once again, he passes from the contemplation of the luminous depths of the spiritual heart to the sacrificial offering of this heart. He sees himself as a creature, recognizes that he is incommensurable with the uncre-

50   *Ascetical Discourse* 19 (PG 90:924).
51   *Ambigua* (PG 91:1112).
52   *Centuries*, suppl. 2, ed. Frankenberg, p. 425.
53   *Oeuvres spirituelles* (*Sources chrétiennes* 5bis, p. 108).
54   *Centuries on Charity* II, 62, *op. cit.*

ated One. Knowledge here becomes encounter, becomes love. This relationship of knowledge and love is, it seems, the reverse of the Indian approach. It is a powerful form of prayer, a "prayer beyond prayer," a thrust toward the inaccessible of the Other, in which the intellect dies in its crystalline splendor which, if closed in on itself, could become demonic.

Then comes the final apophatic stage. It is the encounter with the transfigured Christ, the face of the Father; or, within the soul, it is a kind of interior Pentecost. Or an interior Pascha. Or the total interiorization of the eucharist: "The heart absorbs the Lord, and the Lord absorbs the heart."[55] This is the *enstasis* of real deification in which man, says Maximus, is "submerged in the abundance of glory," in which the fire of divinity, its light, inflames the heart and communicates itself to the very body. It is the *ekstasis* of a love which is ever-renewed, the desire to reach the source of light, which is fortunately always out of reach, in order to achieve an infinite encounter. The created really passes into the uncreated, but without clear boundaries, so that "the one who rises never stops, going from beginning to beginning, passing through beginnings that have no end."[56] This is the experience that St Gregory Palamas suggested by the distinction-identity he made between essence—or rather, super-essence—and energies. "The essence of God cannot be communicated, and yet, in a certain sense, it is communicated."[57] It is manifested, without ceasing to be ineffable, through its uncreated energies. Dionysius' initial hesitation between "light" and "darkness," both inspired by Biblical symbolism, is here resolved by means of antinomy. The "uncreated light" allows and signifies the possibility of a total experience of deification: "Man, remaining entirely human, in

55   An expression attributed to St John Chrysostom by Callistos and Ignatios Xanthopoulos, *Philocalie grecque*, vol. 4, p. 222.
56   St Gregory of Nyssa, *Homily on the Canticles of Canticles* (PG 44:941).
57   *Chapters*, cited by A. Scrima in "Hermes," *Le Vide* (Lausanne-Tournay, 1969), p. 167.

both soul and body, becomes entirely God, soul and body, through grace."[58] But the light is *uncreated*, it springs from a God who remains totally inaccessible even as, in his love for us, he allows us to participate in him fully. "He rises in me, within my poor heart, as the sun," sings Symeon the New Theologian. "What a marvel... that men can be in the form of God, and in them can take form the one whom nothing can contain... so that each one can shine just as my God shone in his resurrection..."[59]

I would like to conclude with two remarks.

The first remark concerns the immensity of the tasks which face Orthodox theology in light of the spiritual heritage I have just described. First of all the spiritual sense of history, the groaning of creation, the difficulties of the present era, whose promises and convulsions we know all too well—in short, the spiritual sense of culture and society. Second is the significance of the encounter between men and women or, in broader terms, the application of the apophatic method to a renewed personalism—for the human being is itself as much unknown as it is known. Third is the light that the contemplation of nature can bring to bear on the scientific efforts of the West, the connection that can be made between the spiritual and rational knowledge of the universe. Finally, it is the light that Orthodox apophaticism could bring to the encounter, now inevitable, between religions.

My second remark concerns the fact that deification brings us to a crucified God. The proper name of God is revealed in his total self-emptying on the Cross. "God is love," writes St John. "He who abides in love abides in God, and God abides in him." This is the mystery, everything else is but a glimmer. Such is the synthesis and the conclusion of these several signposts of life: the difficult, crucifying, luminous exercise of love.

58 St Maximus the Confessor, *Ambigua* 28, cited by A. Scrima, p. 168.
59 *Hymn* 1, *op. cit.*, pp. 161 and 171.

5

Transfiguring the World

The Feast of Creation

For years the relationship between humanity and the earth has preoccupied the patriarch. This may perhaps be due to a childhood spent among peasants who mingled their liturgical life with the rhythms of nature. Humanity has changed, science and technology have immeasurably increased its powers. It is therefore necessary to forge a new nuptial pact between ourselves and nature.

Already on June 6, 1989, the Holy Synod of Constantinople declared September 1, the first day of the liturgical year, to be the *Feast of Creation.* The Church has traditionally prayed that humanity be preserved from natural catastrophe. Now, on September 1, it asks God to protect nature from calamities of human origin! The hymns and prayers for this feast were composed by Gerasimos, an old monk from Mt Athos who was the hymnographer of the Great Church. These call us to repentance because, even though we carry deep within ourselves a nostalgia for paradise, we have tortured the earth, we have destroyed the transparency of the world. In the beautiful texts of this feast, Gerasimos asks Christians to become the voice of creation—which, in the words of St Paul, suffers the pangs of childbirth—by bearing its supplication before the throne of God.

Bartholomew persuaded all the Orthodox churches to adopt this feast; he organized a series of symposia on ecology; and he obtained the support of Prince Philip, the Duke of Edinburgh, and President of the World Fund for Nature. Theologians, ethicists, and scholars from every country in the world assemble annually each June on Halki. A major conference, at which all faiths were represented, was held in Atami, Japan, in April 1995.

Today, the crisis is evident and worsening. A minority of human beings, those who comprise the middle and upper classes of the so-called "developed" societies, live in comfort by pillaging the planet. The prevailing economic system—one could refer to it as "consumerism"—maintains that production, and therefore consumption, is more important than planetary justice, than the spiritual and moral qualities of man, than a respect for the rhythms and limits of nature. Among perhaps a fifth of the world's population, "needs" are increasingly and artificially multiplied, and these needs require immediate satisfaction. The modern ethic, rationalist and utilitarian, maintains an anthropocentric view of nature: the sole meaning and purpose of nature is for human profit. Key biblical texts, particularly from Genesis, are even used in this sense. The sovereignty of man has been interpreted as irresponsible tyranny.

Today, there is a increasing awareness of the risks. But many approach the protection of the environment with the same logic as those who would destroy it. The difference is only quantitative: let us limit and control the exploitation of nature in order to be able do so for a longer period of time. Basically, this is only an improved consumerist rationale, the rational limitation of an irrational practice. Others seek to rediscover the ancient mother-earth cults, seeking in them to forget the transcendence of humanity and its divine mission.

We are thus called to a radical revision of our cosmology.

The Original Meaning of the Cosmos

The world, created by God, by the will of God, has its own reality. At the same time, it reflects divine Wisdom, divine Beauty, and divine Truth. "The Word lays the foundation," says St Irenaeus, "the Spirit makes these diverse forces seek their fullness and their beauty."[1] Uncreated grace, the ever-present glory of God, his energy, are at the very root of all things. "Yes, from the greatness and beauty of creation one can discern their author," for "he is the author of beauty."[2] The covenant with Noah, a cosmic alliance signified by the rainbow, is constantly renewed: "I will make... a covenant on that day with the beasts of the field, the birds of the air, and the creeping things on the ground," says God through the Prophet Hosea.[3] The world is thus not a neutral object. It incorporates the word of the Creator, just as a work of art incorporates the interior word of the artist. Things bear the seal of Wisdom. They are words of God which call humanity to engage him in dialogue. Even the beauty of creation is a gift of God, his *ecstasis* toward us, his offer of communion.

We must therefore regard nature with respect, even with reverential fear, in the same way that we treat an artistic creation which reveals the genius of the artist. This is the source of true knowledge.

In its order and its rhythms, the earth is the sign, the sacrament, of God. Each object has a unique place in the immense symphony of creation. When we become sensitive to God's world around us, we also become more conscious of God's world *in* us. Really to see something is to discover the extraordinary in what is ordinary.

"When I look at your heavens, the work of your fingers, the moon and the stars which you have established," says the psalm; as for man, "you have made him little less than God, and you crown him with glory and honor. You have given him dominion over the works of your hands."[4] Man is called to govern as a king, but also as a priest who receives in order to make an offering. He is also called to be a wise poet whose task is to decipher the revela-

1 *Demonstration of the Apostolic Preaching* 5:9.
2 Cf. Wis 13:3 and 5.
3 Hos 2:18a.
4 Ps 8:3, 5-6.

tion of the cosmos, to render fully conscious creation's song of praise. There is no discontinuity between man and the world; man cannot be separated from the rest of creation; he cannot be saved without it. Man, said the ancient Greeks—and the Fathers picked up this theme—is a "microcosm," who recapitulates all created beings in himself and can therefore know the universe from within.

But the Fathers, going further than the philosophers, also affirm that man is a person created in the image and likeness of God. Man therefore transcends the universe, not in order to abandon it, but to express its meaning, to discern the grace within it—to be, in a sense, its conscience. Man is "the link between the divine and the earthly," says St Gregory of Nyssa; through him "grace spreads to all creation."[5] Through man, the universe is called to become "the image of the image," as is proved in the diversity of landscapes created by old cultures imbued with spirituality.

Humanity does not, therefore, need to be absorbed into some impersonal divinity through the mediation of a sacred nature, of an all-consuming *Gaia*, as our new pagans would have it. On the contrary, it is through man, who stands between earth and heaven, that creation can fulfill its hidden sacramentality. The symbolic Adam of Genesis was placed like a gardener in Eden to perfect its beauty. As *logikos*, he had the task of "naming the living creatures," that is, of discerning and gathering the *logoi*, the spiritual essences of all things in order to offer them to the divine Logos.

Thus the cosmos exists not simply in order that man may fulfill himself. The earth must do more than merely serve our needs. The cosmos and the earth are called to become a dialogue between man and God. The world is the language of God toward humanity. It can potentially become humanity's language toward God.

5   *Great Catechesis* 6 (*PG* 45 25C-28A).

Sin and Redemption

Sin, which is a break in the relation between humanity and God, and therefore between each person and those around him, has degraded and continuously degrades nature, which can only follow man and bear the consequences of his folly. The avidity, the pride, and the ignorance of humanity disfigure and destroy the world. It is not possible here to distinguish between individual and collective sin. Human beings, says the patriarch, created in the image of the Trinitarian God, are interdependent. We are "members one of another," says St Paul.[6] The gap created by our refusal to accept this communion allows the nothingness, from which we are taken, to rise. The dynamics of evolution are henceforth linked with death—entropy, monstrosity, disintegration. "The creation was subjected to futility," says St Paul, "not of its own will but by the will of him who subjected it..."[7] "I looked on the earth, and lo, it was waste and void; and to the heavens, and they had no light," says Jeremiah, "the fruitful land was a desert."[8] Humanity sucks out the blood from the universe, it kills to eat and, by this very act, finds death. Humanity and the world consume each other.

Of course the laws of nature, which make salvation history possible, witness to the cosmic covenant concluded between God and the world after the flood. But this covenant also includes death. It therefore makes necessary the ultimate mystery of Christ: the victory of Christ over death, the work of deification.

The incarnation and the resurrection have brought on the re-creation, the secret, or potential, transfiguration of the world. Patristic and liturgical texts, building on St Paul's intuition, emphasize the cosmic aspect of the Body of Christ. For Christ, says

6   Eph 4:25.
7   Rom 8:20.
8   Jer 4:23, 26.

Maximus the Confessor,

> is the great, hidden mystery, the glorious end for which everything was created, an end which is prior to all existence… With his sight fixed on his goal, God called all things into being. [Christ] is the fullness in whom creatures accomplish their return to God…It is for him, for his mystery, that the universe exists and all that it contains."[9]

Christ assumes the world and transforms its matter into *soma pneumatikon*, "spiritualized body." The Cross becomes the new Tree of Life, making this transfigured modality of creation accessible to humanity. As an anonymous second century paschal homily put it,

> This tree rises from earth to heaven. An immortal plant, it stands at the center of heaven and earth, firmly supporting the universe, linking all things. Held by the invisible nails of the Spirit so as not to waver from its alignment with the divine, touching the sky with the tip of his head, strengthening the earth with his feet, and, between them, embracing the entire atmosphere with his incommensurable hands, [Christ] was entirely in all places, in all things… The whole universe became stable, as if this divine stretching out and this agony of the Cross had penetrated all things…[10]

Despite being illumined in Christ and penetrated by the power of the resurrection, the world remains disfigured by human blindness. Spiritualizing the earth requires not just that God become man, but that man become God. Christ made humanity capable of receiving the Spirit: not just to preserve creation, but to transfigure it little by little, in anticipation of the Kingdom.

Ever since the incarnation and Pentecost, the universe, so beautiful and yet subject to death, carries within itself the

9   *Quaestiones ad Thalassium* 60 (PG 90:612AB).
10 Anonymous paschal homily inspired by Hippolytus' *Paschal Treatise* 34:49-51.

Church; but in reality, it is the Church that bears and transfigures the universe. For the Church, understood in all its evangelical, baptismal, and eucharistic profundity, seeks the salvation not only of humanity, but of all creation.

The "mysteries" of the Church, and the Church as the "mystery" of Christ in the Holy Spirit, constitute the very heart of cosmic life. "In all this," says St Gregory of Nyssa, "dead and insensible matter... receives the power of God within itself."[11] Separation and darkness are exorcised. In the sacraments, matter responds to its original vocation of being the means of communion between man and its God, and therefore among all men. The epiclesis[12] of all the sacramental actions are a continuation of Pentecost, infusing the Holy Spirit who renews creation. Everything culminates in the eucharist, at which bread and wine, the fruits of creation, expressing both human work and human celebration, are liberated, made capable of receiving the divine Presence, and thus of being transfigured. According to St Irenaeus, we offer all nature in the holy gifts, so that it can be "eucharistized."[13] As St Cyril of Jerusalem recalls, in the offering "we remember heaven, earth, the sea, the sun, the moon, and all creation."[14] The Armenian liturgy proclaims: "Heaven and earth are full of glory because of the manifestation of our Lord, God, and Savior Jesus Christ... for by the passion of your only Son, all creatures are renewed."

A Eucharistic Ethos

In the Church, humanity is called to a eucharistic apprenticeship, to learn to use natural resources with gratitude, to offer the world and itself up to God.

Orthodox asceticism focuses not merely on the soul, but on the

---

11 *On the Baptism of Christ* (PG 46:581B).
12 Prayers addressed to the Father asking him to send his Holy Spirit on the matter of the sacrament in order to transfigure it.
13 *Against Heresies* IV, 18:5.
14 *Mystagogical Catechesis* V, 6.

body as well. And the body, imbued with divine light, communicates it to the rest of creation, to which it is inseparably linked. Even the most isolated hermit in fact covers the whole earth with his prayer and prepares its transformation. "Glorify God in your body," says the apostle.[15] The rhythms of our breathing and our heart were given to us so that the Spirit can penetrate to our very roots, in order to transform our heart into an "eye of fire," an "eye of light" which can see the Light of Mt Tabor—not only in itself, but also in the external and hidden reality of creation. The "contemplation of nature," "of the glory of God hidden in all creatures," is a major aspect of Orthodox mysticism. The spiritual man no longer objectivizes the world through his own covetousness and blindness, but identifies it with the "body of Christ." His presence exorcises, alleviates, and pacifies. He understands, and liberates, the language of creation. This is the language that Nectarios of Aegina, a saint from our own century, allowed his nuns to hear.

> One day, we asked our father… to tell us how creatures who have no voice or reason…, whom the psalmist invites to praise the Lord, can do so. The saint said nothing. Several days later, he said to us: 'Several days ago, you asked me to explain how creatures praise God. Here, listen to them.' We were then introduced into the transfigured world in which we heard each creature distinctly singing and praising the Lord and Creator in its own fashion.

The holy elder Silouan of Athos, another great 20th-century mystic, said: "For the man who prays in his heart, the entire world is a church."

The Church teaches us the necessity of *metanoia*, of a change in our perspective, in order to discover the world of God, to limit ourselves, to live more simply and less destructively. Fasting, in particular, allows us to separate ourselves from the self-centered

15 1 Cor 6:20.

voracity characteristic of our fallen condition. Fasting reduces our enslavement, lightens our physical being, and enables us to share with those who have less than we do. The liturgical *ethos* underlines the communal nature of the eucharist: it consists of sharing, of communion with Christ. And, in Christ, we can achieve a communion with the neighbor that has no limit. It is in a spirit of fasting, of self-limitation, that Christians must face our so-called "consumer society," but which in reality encompasses only a minority of the human population. Indeed, it is in this spirit that we must collaborate with all those who work to achieve this planet-wide community of sharing.

In Other Faiths and in the West

The preservation of creation, if not yet its transfiguration, is found in all religions. The covenant between God and man is a fundamental theme of the three Abrahamic traditions. All three believe in one single Creator and Source of all things. For all three, humanity's power over nature must be exercised with moderation, justice, and compassion. We have already recalled the covenant with Noah, which also affects the earth, and which God renews several times in the course of the First Testament. In transforming feasts of nature into historical feasts, though without forgetting their agricultural origin, Israel weaned humanity from the archaic nature cults. One could say that Israel delivered humanity from the womb of Mother-Earth. In the Cabalistic movement, it rediscovered the cosmic sense of Scripture. And, in Hassidism, Israel found the childish joy of humanity playing with God's creation.

The patriarch's Moslem friends tell him that, in the Koran, all living creatures form an immense community, for which man, *khalifa*, vice-regent of creation, is responsible before God.[16]

16 *Koran*, surat 6:38.

Do you not see that it is the praises of God that all creatures celebrate in heaven and on earth, even the birds in flight? Each creature knows its prayer and its praise, and God watches over each one. Do you not therefore understand that creatures proclaim his glory?[17]

Bartholomew admits that he knows the Asian religions less well, but he thinks that for India, as Mircea Eliade has shown, the world is an immense theophany—a "game of God," say the Tantras, taking up the ancient Vedaic intuition. And Buddhism is reported to have been born of Buddha's smile as he contemplated a flower. In Shintoism, when one thinks of the forest of Ise, in which deer and white horses wander freely, one has a strong sense of the world as a sanctuary.

The Orthodox theology of divine energies, as well as the "contemplation of nature" which it allows, and the Orthodox perception of the "cosmic liturgy" could also give a meaning to the search for a *wonderland* that characterizes western poetry, particularly English and German romanticism. It is as if the most spiritually sensitive westerners, fleeing a pietistic and moralizing Christianity, were searching for new names for God in "fidelity to the earth," in the mysterious quality and density of beings and things. It is Nietzsche writing, in *Ecce homo*, "Here all things approach…, they wish to be carried in your flight… Every existence here wants to become word, every growing thing wants you to teach it to speak." It is James Joyce, in *Dedalus*, evoking "the soul was all dewy wet" in the light of dawn, celebrating "a morning inspiration," when "a spirit filled him, pure as the purest water, sweet as dew, moving as music."[18] And even though the patriarch does not much care for Heidegger, who celebrates being but refuses to see its source in communion, he likes to cite the last few lines of his meditation on the "mystery of the belfry," *Vom Geheimnis des Glockenturms*—which, the patriarch says, is almost Christian:

17   *Ibid.*, surat 24:41.
18   James Joyce, *A Portrait of the Artist as a Young Man* (1916), Ch. 5.

The juncture full of mystery in which Christian feasts, vigils, as well as the passage of the seasons and the hours of each day, morning, noon and evening, joined one another, so that *one single sound* continuously filled young hearts, dreams, prayers, and games—this juncture also shelters one of the most enchanting, most salutary, most durable mysteries of the belfry, so as to offer it, until the very last sound, in the collective shelter of Being.

A Call to Action

The time for patient action is now here. An alliance must be created between the Church, the churches, and different religions on the one hand, and the saner ecological organizations, unaffected by paganism, on the other, in order to pressure our governments. Orthodoxy, whose message on these issues bears great weight, must raise the general consciousness. Among the young, who already enjoy walking through forests and mountains and by the sea, it must instill a sense of the mystery of the presence of the living God in all things, of the sacramentality of nature through the breath of the Spirit. They should be taught to plant trees, to preserve forests, to clean our polluted lakes and seas. It would also be possible to restore to cultivation, or cultivate anew, wild or abandoned lands while respecting the natural rhythms, refusing to poison them with chemicals, creating places of beauty. Followers of the *New Age* do this, why can't we? All this can be done in the atmosphere of a simple and powerful liturgy, renewed, perhaps re-created, which would bestow on existence an odor of resurrection.

We need prophets capable of criticism and denunciation, but also of articulating meaning and proposing solutions. A human consciousness open to the celestial is capable, little by little, of regularizing, spiritualizing, and embellishing nature. The humble and necessary production of food—both physical and spiritual—and therefore our link to the earth, requires an *ethos* of gratitude and respect, a "eucharistic *ethos*," if we dare to use the expression. We will also need to rethink the relationship between city and countryside, to eliminate the megalopolises of vulgarity and violence—not every city, like Istanbul, has the fortune of being crossed by two branches of the sea! The increase in productivity, which leads today to so much unemployment, could also free us from mechanically repetitious work, from our compulsive attitude before computer screens, thus restoring a proper relationship with creation, as well as allowing time for enjoyment and contemplation!

Let us have confidence, the patriarch concludes. In the words of the ancient Greeks, "Drops of water ultimately pierce the hardest rock."

PART III

In History

6

On Freedom

Liberty, liberator: these words are at the heart of our modern age. But they have varying, and at times contradictory, meanings. For this reason, we will speak in succession about:

— the existence and tragedy of freedom;
— Christ the liberator;
— the courage of freedom.

The Existence and Tragedy of Freedom

Freedom is present in the human heart and is inseparable from the awareness of the value of one's life. It could be said that the original human experience is mingled with the experience of freedom. Freedom is like the air: we are not aware of it, but we live by breathing it. If there is no air, if liberty is trampled, then man risks death. Even before reflecting about freedom, man risks his life to defend it. Freedom is one of the reasons for living, and therefore worth risking one's life to preserve. Every person who stands boldly before his executioners, every person who, in a world full of hatred and violence, refuses to capitulate—bears an irrefutable witness to freedom.

At the same time—and in this contradiction lies the whole tragedy of freedom—our modern age stresses that humanity is conditioned, that its future is determined. We need not even speak of totalitarian ideologies, which now appear to be mortally wounded, which reduce humanity simply to productivity or to racial conflicts, and which reduce the concept of freedom to the utter lack of awareness that a locomotive might have as it rolls down the tracks. Today, a multi-faceted positivism insists that man is conditioned by his genetic make-up,

by his biology, by the interplay of his impulses, by the stratifica-
tion of his subconscious, by his family, social, and cultural sur-
roundings, by the interiorized structures of his education.

Affirmation of freedom, negation of freedom. Responding to
this dilemma are the claims of what might be called *libertarian
freedom.* Since our future is determined—and we are aware of the
fact—we may as well do whatever we want, follow our impulses,
abandon ourselves to our conditioning. A libertarian freedom rejects any constraints, any preexisting order. It accepts to do only
what is dictated by momentary urges. This is the modern solution: "I do something only because I want to." What I think, but
do not express, is: "And, in any case, I cannot do otherwise!"

Is not gratifying one's impulses, however, becoming a slave to the
self at the same time that one rejects slavery imposed from outside?
Other forms of slavery arise under the guise of the freedom thus
"achieved": for the ego is fragmented and contradicts itself in the hall
of mirrors of narcissism. In the heart of man lurks the secret and un-
controllable fear of annihilation. All of our transgressions derisively
mimic the only transgression that could liberate us, the transgression
of death. Paroxysms—of eroticism, of torture, of drugs, or the absolute power of the terrorist—always lead to death, death of the
"other" and of the self. Death is the absolute form of slavery.

Faced, on the one hand, with the ravages of libertarian freedom, and, on the other, with horrors justified by various ideologies, our societies are rediscovering the need for Law. Law limits
the expressions of evil, balances relations between the individual
and the group, and limits one's freedom in order to respect that of
others, for both good and bad. The Law humanizes humanity by
partially rescuing it from its impulses. But the Law remains external. It feeds the pride of "the good" and their desire for revenge
against "the bad," who become the scapegoats for our collective
anxiety. The Law does not change the "heart." The Law greatly
frustrates libertarian freedom in a never-ending and constantly

intensifying cycle. From these remarks, we can discern one accomplishment and one possibility.

The positive achievements are our refusal to be considered as objects which can simply be used, and the necessity to respect differences in others, an issue that is particularly dear to Patriarch Bartholomew. The person who senses freedom awakening within himself refuses the right of any one, even of God—in reality, a caricature of God—to shape him from without. The prophets of modernity have tried to break the confidence of the powerful, and to kill off a God perceived as a rival. In accordance with the Marxist dialectic of master and slave, the Freudian notion of the castrating father, or the Nietzschean attack against the heavenly spy whose gaze petrifies man to the very depth of his existence and his future, modern humanity often perceives God as the enemy of his freedom. Theologies of predestination and the western debates about liberty and grace have paved the way for modern atheism. As Kierkegaard also noted,

> A time came when the Gospel, "grace," changed into a new law, even more severe toward men than the old. Everything became subject to painful and incurable torments, almost as if, despite the song of the angels at the dawn of Christianity, there was no more joy in heaven, nor on earth. Through the cruelty of the torments we inflicted on ourselves, we made God—what poetic justice!—equally cruel…[1]

The suit brought against God by contemporary atheism, and presumably definitively won by libertarian freedom, implies that omnipotence and omniscience, conceived according to our overly human categories, reduce history, and each of our destinies, to a puppet game. In this way God, who would alone be free, is guilty of all the evil in the world; and therefore he does not exist.

The conflict between freedom, which is perhaps not of this world, and death, which imprisons this world, can also open up

1 *Towards an Examination of Conscience* (1851).

humanity to the revelation of the Gospel, to the revelation of the incarnate and crucified God. Anguish is the opposite of desire, because desire, while it provides motivation, also reveals a lack of something. And desire prepares a proper spiritual context for freedom: interiority, self-transcendence, and communion. This is not the subjectivity that we project onto others, but the interiority which allows us to perceive the irreducible interiority of the other.

That interiority which seeks transcendence and desires communion exists within us as a promise and a call. Animals have an interiority that is almost entirely self-enclosed, consisting of regulating organs and elementary cognitive faculties. It functions in a closed circuit. Man, by contrast, if he is immersed in the world, when he stands before love and beauty, perceives an open interiority in himself, an inner transcendence. This is what can be called, more broadly, the life of the spirit. At times it allows him to make a gesture of unselfish goodness, however small, even at the risk of his life—perhaps a meeting of the eyes that leads not to seduction, to confrontation, to objectivization, but to humble acceptance and welcome.

Interiority awakens only in a personal encounter. But encounter is always precarious. Only the revelation of the hidden God, of the God who is more interior to me than I am to myself can strengthen my own interiority, can give it infinite depth. "Very late did I come to love you, O Beauty both so ancient and so new, very late did I come to love you!" cries out St Augustine. "What! You were inside me, and I was outside myself, and it is outside that I was looking for you…"[2] Freedom, which "outside the self" always risks becoming libertarian freedom, becomes absolutely limitless in this interiority of communion.

We can no longer speak of freedom without invoking the Christ who liberates, who bestows the Spirit of life, the Spirit of freedom. For "where the Spirit of God is, there is freedom."[3]

2   *Confessions*, Book 10.
3   2 Cor 3:17

The Liberating Christ

Whatever the risks, we must abandon the images of God created by our enslaved selves, by the terrorized robots we have
become.

In the "apophatic" approach to the mystery—which consists
first of negative theology, then of silent expectation—our categories of power do not apply.

Our Fathers in the faith, meditating on the words of Jesus in
the Gospel of John, "I and the Father are one," have pointed out
that the very being of God is communion. The Trinity is primordial, God exists only as an act of communion. And from all eternity, communion originates in one Person, the Father. The
infinite depth of divinity surges from the "bosom of the Father";
it is a paternal abyss, an abyss of love, a theme the patriarch apparently borrows from the theology of Metropolitan John (Zizioulas)
of Pergamum. In the final analysis, personal freedom and personal love are identical and constitute true being. Being proceeds
from the Person who is free, from the Person who loves freely,
who affirms his identity in his relation with other persons,
through his joyfully sacrificial gift to other persons. True being,
absolute being, comes from the Father who loves the Son and
makes his Spirit to dwell in him. This is a loving, liberating paternity, a far cry from that alienating and oppressive paternity about
which libertarian freedom constantly speaks and which it ceaselessly denounces.

The creation of personal beings means the creation of freedoms, in the image of God's freedom. "Man is free from the beginning," wrote St Irenaeus of Lyons, "for God is freedom, and it
is in the resemblance of God that man was made."[4]

If God, Father-Son-Spirit, is *freedom of love*, he cannot be, in
relation to us, only *love of our freedom*. The creation of a personal

4 *Against Heresies* 37, 4.

being—i.e., a free being—is the masterpiece, the greatest achievement of divine power. But it also carries within itself a voluntary
limitation of this power in order to give the creature the space to
exercise its freedom. When God creates the existence of another,
who is truly other, "outside" himself, his omnipotence fulfills itself by crucifying itself in the passionate, unconditional respect of
that freedom. The free creation of freedoms implies the risk of the
Cross. God makes himself vulnerable to his creature. "The
Lamb," says the Book of Revelation, "is immolated from the beginning of the world."

God is so free that he can transcend his own transcendence to
engage humanity in a genuine drama of love. God is so free that
he can love with the respect, the discretion, the humility, and finally the humiliation of one who awaits the free response of the
beloved. He has no wish to constrain his human creatures, for
that in itself would destroy the nature of his free response. God is
so free that he allows humanity to challenge his omnipotence.
The great spiritual masters have called this freedom of God the
"folly of love." It finds its ultimate expression on the Cross. The
incarnate and crucified God takes upon himself all our enslavement, he takes on death in all its spiritual depth: death as hell, as
the absence of God, as the absence of love, as the "wages of sin,"[5]
the wages of separation, of hatred, of murder and suicide. Everything is transformed. The despair which stood between God and
the God-made-man, between God and man, is abolished in the
unity of Father and Son. From that point on, life, light, the Spirit,
and true freedom spring forth for us. They come to us not from a
God who is outside us, for that would be unbearable and would
crush us. They come from a crucified God who has "emptied"
himself (this is certainly the best expression for "kenosis"), from a
God filled with love, in the desire that humanity find its liberated
and newly creative freedom in him.

5   Rom 6:23.

Contrasted with the mortal deviation of libertarian freedom, Christ is the truth—not God against man, nor man against God, but the fullness of what Orthodox religious philosophers call "divine humanity," in which man's interiority succeeds in becoming transparent, in which freedom discovers its content, which is love. In Christ, says the Gospel,[6] we know the truth, and the truth will make us free. For the divine humanity is the locus of the Spirit, the hypostasis of freedom. The Spirit tends as much as possible to reduce exteriority, which is the essence of constraint, the law of this fallen world. He reveals "the glory of God hidden in beings and things" by transforming object into subject, thing into presence, and, the Patriarch specifies, the *it* into *thou*. Our awe before the life-giving Cross, before God's tremendous love, opens us to the Spirit. And the Spirit liberates our freedom from within. He illumines our freedom as creative inspiration, as life, as fire; for he is himself the interiority of all that exists, the Life of life, the spiritual fragrance of every being and all things, the true visage behind every opaque human face.

This liberating presence of the Spirit, the gift of the Resurrected One, is bestowed only on those who have faith. But faith, which is confidence, the personal adhesion to a personal presence that is simultaneously both veiled (so as not to impose itself) and unveiled (so as to solicit love)—faith is identified with freedom in the tradition of the Christian East. When God becomes incarnate, he does so not in the Holy of Holies, where the Sacred dwells, but in a stable, among the outcast. In the desert, he refuses the temptations of magic, of possession and power, which would attract people to him like fascinated slaves. Blindfolded and beaten—"Prophet, prophesy!"—he does not open his mouth. He refuses to come down from his cross: "But then we would believe in him!" He rises from the dead in secret and appears neither to the Sanhedrin, nor to the Senate in Rome, but only to those who

6 Jn 8:31.

place their trust in him, to those whose heart begins to burn, such as the travelers on the road to Emmaus, to those who weep and whose eyes suddenly open when he calls them by name, such as Mary Magdalene. It is in the royal freedom of faith that we discover that the Crucified One is now the Resurrected One, who raises us. It is in the royal freedom of faith that we discover that the world, which is a tomb, is in fact an empty tomb, filled with light. We discover the Kingdom which comes furtively among us in the peaceful beauty of the liturgy and the icon, in those moments of peace, of light, of joy, of spiritual lightness, where nothing is either exterior or hostile, when there are only faces, when the earth is truly a sacrament.

A post-ideological Christianity must strongly affirm that *God is the freedom of man.* If God did not exist, then man would be nothing more than a derisory fragment of society, of the universe, of fate, the destiny of Greek tragedy. The law of inevitable failure and disaster would reign over us and we would have no hope. If God existed, but as a heavenly despot who ruled arbitrarily over us, man would be nothing more than a slave, with no escape other than the revolt of Lucifer or Prometheus. But the God who reveals himself to us in Jesus Christ is a crucified and liberating love. In "The Legend of the Grand Inquisitor," Dostoevsky has shown that Christ calls us to the freedom of faith. Thinking to insult Jesus, the Inquisitor—a figure representing both totalitarianism and our hedonistic nihilism—in fact celebrates him as the founder of true freedom: "Instead of the burdensome old law, man now has to discern between good and evil with a free heart, having no guide but your image."

And this image—which is in reality his model—awakens in man the impulse toward liberated freedom. "The heart [of Christ] is aflame with love. His eyes release... the Power which illuminates and awakens love in our hearts." For he "thirsts for freely-offered love, and not for the servile behavior of the terrified slave." In Gethsemane and on Golgotha, he inaugurates in himself, in his humanity which is ours, and thus in all men, the true vocation of humanity to be the "child of sacrifice and of freedom." Yes, we are finally free because we discover ourselves to be loved, for ever, with a love that is stronger than death, and because we in turn are able to love, for ever. Then, with the courage of our freedom, we patiently become laborers for human communion and the transfiguration of the world.

The Courage of Freedom

The Church, through Word and Sacrament, offers us the possibility and the power of new and free life. But we have the task of conforming ourselves to it, of letting it grow in us, allowing it to mature in us through life-giving ascesis. We must remove our dead skins by taking off our masks and the personae we put on. Thus, little by little, we can pass from the psychological "I" to the truly personal "I," the image of God "magnetized" by its model, which transcends this world in order to liberate our desires centered on illusory idols and in order to restore the spontaneity of our attraction—in "fear and trembling"—to God and to our neighbor.

Christ shows us that real freedom is obedience "unto death, even death on a cross."[7] And this obedience of Christ expresses no subordination, no destruction of freedom by any external authority, but rather mutual love with the Father. For this reason, in the Church freedom should mean confidence, service, and, we might say, the obedience of all to all. The Christian acquires freedom by becoming the "servant of Jesus Christ," a servant called to become a friend: "I no longer call you servants, but friends." In this way, one becomes the servant, and perhaps one day the friend, of the brother, for "after God, you should consider your brother as your God," in the words of an old monastic saying. Here, freedom is

7 Phil 2:8.

the desire for the good of the other, just as Christ desired it—even to the cross.

In the classical ascetical perspective, obedience requires *parrhesia*, confidence, as well as placing ourselves in the hands of someone who respects us, welcomes us, and appears to be further advanced on the path of salvation than we are. Obedience is our free decision to be adopted by a "spiritual father," in whom is manifested the liberating paternity of God, who bestows the Spirit. In this way, we can little by little become capable of blessing and serving life, capable of a fully-responsible freedom.

Let Christianity therefore be the life-giving Breath, a responsible and creative freedom. The task of the Church, of the Mother Church, is to produce such liberated persons, who together will be able to reinvent love, beauty, and culture. A few words are sufficient to summarize everything: non-possession, interior poverty, the humble courage of sanctity.

Real freedom is realized in the form of poverty because it constitutes an impulse toward the "other," the respect of his otherness, the risk of his estrangement and his refusal. Poverty signifies the passage from a self who appropriates the finite—and this appropriation stifles and destroys its object—to a disappropriated self oriented toward the beyond—and this disappropriation is a generosity of being, the multiplication of life.

Disappropriation begins with respect for things. Such renunciation frees us from avidity and makes us good stewards, true artists of nature, joyful celebrants of the "Canticle of creatures." Such an attitude is essential today, the patriarch stresses, and it must be held not only by individuals, but by all of society, if we wish to save the earth from environmental destruction and from "nuclear winter."

But disappropriation is applicable most particularly with respect to the self and to others. Man in the image of God cannot be an object—of ideological manipulation, of commercial manipulation, of genetic manipulation. Unconditional respect alone allows us to accept man as someone *who cannot be possessed*, but *who reveals himself.* St Seraphim of Sarov greeted those whom he met with these words: "My joy, Christ is risen!" For if Christ is risen, we are no more afraid. If he is risen, then we also escape from the parade of narcissism, from possessiveness, and freely and joyfully accept the "other" in his freedom.

Let us conclude with a basic example, that of culture. In the development of European culture, three stages can be distinguished. During the Middle Ages, Christian societies exhibited an absolute identity between culture and religion. Then, beginning particularly during the Renaissance, in a frenzy of liberation, various aspects of culture were emancipated. This made possible, and continues to do so, a rash of amazing developments which would not have been possible had clerical power been maintained. But this also led, either through ignorance or out of refusal (the "death of humanity" after the "death of God") to a spiritual collapse which could ultimately lead to knowledge and power without meaning, to an empty freedom.

Hence the third stage, which is our present task. We must light and stir up a humble fire which might give off a unifying light. This would consist not in power, but in a deepening of freedom to face the ultimate questions, and to provide an unexpected and simple offer: "Come and see." It can be done only through a renewed sanctity, a sanctity open to all the complexities of the life of the modern world, a sanctity of transfiguration.

The *person* and *freedom* are, inseparably, the greatest, though yet incomplete, discoveries of our tragic century. Personhood comprises the unique way in which every one has the vocation to make humanity exist through a process of offering and communion. The person is freedom and love. It is the image of God restored by Christ, an image we are called to realize by opening ourselves up to the grace of the Spirit. The ultimate freedom of the person stems from Christ's victory over death, which transforms our anguish into confidence, our aggressiveness into creative power. In the early centuries of our era, Christians were called "those who do not fear death." Today, we are all haunted by emptiness, which seems to rise again to the surface of history. It surrounds our civilization. Freedom consists of remembering that Someone always stands between ourselves and the abyss of nothingness. Remembering that, if we desire it, the crucified God can create us anew. In this world, where the fear of annihilation manifests itself in a multitude of fears—one sometimes hears of the "terrors of the year 2000"—let us pray that we might be free of fear, truly free—that is, capable of love. Today, the most radical freedom seeks after the ultimate transgression, that of death, and it is Christ who offers it. Today, freedom is called *Resurrection*.

7

On Love, and Other Subjects That Preoccupy Young People

Freud Did Not Say It All

"God is love," says St John. And therefore "he who loves is born of God and knows God."[1]

This is no doubt true. And yet, as the patriarch remarks, "love" is a difficult, ambiguous word, a word with many meanings.

Let us try to clarify things a bit. Freud's theories have become a commonplace in our culture. But his atheism did not serve him well. He confused *eros* with its sexual expression. But *eros*, as Plato said in *The Symposium*, is an impetus toward the divine that can certainly be expressed in sexual life, but which also goes far beyond. There is, for example, an artistic *eros*, a theological *eros*, and particularly a mystical *eros*. Perhaps it is only the monks who know the secret of love. Through their ascetical efforts, they separate desire from need, including sexual need. They unite their desire to the immense impetus of the life-giving Breath, which they transform and fulfill in divine *agape*. *Agape* is a tender and compassionate love, a properly personal love which remains *disinterested*—we risk using this word despite the sneers it provokes from the innumerable partisans (or slaves) of popular psychology. The spiritual person whose ascetical efforts have borne fruit is capable of encountering others without any carnal or psychological possessiveness. And this is true not only for monks! Compassion and goodness exist among apparently random people (in reality, seen through the eye of the heart, no single person is random). In the

---

1   1 Jn 4:7.

accounts of the Desert Fathers, we find the story of the robber who captures a beautiful woman, desires her, and wants to force himself on her. But she supplicates him with tears. She goes to the neighboring town to try to pay off her husband's debts, because he has been thrown into a debtor's prison. The robber, touched by this, not only hears her pleas but gives her the money she needs. This man, concludes the account, is greater than a good many monks! Fear and hunger are as important for humanity as sexuality. This is something that Freud, who lived in a well-fed society, doubtless forgot. And yet in concentration camps, Nazi, Communist, or other, in which people were and still are starved and terrorized, there are always some who resist—who share or give up the piece of bread that would allow them to survive, who take another's place in the line marching toward the gas chamber. The concentration camps are the peculiar monasteries of our age.

At the level of our nature, which is subject to death and to biological individualism, sexual polarization always interferes. And yet friendship, a love which the ancient Greeks called *philia*, surpasses this division. It is the same for the relationship between parents and their children. Parents must bring children into this world not only physically, but also spiritually. The sentiments they bear for the child demand no reciprocity; the child, the Ten Commandments say, must only "honor" his parents. Parents must protect when necessary, step back when necessary, in order to teach the child to be independent. Love here is not turned in on itself. Incest, even if only psychological, as well as the homosexuality to which it sometimes leads, confuses that which must remain distinct. If not, then the child's sense of identity is compromised.

The Meaning of Love?

In light of what has been said, it is evident that, for most of our contemporaries, love is primarily the strong attraction that draws a man and a woman together. There is today a spiritual void; our computerized work life irritates our nerves more than it tires our bodies. Far from the earth and the physical labor which leave us with a sense of peace, the suburbs of our major cities give us a life of solitary promiscuity and ugliness. Everything seems regulated, in the style of Kafka, by a blind bureaucracy. Love thus appears as the great adventure, the only poetry left in life, the ultimate miracle. Here life then reaches its most intense state. Love provides an encounter which breaks down our agonizing solitude.

And what can we, who are men of the Church, say? If you want lessons in morality, I am not the one you should ask, the patriarch replied to journalists in Strasbourg when, in April 1995, they questioned him on these issues. Lessons in morality, prohibitions, too much intrusion by old, celibate men into the intimate lives of couples can only get in the way between modern humanity and the message of the Gospel. For us, this message consists of the resurrection and, in the resurrection, in a life finally freed from nothingness. It marks the advent of the person and of the communion of persons. To young people, the patriarch wishes to say: What you are living—when you seek not just your pleasure but a sincere encounter with another—is a quasi-mystical experience, an experience of the presence of God. So you must be careful, as there is much at stake! Do not be carried away like a straw in the wind by the anonymous billows of life. If you move ceaselessly from one brief encounter to another, you will break yourself and others apart. What the Church proposes—it imposes nothing, you are free!—is to integrate the immensity of life into a real encounter. To "know" a person, as the Bible says, to become "one flesh," as Christ repeats, requires time. One comes to know someone only after many years, through a combination of both work and leisure, of sharing and common service. Passion then becomes patience, mutual respect, true love.

Love and the Church

But one cannot achieve this type of love alone. Some people never reach it, because death comes first. There are so many deaths in our lives! For this reason, the Church proposes that you take charge of your love—through the sacrament, the "great mystery" of marriage. The relationship between man and woman is then inserted into that between Christ and the Church; and the Church is the world on the path of transfiguration. The baptismal sacrament of death and resurrection teaches you to die to yourself so that the other can exist. And the eucharist, as well as the common cup that you share in the rite of marriage, the Gospel reading about the wedding at Cana—all this can help you find great joy in the patience necessary in daily life.

But if the man and woman cannot align their lives with this "great mystery," if they end up destroying one another, then the Church understands and forgives divorce. It allows both second and third marriages, though these rites have a penitential tone.

Love is not justified by the bearing of children, but the child is the normal consequence of the superabundance of love. Do not expect from a patriarch orders or prohibitions about how to love each other! As both Bartholomew and his predecessor, Athenagoras, have stated: if a man and a woman truly love one another, I have no business in their bedroom! Regarding birth control methods, they have their own consciences, their physician, their spiritual father to guide them. It is not my business.

As for abortion, this is always profoundly dramatic for a woman and deeply injures her femininity. For this reason, abortion for the sake of convenience is, we cannot deny it, extremely serious and must be strongly discouraged. But there are situations of extreme distress when abortion can be a lesser evil, as, for example, when the life of the future mother is in danger. In a number of cases, the woman is less responsible than the man, who either commits rape or simply abandons her; or she is less responsible than a society in which the children of the poor are massacred or mutilated to harvest their organs, as happens in many places. The woman needs help, needs reconciliation, needs the healing of her body, of course, but also of her soul. And, when there is yet time, she, together with her child, must be offered assistance—this is today the duty of the Church, of the Churches.

We Orthodox, the patriarch points out, are fortunate to have a married clergy. This has been the case since the beginning of the Church, as the First Epistle of Timothy proves: "Now a bishop must be... the husband of one wife, temperate, sensible, dignified, hospitable, an apt teacher... He must manage his household well, keeping his children submissive and respectful in every way."[2] The western argument that a celibate priest is more available seems highly debatable. First, many of our priests, in order to be available, are greatly assisted in their ministry by their wives. Second, history shows that priestly celibacy arose in the West for entirely different reasons: the Levitical prohibitions which affirm the incompatibility of sexuality and service at the altar.

Celibacy is meaningful only when it is part of a broader asceticism of a monastic type. We cannot confuse the way of life of a monk with that of a parish priest. The Church must be free to choose its priests from either married men or, if necessary, from among the monks.

The Ordination of Women?

The Gospel has unequivocally affirmed the equal personal dignity of man and woman. The wife of the priest—without whose agreement a man cannot be ordained—in her own way, with a discreet efficacy, shares in her husband's pastoral work.

2   3:2-4.

The East has also known deaconesses, at least until the 11th century. These received a true ordination, and not a simple blessing. This is a ministry that should today be restored, and its role redefined to fit modern needs.

As for the ordination of women to the priesthood, Bartholomew at present believes that a 2,000-year-old tradition should be taken seriously. He is aware that quite a few theologians say that this discipline has no theological basis. But there are, he believes, symbolic reasons. Unfortunately, symbolic language has for us become foreign or has, in Orthodoxy, been twisted into explanations that make the woman inferior. Its true meaning must be restored through our contemporary research in all fields, and also through a more careful reflection on the teaching of the Gospel, in which the woman whom Jesus freed from her "impurity" appears not as an apostle, but as an "apostle to the apostles," to use a liturgical expression. It is also necessary to "declericalize" the Church, to remove all connotations of power from priestly service.

In any case, in both the theological and symbolic realms, the question remains open.

About AIDS

I am often questioned about AIDS, says the patriarch, particularly by journalists. I am not among those who judge and who condemn. Christ teaches us compassion without limits. This disease, it seems to me, reminds us of three things.

The first is that medicine, as advanced as it may be today, does not always heal. Certainly, research should be maximized, but the AIDS virus hides and mutates. In the meantime, the most important things are a staunch refusal to exclude its victims and the human and spiritual comfort provided them.

The second is the inseparable character of love and death. And only spiritual life, about which we spoke earlier, can transform this death into resurrection. AIDS is a strange sickness and takes its time. It is therefore possible to contaminate others, to transmit death in the very act of love.

The third is the inevitable and imminent aspect of death, which we nearly always forget. When sickness strikes, the aging process accelerates, and the confrontation with death becomes precipitous. All the important issues now come to the fore: our attitude toward time, our relationship to others and to the self, the meaning of our life, or the lack of it. We cannot flee; every minute counts. Our spiritual growth is tremendous.

For us, there are two challenges.

First, we must accompany these victims with a great deal of care, with tenderness, and sometimes, when and if barriers break down, with the brave simplicity of our witness.

Second, we must fight the spread of this epidemic. If we do not, it will devastate Africa and Southeast Asia. We must be realistic: "protecting" ourselves and "protecting" our partner is essential.

It is certainly good to preach to Christians about continence and fidelity. But what about everyone else? What about half-Christians? What about our adolescents, who cannot live up to these virtues from one day to the next? What about those adults who, hurting from a broken relationship and feeling totally alone, seek solace just once in a one-night stand that could leave them infected?

It is also important for us to develop sex education, but we cannot reduce such education to pure mechanics—man is not a machine. Sex education must include teaching about love. Adolescents are passionately attentive, and the patriarch knows this well, when they are told that freedom requires responsibility, as well as respect of both others and the self.

Having said this, and it needed to be said, we must go further. Just like drugs, sexual promiscuity ultimately reflects a deep unease. One never goes beyond the self, one loves neither the "other"

nor the self. One seeks only immediate satisfaction, which can itself become a drug. We must listen to such persons, understand
them, love them, and, when the time comes, witness to them. So
many souls are famished. Will we know to give them the nourish-
ment they ignore, but for which they wait nevertheless? What
kind of face, or mask, or caricature of itself—or, alas, of
God—does the Church offer them?

About Drugs

Drugs have always existed in western culture, but they were
chiefly confined to a small group of aesthetes. What is new in
our times is that drugs affect many young people from all walks
of life.

We could broaden the problem by asking ourselves whether
contemporary civilization is not, in fact, a civilization of drug addicts. Millions of people consume drugs under the guise of tran-
quilizers or stimulants, not to mention certain abuses taking the
form of excessive speed, alcohol, or sex.

Our civilization is also based on impatience. Rapid technical
advances make transition and preparation useless. Air travel abolishes space. A tiny movement of the hand suffices to light up an
entire room. The time between desire, its gratification, and renewed exasperation grows ever shorter. Initiatives patiently
brought to fruition have disappeared. Drugs, then, offer the illusion that we have everything, immediately. They dissolve the
"principle of reality" into the "principle of pleasure." We do not
know whether the use of "soft" drugs really has no psychological
effects, but we clearly see the extent to which it halts the maturing
process among adolescents.

At the extreme, a person uses drugs to forget an anguish that
has become unbearable. Needless to say, adolescents are nearly always haunted by anguish. This anguish is caused by the society in
which they must find their place; it is caused by death and sexual-

ity, which attract and repel them simultaneously. But adolescent angst becomes unbearable only when it is combined with and magnified by that of an entire culture—a culture that offers no refuge, no values, no meaning, and, ultimately, only nothingness. The result is drug abuse, the denial of death, the return to the maternal womb, the incredible explorations into the subterranean mind and world, the discovery of alternate states of consciousness—but all this never transcends this world, whose end is death. "Often, for several hours," writes Dostoevsky, "one can sense the paradise of love, or life in its entirety, enormous, incredible, marvelous, like a great, beautiful dream." But then he also adds: "But the minutes when one regains sobriety are horrible. The miserable creature cannot bear them and immediately takes an even stronger dose of his poison."[3] It all leads to an extreme coldness, that icy feeling described by Baudelaire, which led him to say that drugs were a weapon of suicide.

Detoxification is easy, but by itself it means nothing. It must be followed by acceptance, protection, and guidance. Persons who have lost their connection to the structures of life, who have become like ghosts, but who have shown that they await something, need something, those who have made the initial effort to move beyond their present state, need structure and growth. The only true solution for the long term is the rediscovery of an authentic spirituality. Hesychasm, for instance, rejects extraordinary experiences, unusual visions such as those that drugs can provide. It is one's entire existence which, little by little, becomes aware that it lives "in the mystery." If the light of the resurrection can set the heart on fire—i.e., transfigure the body—it can be received only in faith and humility, and through patient service toward the "other." One moment of silence with God, and the heart is touched by peace. A blade of grass sways in the breeze, and the heart beats to the rhythm of universal celebration. At times, we

3   *St Petersburg Gazette* (1847).

perceive the real visage beneath all the scars and masks—"the one who sees his brother sees his God"—and we weep with the one who is suffering, we rejoice with the one who is happy.

Are we aware of the extent to which the invisible about which drug addicts speak is, in fact, a desert in which they see no one, in which no one comes to them? In the mirror, or on its other side, there is no one but themselves, and nothingness. They emerge from this state with a terrible sense of need, only to steal or prostitute themselves.

For the Christian on the other hand, the world is one immense dialogue.

"What is immortal life?" asks Isaac of Syria. His answer:

> To feel everything in God. For love comes from encounter. Knowledge, uniting itself to God, fulfills all desires. And, for the heart which receives knowledge, it consists entirely of sweetness overflowing the whole earth, for there is nothing like the sweetness of the knowledge of God.[4]

Becoming Responsible

As the patriarch told a group of high school students he met in Athens in April 1995, he is well aware of the "snares" facing modern youth: alcohol, drugs, AIDS. Prevention is needed, but it will mean nothing unless it is accompanied by an awareness by young people of their responsibility. We must transmit to them, first of all through our own example, the need to respect the "other" and the self. They must become responsible toward those around them, their parents, toward society, and, if they live in a Christian community, toward the Church: but they must particularly be responsible toward themselves. Then the risk of falling prey to these snares will diminish, not be-

4   *Ascetical Treatise* 38.

cause society or the Church prohibits certain things, but because young people, out of respect for and faithfulness toward themselves, will themselves reject them. What is important is not to impose rules, but to convince them of their vocation to be personal beings, capable not of wasting life, but of truly loving it through friendship, love, and creativity. If the Church says nothing, does nothing in this regard, the damages risk being even more severe. Instead of accusing and condemning, let the Church counsel. Let it welcome persons into real communities. Let it become, and never cease becoming, what it is: a place of rebirth.

8

Church and State

The Christianized Roman Empire and the Orthodox Commonwealth

In the political history of the Christian East, the empire, potentially universal, preceded the nation. The empire expressed the diverse unity of the Christian people—it was the Christian *res publica*, the *politeuma* of the baptized. The "Roman" Empire, centered on the two Romes, old and new, disappeared in the West at the end of the fifth century; but in the East, it remained for another millennium, marked by several periods of great power and expansion. The Empire was the rampart of the Church, the baptismal crucible and civilizer of nations.

In this "Roman" Empire, miraculously christianized during the fourth century, church-state relations were marked by a "symphony," a "harmony" between spiritual authority and secular power, two functions of one single organism. Against the "cesaro-papist" temptations of the emperors, the patriarchs were able to maintain the spiritual independence of the church, so that neither doctrine nor morals were bent by political interests for any extended period of time. The patriarchs, sometimes weak before imperial power in the short term, ultimately won out thanks to support from two sides: first, that of the humanists, who maintained the freedom of the spirit; second, particularly that of the monks—and of the populace they brought with them—who maintained the eschatological freedom of the Spirit. The structure of this seamless society was therefore truly "bipolar."

Gradually, the borders of the empire stabilized, then retreated. But the mission of the church continued to expand, eventually extending from the Balkans all the way to the Polar Circle. This led to the development of a new structure, which could be described as a *commonwealth*. Around the empire, still prestigious even in its weakened state, arose young nations. These new states were politically independent, but their churches, while flexibly autonomous, had their primates confirmed or appointed by the ecumenical patriarch. This procedure in fact ensured a real independence of the primate with respect to the local sovereign. It is in this context that the first "autocephalies" appeared in the Balkans, with no conflict or turning in on the self, a kind of interdependence rather than independence...

Had such a process been followed in the West, as the 14th century "conciliarist" movement sought at one time, the Reformation might well have been avoided. In the East, the process was halted as a result of two concomitant factors: the collapse of the center, and the progressive invasion of southeastern Europe by the Ottoman forces. The disintegrating empire, now composed solely of Greeks, transmitted a universalistic dream to Hellenism. The Balkan Slavs, Bulgarians and Serbs, affirmed themselves as totally independent nations and as candidates to succeed the empire. Later, the same thing happened in Russia.

National Awakenings, Imperial Dreams, Messianic Temptations

In this way, the imperial dream projected itself on national awakenings. The notion of the "people of God" was confused with the nation, which considered itself as elect, vested with a quasi-messianic mission. The Turkish invasion buried these aspirations in a new, multi-national—but also alien and non-Christian—empire, where these ideas remained within the collective memory and gradually turned into obsessions. In 1389, for example, King Lazarus of Serbia consecrated his people to God with an oath on the eve of the Battle of Kossovo, at which he lost his life and his country its independence. Ever since, the oppressed Serbian people have remained faithful to the notion of a "Heavenly Serbia," charged with a special mission to defend Orthodoxy from assault by the Roman Catholic world from the West, and Islamic attacks from the East.

After the Ottoman capture of the Balkans, Russia remained the only independent Orthodox country, the "Third Rome," whose destiny was to save Orthodoxy. In this capacity, it was often able to assist the Orthodox population in the Balkans in a truly disinterested fashion. But, in contrast with Byzantium, the Russian Empire was not truly multinational, for it was based on the domination of only one people, the Russians. Thus we find once more the perversion of nationalism by a kind of messianism.

In the Balkans, the ecumenical patriarch has been able to preserve the supranational character of the Church. This is, for example, evident from the presence of monks of all nationalities on Mt Athos, or from the active role of the Romanian Church at the crossroads of Orthodoxy and Europe. Constantinople was able, outside the borders of the Ottoman Empire, to preserve Ukrainian Orthodoxy and to strengthen the bond between the Church and the Christian population of this area. The Church, in fact, succeeded in preserving the language, the culture, and the customs of the Greeks, Bulgarians, Serbs, and Romanians. But this also completed the fusion—or, rather, confusion—between ethnic and religious identity.

In the 19th century, the rise of nationalism in southwestern Europe partly inherited this symbiosis in its aspect of diversity. But, under western influence, it ignored or rejected its unitive aspects. This was an ideology elaborated by the French Revolution (one belongs to a nation because one knows it and desires it) and by German Romanticism (one belongs to a nation because of links to the land, ties of blood, and social conditioning, even if one is not aware of it). This remained a secular ideology in the

realm of simple patriotism, but it became pseudo-religious when
patriotism turned to rabid nationalism and awoke messianic tendencies, in the West as in the East.

In 1833, in a Greece that had barely earned its independence,
a westernized elite imposed the autocephaly of the Church, thus
causing a break with Constantinople. The rupture was strongly
felt both by the mother-church and by the most pious Greek Orthodox believers.

The same phenomenon occurred in other Balkan countries
(only the Serbian Church did not present the ecumenical patriarchate with a *fait accompli*). The model, more or less everywhere,
was Lutheran. Autocephaly was no longer conceived of as interdependence, but as absolute independence. The trend was to an absolute "autocephalism."

The Ambiguous Link Between Church and Nation

Thus the growing link today between church and nation is
deeply ambiguous. It is certainly good that the Church, in contrast with what took place in Catholic Europe, did not present
itself as a state within the state, at the risk of fracturing the national community. It is good that it enriches national life
through a discreet osmosis, and that it calls for the defense of
the nation under threat. This happened in 1949, when Italy attacked Greece, and in 1941 when the Germans assaulted Serbia and Russia. But the essential and evident separation from
the external enemy could not be maintained with respect to the
state. Nationalism, so long frustrated by centuries of subjection
to more or less multi-national empires, now tried to appropriate Orthodoxy, to turn it into its instrument, to instill in it its
hatreds, its fears, its phobias. Orthodoxy has often become the
sign of belonging, a little bit like Judaism in the State of Israel.
One can love the forests of one's native land, the singing in its
churches and the light of candles, without ever having read the

Gospel. One can call oneself Orthodox (specifying also the nationality) without any awareness of being a Christian. One can even call oneself Orthodox while remaining an atheist!

An improved relationship between church and state began in Russia and in other East-European countries at the end of the 19th and the beginning of the 20th century. The Council of Moscow in 1917-1918 began—too late, through the fault of Nicholas II—to develop new structures. But the spread of totalitarianism put a stop to everything.

Against Stereotypes

In reflecting upon this long history—we will speak below of the current situation—we must reject the stereotypes about Orthodoxy long held in the West. No, the Orthodox Church has not always been a tool of the state. We have already mentioned the situation in Byzantium, and the bipolarity between the empire and the monks (from among whom bishops and the patriarch were recruited). In Russia, the church maintained its right to protest and intercede until the secularization promulgated by Peter the Great. The "fools for Christ" confronted the most absolute rulers with their bitter humor and condemned the pharisaism of a ponderously ritualistic society. We should not forget the witness—often to the point of death—of Philip of Moscow before Ivan the Terrible, of Benjamin of Petrograd before Lenin, of the Greek and Serbian bishops before the puppet regimes installed by the Nazis. Certainly, the Orthodox Church often taught the faithful to be resigned, at least openly. But the Greek Church, for example, opened "secret schools" despite the Turkish occupation; the Romanians printed books in Venice; Nicodemos of the Holy Mountain published fundamental writings about the faith in Vienna. Significant revolts also erupted in the Orthodox world, revolts not

against God, but against caricatures of God: those of Avvakum
in 17th century Russia; and Papoulakis in the 19th, opposing a
German-style regime in the Peloponnesus which enslaved the
church; to Berdiaev who, on the eve of World War I, denounced the "stiflers of the Spirit" in the Holy Synod and the
Russian Empire. And what of Solzhenitsyn and the great Russian dissidents of our own era? Even in the darkest of times,
there was light. A report prepared by a high Soviet functionary
during the era of "stagnation" indicated that only one third of
Russian bishops were considered fully satisfactory; another
third, while maintaining their loyalty to the government, did
their best to sustain and develop the faith; and the last third did
the same, but were not politically trustworthy!

Another stereotype has it that Orthodoxy and democracy are
incompatible. But this is to forget the role of the church in the
merchant republics of Novgorod and Pskov, and then later in
Russia between 1905 and 1922, when Lenin expelled the great
Orthodox thinkers who wished to participate in the building of a
new society. This is also to forget the church's role in the constitu-
tional monarchies of southeastern Europe from the late 19th century to World War II.

It is true that Orthodoxy rejects both western individualism
and totalitarian expansionism. It places its accent on personhood
in communion, on diversity in unity, on the preeminence of contemplation and creativity. Berdiaev wrote of "communitarian personalism." Solzhenitsyn spoke of a "democracy in small places."
Christos Yannaras speaks of the need for a new theological paradigm which would, within the realm of Orthodox conciliarity,
promote structures thoroughly conducive to concrete expressions
of fellowship and cooperation.

Throughout its history, the Orthodox Church has encouraged
numerous local democracies, with elected leaders; and it is these,
for example, that enabled Russia to overcome the "Time of Trou-

bles" (and the massive Polish invasion that accompanied it) through the creation of an "Assembly of the Land" which appointed a new tsar and worked with him.

In the 18th and 19th centuries, village communities in the Greek world were vigorous and able to stand up to the Turkish authorities. It is in this context that St Cosmas the Aetolian was able to conduct his campaign for justice, education, and improved conditions for women and children. The patriarch himself was elected, not just by bishops, but also by numerous lay persons representing the most active elements of the Orthodox *millet*.

The Current Situation

After the long period of communist domination, which, despite numerous martyrs and confessors, left Eastern Europe dechristianized to a degree that we can hardly imagine, the Orthodox Church has reached the era of freedom—a century or two later than the western confessions. It must now develop a new style of witness within society. In some places, the faith has been deepened; it has become conscious and personal. But among the masses, the spiritual void is made even worse by the intrusion of the most mediocre elements of western culture. Sectarian incursions accompany the agony caused by the destruction of values and standards. It is out of this context that there arises a rabid nationalism which takes the form of a pseudo-religion and appropriates Orthodox trappings. Its hatred of the "rotten West" at times leads it to rehabilitate, at least partially, the discredited totalitarianism of our century: communism, of course, or a nostalgia for national and imperial greatness, but also Nazism, that great opponent of a mythic "Judeo-Masonry," conveniently failing to remember Hitler's attack on Russia!

This pressure of nationalism has divided the Orthodox. It reduces Christianity, exerts strong pressure on the hierarchy, and spreads its xenophobic, anti-Semitic, and anti-democratic ideas among the mass of the faithful, who themselves tend to be very ritualistic, on the defensive, and to avoid politics. But there also exists an open and intelligent minority which desires, within a democratic context, a real separation between church and state. It believes that the church must act discreetly, primarily by example, like leaven. This fervent minority also influences the masses by uniting an intense spiritual life to a renewed liturgy. Moreover, all sides have joined together in vigorous social action, assisting prisoners, drug addicts, the handicapped, the sick and the dying, all those marginalized and abandoned by society. Patriarch Alexis of Moscow—a man of great worth, says Bartholomew—resists the nationalist and extremist trends, supports democracy, refuses any "political marriage" between church and state, and condemns violence and anti-Semitism. But he fears a schism, and for this reason he acts very prudently.

At this point, we cannot avoid speaking of the Serbian problem.

The Serbian Drama: Several Statements

It is well-known that the western media have demonized the Serbs and blame the Orthodox Church for the horrors of an abominable war.

Bartholomew would first like to bring up several statements. On Christmas 1992, he wrote:

> We dare to raise our voice to ask all those responsible once and for all to put an end to this frenzy, to this madness, to this triumph of death which can leave only heaps of ruins, tears of the innocent, and a memory of hatred. We raise our voice—a voice of agony and of extreme suffering—at this moment when we approach the anniversary of the birth of Christ, the God-man, who is venerated not only by Christians... but also by our Moslem brethren, who consider him to be a great prophet who was pleasing to God....

In February 1994, the patriarch sponsored a meeting in Istanbul of numerous leaders of the three great monotheistic traditions, chiefly from southeastern Europe. Together, they crafted the "Bosphorus Declaration," which was unfortunately largely ignored by the western media. It denounced the crimes against humanity committed in Bosnia, as well as the use of religion for nationalistic purposes.

> The exploitation of religious symbols to support the cause of aggressive nationalism is a betrayal of the universality of the faith... We demand an end to the confiscation, profanation, and destruction of places of worship... We abhor and absolutely condemn ethnic cleansing, rape, and murder... We condemn those who forcibly remove families from their homes, separate children from their parents, husbands from wives, in the name of senseless nationalism...

Does the world know, Bartholomew insists, that Patriarch Pavle of Serbia, a real monk, an old man purified by fasting and prayer, speaks a different language? He has distanced himself from the regime, arousing considerable criticism. "Evil," he says, "can never engender good." "No national interest... gives us the right to respond to crime with crime."

> I have said: if the question is put in these terms, to maintain a Greater Serbia at the cost of crime, I would never accept it. Never. Let Greater Serbia disappear if it can be maintained only at this cost. And even if no longer a Greater Serbia, but a lesser Serbia were maintained at the cost of crime, I would not accept that either.[1]

> I was asked my opinion about the rape of 30,000 Moslem women. I answered that the Serbs who committed such acts are not human beings...[2]

1   In the *Serbian News*, published in California and reprinted in the journal of the Serbian Patriarchate, *Pravoslavlje*, October 1994.
2   Interview in the Serbian bi-weekly *Duga*, July 28-August 13, 1993.

In the Koran, it is written that whoever attacks a single man
attacks all of humanity. And this is true: an injustice committed against a single man affects everyone. We are all
brothers, we all have the same heavenly Father.[3]

Patriarch Pavle has repeatedly met with Cardinal Kuharic of
Zagreb, and, in England in 1993, with the Reis-el-Ulema Jakub
Selimoski, representative of the Bosnian Moslems. Jointly with
them, he condemned "ethnic cleansing."

The Serbian Church has often announced—without ever being heard in the West—that close to 400 Orthodox churches have
been profaned and totally or partially destroyed. With a sad irony,
Patriarch Pavle recounts how the Croats, when they invaded western Slovenia, destroyed the church in his village, for the simple
reason that this was the village in which he was born. He has
asked for international assistance for the 700,000 refugees in Serbia, among whom the mortality rate continues to rise, particularly for children and the aged. These refugees, to whose number
are also added those who come from *Krajina*, have also been the
victims of ethnic cleansing—unfortunately a typical phenomenon in the Balkans for centuries.

But the patriarch has not concealed the fact that

the Serbs, on their side, destroy places of worship belonging
to Croats and Moslems. For example, in Banya Luka, the
Ferhadjia and Arnaudija mosques, masterpieces of Islamic
architecture dating to the 16th century; and the Alaça
mosque was destroyed in Foca. Even the name of Foca has
been suppressed, even though it derives from an old Slavic
place name, Hodja.[4]

Finally, the patriarch insists on a *sharing of responsibility*, and
Bartholomew shares this view.

3   *Ibid.*
4   Interview in the newspaper *Nin*, Belgrade, January 27, 1995. In Islam, a *Hodja* is
    someone who has sanctified himself by making a pilgrimage to Mecca.

The Serbian Drama: Historical Remarks

The present crisis was born of the hasty dismemberment of the Yugoslav Federation, too quickly recognized by Europe and America. The foreign powers should first have mandated negotiations concerning the status of people who would become minorities (which they were not in the former federal context), as well as about the location of borders—borders originally fixed for the most part by the hazards of history, by blind collisions between empires. A third of the Serbs in Yugoslavia live outside the borders of Serbia proper. Tito restrained and parceled Serbia because, during the war, it had been hostile to the communist partisans, siding with Mihailovic's *Tchetniks*. In Croatia, the Serbs comprised 15 percent of the population. A number of them lived in a distinct settlement in the *Krajina*, literally a "fence," a buffer zone against the Ottomans, installed there by the Hapsburgs four centuries earlier, where they had been given guaranteed rights (the Croatian state did not yet exist). During World War II, the Germans and Italians created a Croatian state. Within this "independent" Croatia, the *Ustashi* (together with Moslem members of the SS) carried out a genocide, with the agreement of their sponsors, massacring 700,000 Serbs (together with Jews and Gypsies) and forcibly converting 240,000 Orthodox to Catholicism by rebaptism. The chasms of Karst were filled with cadavers which Tito walled in without those responsible ever being held to account.

The Serbs of *Krajina*, therefore, were neither invaders nor occupiers—contrary to what might have been heard in the West. This was their home. When, in 1991, Croatia became fully independent, and this was internationally recognized on German initiative, the Serbs of *Krajina* were worried. Certain emblems from 1941 reappeared, and Germany's role left an impression that World War II was resuming. Certainly, propaganda by the Serbian Communist

Party, now converted into an ultra-nationalist party, systematically aggravated this concern. The "anti-secessionist" war launched by the federal army was conducted according to the terrorist methods of the Soviet military school. The strong pressures to flee exerted on the Croatian inhabitants of *Krajina* must also be loudly condemned, as well as the breaking of communication links with Dalmatia, which was carried out without warning. And finally, it cannot be denied that *Krajina* was a chiefly Serbian state which, for centuries, had never depended on Zagreb. For these reasons, the recent exodus of a majority of its inhabitants is a disaster in Serbian history. A disaster that cannot be justified.

As for Bosnia, it is not a nation, but the fragment of a multinational empire, one of those empires the West destroyed during World War I. Bosnian history has been marked by more than 500 years of foreign domination, by resettlements of entire populations, by very hostile conditions for Christians, and by kidnappings of young boys who were made into "janissaries." Mass conversions to Islam took place in the 15th and 16th centuries, and individual conversions continued subsequently, more out of self-interest than from constraint. In particular, large landholders were thereby able to consolidate their domination over the peasantry.

There is only one ethnic group in this country, the Slavs. Differences arose as a result of social, psychological and cultural factors; and religion, the patriarch emphasizes, signifies an identity and not a faith. It was Tito who made the Moslems into a "nation." Before that, they considered themselves to be Serbs, or Croats, of Islamic faith.

When the Yugoslav federation broke apart, a pact was reached among the three groups comprising the population, according to which all major decisions required their common agreement. But this pact was violated when the Moslems and the Croats proclaimed their independence after a referendum on this subject, from which the Serbs abstained *en masse*. An agreement, however, was signed in Lisbon by representatives of the three Bosnian "nations," and this is a point to which Patriarch Pavle often returns. He foresaw the transformation of Bosnia into three separate districts. But America and Europe immediately recognized the new country, again without much preliminary reflection, as a "unified" Bosnia: Izetbegovic immediately retracted his signature. Civil war was inevitable.

In the words of Patriarch Pavle,

> Because of this international recognition, those who rejected it automatically became aggressors. In the eyes of the world, the Moslems were now the "Bosnians," and the Serbian natives were "aggressors."

Questions

We would be remiss if we did not at this point raise several questions.

Why did the West recognize the right of self-determination for the Croats and the Moslems, but did not recognize it for the Serbs?

Why did the West, which strongly condemned the notion of a "Greater Serbia," say nothing when the Croatians *de facto* annexed that part of Bosnia in which they form the majority, expelling the Moslems and creating the Republic of *Herzeg-Bosnia*, with the Croatian flag, currency, and army?

It is, of course, not possible to justify the horrors that some Serbs may have committed, the massive expulsions or terrible massacres of Moslems, particularly in Srebrenica, or the endless suffering inflicted on Sarajevo. Some Serbian militia leaders and certain highly-placed military officers are incontestably war criminals. But then arises another, much more serious, question, formulated by Patriarch Pavle himself: How did things get to this point, after he himself had always demanded that the Serbs fight loyally, limiting violence and, in particular, respecting civilians? Why were so many mosques destroyed, while those in territories conquered during the Balkan wars in 1912 were left untouched?

The patriarch answers that this stems, on the one hand, from the extreme moral degradation caused by the aggressive atheism of Communism, and, on the other, from the pleasure-seeking nihilism which, today, comes from the West. Taking up the well-known argument of Dostoevsky, he notes that "terrorists are spawned by the dominant ideology of our day, according to which all is allowed, since there is no God."

Clearly, the interpretation of this war varies greatly in Eastern Europe and in the West. For the western media, which seek a substitute enemy ever since the collapse of the Iron Curtain, the Serbs, and perhaps the Orthodox, are fascists. For the Serbs and the Greeks, who heroically combated fascism during the last World War, while the Croats collaborated with it, the recent war has revealed the hypocrisy of a West which, under the guise of human rights, knows only power and money. And there is sufficient blame to pass around that each finds support for its argument.

The Task of Constantinople

The role of the ecumenical patriarchate, located at the juncture of East and West, is to help them understand one another, help them disarm in spirit. Negotiation cannot come from force alone. It requires an opening of hearts. The spirit of the "Bosphorus Declaration" must be reclaimed and deepened. The world marches irresistibly toward unity. God "made from one every nation to live on all the face of the earth..."[5] This unification, if it is carried out exclusively through technological and market forces, will only lead to greater crises of identity. Only love, which seeks diversity in unity, an active, creative love, can gradually surmount these obstacles. As St Paul says in his speech on the Areopagus: God, "having determined [for the nations] allotted periods and the boundaries of their habitation, that they should seek God, in the

5   Acts 17:26.

hope that they might feel after him and find him. Yet he is not far from each one of us."[6]

It is the task of the Church to provide an example. But if an extreme Roman centralization weighs on Catholicism, Orthodoxy appears today to be torn apart by the rise of nationalism. The condemnation of phyletism by the Council of 1872 seems today forgotten, or insufficient. More efficient steps need to be taken to enable Orthodoxy to overcome its divisions, so that it will no longer appear to the world as a conglomerate of churches which, though sharing the same faith, live in isolation, or even confront one another under the impulse of excessive nationalism.

The Church must become not a passive instrument, but the critical conscience of the peoples it is charged with evangelizing. *Orthodoxy must be able to speak with one voice* for its witness to be heard. Hence the importance of the ecumenical patriarchate, the importance of the pan-Orthodox conferences it convenes, the importance also of the "synaxes" of all the primates that the patriarch tries periodically to organize. In the *diaspora*, which this pan-Orthodox collaboration will allow to organize, parishes exist which celebrate in the local language: here one finds Orthodox of all ethnic backgrounds praying and working together. In this way, they discover Orthodox unity. "I support them with all my might," Bartholomew affirms.

As for the notion of an "Orthodox political axis" in Central Europe, it is totally foreign to the patriarch. A congress of Orthodox parliamentarians took place in Thessalonika in 1993. He sent them a message rejecting any political alliance in the name of Orthodoxy. Certainly we belong to the same family and have common spiritual and cultural interests. But the notion of an "axis" or a "bloc" is purely secular, reducing spirituality to politics, just as does nationalism! This has nothing in common with the "conciliarity" of Orthodox ecclesiology. Let us not put the cart before the

6   Acts 17:26-27.

horse. Our primary task is to bear witness to the resurrection. Later, if there are indeed some resurrected ones in the Resurrected One, then we can begin to speak of a "third Orthodox way," and other such things. Or rather, about an evangelical and resurrectional path for all humanity!

NB: Regarding the Yugoslav crisis, this chapter was written before the Dayton accords and their difficult implementation. This does not, however, lessen its import.

9

On Europe: Secularization and How It Might be Overcome

The Origin and Meaning of Europe

The origin and meaning of Europe is the person. And, let us not forget: a person requires communion.

In ancient civilizations, which we call "traditional," everything is seen to exist and relate in a sort of *magical sphere*. Everything, i.e., humanity, the gods, the cosmos. The world is sometimes perceived to be an illusion, sometimes as a divine game, but always merely as an "appearance," which has no consistency of its own. In this context, time consists of cycles in which the "golden age" always lies in the past, in which history is only oblivion and decay, in which we advance backwards. Any innovation is always bad, and the most we can hope for is restorations, which are themselves increasingly precarious. The psychological envelopes of the supra-personal Self move forward from one existence to another, a fatal "cycle" from which one always seeks escape. *The "other" as such does not exist.* Society is cemented by a ritual conformity. One who deviates, the "scapegoat" who is demonized (and sometimes sacralized), is subjected to violence, which purges the community of its own destructive impulses.

Toward the seventh, sixth, and fifth centuries BC came, more or less everywhere, what Karl Jaspers has called the "axial period" in human history: individual awareness moved outside the sacred collective, philosophical questioning appeared, concepts began to challenge myths, prophecy opposed an immanent sacredness. This was Confucius in China, Buddha in India, Zarathustra in Iran, Socrates and Antigone in Greece, the great Jewish prophets in the Middle East.

This universal upheaval had lasting effects only in the Biblical and Greek worlds, which soon expanded into Hellenistic culture through the conquests of Alexander the Great, and then of Rome. Elsewhere, a kind of immobility returned. In the Hellenistic world, a concern for the individual developed, as is evident from the numerous portraits from the last centuries before the Christian era—a concern which was poorly answered by the hardened serenity of the Stoics or the self-divinization of the man with power or fortune, such as Alexander or Caesar.

Between the Asian East, where humanity was fused into the divine, and the ancient West, where there developed a concern for the individual, came Biblical revelation: a personal God, who could no longer be confused with eros and the cosmos, together with man in his image, called to become a unique, incomparable person; the universe as creation, both autonomous and imbued with divine wisdom; time as history, leading toward a particular goal. The revelation of the Gospel provided something both deeper and new: God is Love; the human person, after the image of Christ, becomes rooted in the ontological unity of humanity. The Fathers and councils of the fourth and fifth centuries developed further the great affirmations about Jesus in the Gospel of John: "That they may all be one; even as you, Father, are in me, and I in you, that they may also be in us." In the image of and by participation in Trinitarian existence, we are called simultaneously to diversity and communion. In both God and man, being is relational.

The fruitful persistence of Judaism, then the rise of Islam, both of which confess the living, personal God, but who ignore the Trinity (or think they do, as we shall see later), completed the division of humanity into two spiritual hemispheres: the "Asiatic" hemisphere, arising out of India, with the immense spread of Buddhism throughout the Far East, and the "Semitic" hemisphere, which today encompasses Judaism and Islam. The Asiatic hemisphere emphasizes interiority and the omnipresence of the divine, into which the universe is fused. The Semitic hemisphere rejects this absorption, but sees no encounter between God and man other than through human obedience to a revealed Law (except in esotericism: certain forms of Kaballa and Sufism, in which there appear tendencies toward fusion, often through Neo-Platonic influence).

Between the two lie Christianity and Europe (from which the Near-Eastern matrix cannot be eliminated)—i.e., the mystery of the "Other" inscribed in the heart of Unity.

The Ambivalence of "Christian Societies"

The Gospel has indeed been the leaven of history. But it has also been abused by history. Hence the manifest ambivalence of "Christian societies," that is, of groups that call themselves Christian.

In the East, the Roman Empire was christianized quite deeply. The rights of women and children, laws regarding property, and the status of servants were all humanized. The monks maintained the freedom of the spirit. Culture remained open, with a lay, imperial university, the persistence of non-Christian philosophical movements, the influence of Homer alongside that of the Bible. One even finds a thread of democracy, both within church structures, with large, local autonomous churches, and within the state, because the empire—long ago multi-national—was not hereditary and, theoretically at least, anyone could be elected emperor by the people, the army, and the senate. War was conceived of as strictly defensive, with precise rules about allowing a defeated enemy to withdraw. And the Byzantine Church never accepted any notion of holy war or of crusade.

In the West, a nearly steady evolution leads from slavery to serfdom, with its guaranteed rights, and finally to freedom. The Church turned the savage warrior into a knight (the East similarly had its "holy princes"). War, here as well, was limited by the "peace of God" and the "respite of God." Democratic structures arose in the communal movement and in the mendicant orders, particularly among the Dominicans.

In the West as in the East, the harvest of beauty is immense, and we would not exist without it.

Nevertheless, on one side as on the other, the intimate connection between Christianity and power tended to turn "religion" into an ideology imposed within a closed society. *Christian societies have sinned against the freedom of the spirit.* They have denounced, persecuted, or attacked the *"other,"* the heretic, the Jew, the Moslem. The Inquisition of the western Middle Ages was a model for 16th-century Russia, and later for what Solzhenitsyn has called the "Russian Inquisition," which persecuted the Old Believers to the dawn of the 20th century.

In the modern era, the Orthodox world has by and large retreated into a rural form of existence, manifesting some interesting forms of community life both in Russia and the Balkans. The Ottoman Empire, more hospitable than Roman Catholic Christendom, welcomed the Jews expelled from Spain. On the whole, however, it is in Western Europe that new values developed. And these values, both positive and negative, were to awaken Russian thought in the 19th century and lead it to formulate the theme of *sobornost* more precisely as communion in freedom, not without a touch of idealism about rural life.

The Origin and Meaning of Secularization

In the West, a revolt against clerical totalitarianism, after a thousand years of religious wars and of "teaching through fear," led to claims about "the rights of man." The "Declarations of the Rights of Man" of the late 18th century certainly had Christian roots, but they opposed ecclesiastical institutions. "Christians without a church," in the words of Leslek Kolakowski, played a major role in their formulation. The desacralization of power by the Reformation (for the Reformers, power corrupts everything even while remaining indispensable, hence the need for "checks and balances") converged during the 19th century with a finally emancipated Judaism and a humanism which remained open to Gospel values, leading to the creation of government based on civil rights. Faced with currents of totalitarianism, the influence of the Gospel continued in the existential and personalistic passion of a Kierkegaard or a Dostoevsky: in the creation of more or less balanced democracies, and in the social contract of France and England (that "exterior Christianity," in the words of Péguy), whose Christian roots are evident. Modern Europe, highly complex, often tragic, was thus born from a double opposition: that of the "rights" of God versus man, and that of the "rights" of man versus God. Free human creativity, following the steps of Prometheus, rose up against the "God of morality," all too often a police God, a sadistic, castrating father.

Little by little, various aspects of existence—political, social, cultural—were emancipated, while the "religious" became simply one dimension of the cultural domain. There is no more "dominant" authority or ideology, but only independent authorities, each in its own domain. The state does not regulate the churches—as was often the case in the East, where the laity was virtually ignored. But the churches, on their side, can no longer regulate the state or society. Science and philosophy are no more "servants" of theology, which, by the way, is completely free to develop on its own.

In this fashion a new culture was formed, heterogeneous, multiple, never complete, self-critical by nature, never self-assured, hardworking, energized by research, by polemics, by diversity—all of which create tensions at the same time that they provide the impetus for change. Always in the process of reinvention, the modern state, based on law, guarantees freedoms and limits manifestations of violence.

Particularly since the 17th century, instrumental reason has imposed itself. Its goal is no longer to know and admire the connection between things, the order of the cosmos, as in ancient thought, but to transform nature, to appropriate it. It is precisely the biblical, Judeo-Christian tradition which enabled this passage from Greek thought, which sought to contemplate the order of the universe, to experimental and instrumental reason. God is not drowned in sacred nature; Genesis reveals him to be the creator of the heavenly bodies and of beasts, which other traditions divinize. The battle waged by the prophets against the Baals and cosmic magic has been continued by the monks. Christ's words affirming that "My Kingdom is not of this world," and abolishing the material distinction between pure and impure, have opened the way to secularism.

The Consequences of Secularization

Secularization, therefore, is simultaneously the daughter of Athens and of Jerusalem. Its beneficial effects are obvious. In the West, liberation from clerical control has permitted the exploration of the physical universe and of the human psyche. In the artistic realm, painting and music have flourished. Life expectancy has increased, the human population has grown, women have been emancipated, and the planet has been unified by the formation of what Teilhard de Chardin called the "noosphere." European culture appears today as the first *open* culture in history, recapitulating all the arts, all the human myths, with no other implicit philosophy than a *philosophy of the "other" welcomed in his otherness.*

Little by little, however, other, fearsome consequences become apparent: the loss of meaning and of the desire to live, the disappearance of traditional symbols concerning relations between men and women, between father, mother, and child. In assuming all the human experience of time and space, European culture destabilizes other cultures, and ultimately its own rich and complex heritage, that of its abandoned villages, its overgrown cities. The culture of unlimited production turns the Third World into a proletariat, and western societies themselves explode with unemployment and urban terrorism.

On Nihilism

Thus nihilism was born. Nietzsche and Dostoevsky say the same on this point.

"Where is God?" Nietzsche has his madman say in his *Cheerful Knowledge.*

> Where is God? he cried. I will tell you: We have killed him, you and I! ...But how could we have done this? How could we have emptied the sea? Who gave us the eraser to wipe off the entire horizon? What have we done, to detach the earth from its sun? Where is the earth going now? Far from all the suns? Are we not cast into a perpetual fall? Backward, sideways, forward, to all sides? Is there still up or down? Are we not crossing an infinite void? Do we not feel the breath of emptiness? Is it not colder and colder, is not the night growing deeper and deeper?

And Dostoevsky, in *The Gentle Woman,*

> Men are alone on earth, that is the tragedy. "Is there a living man on the plain?" shouts the valiant warrior of Russian legend. I also shout, and no one answers. They say that the sun makes the universe to live. Let it rise, the sun; look at it, is it not a corpse? Everything is dead, there are dead everywhere. Only men, and around them silence—such is the earth!

Nihilism was at first collective and, we might say, "warm." The totalitarian movements of our century actually mobilized the religious instinct of the masses. But the ashes of Auschwitz fell on Hitler's folly, on the announcement of the millenarian Reich. And on the dreams of Lenin (Stalin, for his part, consisted of nothing more than the raw desire for power) fell the snows of Siberia, where so many corpses lie mummified, a little wooden board attached to their ankles.

Then came individual nihilism, filled with a cold fire. Death has never been so rejected and so naked. The biblical revolution has forcibly removed Western Man from the impersonal, almost vegetative, peace of the "magic sphere," often more or less christianized. Machines have removed him from the maternity of the earth. "What good is it to go to the moon if it is only to commit suicide there?" asked André Malraux. For the Western Man seems to have forgotten the resurrection. And now here he is, knowing himself to be both unique and derisive, alone in the infinite prison of the universe. The very experience of freedom opens in him a chasm. Hence the search for violent emotion and escapes; hence the popularity of sects and the supposed "return of the religious," with its techniques of interior meditation, reinforced by Asiatic religions, that efface the person.

In Eastern Europe, Christians witness the collapse of the cultures which their faith had, to some extent, inspired—the art of living together, which is brutally destroyed by money, individualism, and an often coarse hedonism. More than half a century of persecution has often transformed the church into a liturgical ghetto, where the faithful are more "liturgized" than properly evangelized. Orthodoxy then becomes a sign of proud belonging rather than a personal, compassionate faith. Hence the emphasis on identity, the exaltation of what remains when all else has collapsed: the earthly, "ethnic" community, bonded by a kind of "religious" folklore. The real wounds, anesthetized by tyranny, now begin to bleed once more. *This religious nationalism is the Orthodox form of secularization.*

The Orthodox Position

Over these last years, the Orthodox Church, as a living Church, has ceaselessly denounced this modern ambivalence—"and I have tried to help in this regard, the patriarch repeats."

The message of the 1992 "Synaxis" of Orthodox primates assembled in Constantinople declares:

The 20th century can be considered as the age of major accomplishments in the realm of knowledge about the universe and in the effort to submit creation to the will of man. During this century, both the power and weakness of humanity have manifested themselves. It is evident that man's domination over his environment does not automatically bring happiness and the fullness of life... Scientific and technical progress can become an instrument for the destruction of nature and of social life. This is particularly clear after the ruin of the Communist system.

More broadly, there is also the failure of all anthropocentric ideologies, creating in humanity a spiritual void and an existential insecurity, and leading many to seek salvation in new religious or pseudo-religious movements, in sects... and all sorts of proselytism which reveal the profound crisis of the contemporary world...

And in the social sphere, only one part of humanity accumulates privileges and powers stemming from the rapid progress of technology and science, while the misery of other peoples increases, thus creating tensions and provoking wars...

The risks also increase that man will not survive as a free person, made "in the image and likeness of God." Developments in the field of genetics, while they can certainly be immensely helpful in combating disease, can also transform the human being into a thing, a controlled object, manipulated by those with power.

It is ridiculous to think that Orthodoxy opposes the West, the patriarch affirms. Orthodoxy believes—as do many westerners, particularly among Christians!—that the West places an excessive value on material progress, a progress that also harms the spiritual life of humanity. The spiritual treasures of Orthodoxy belong to every one. Orthodoxy shares the responsibility of creating a unified Europe. It is an integral part of a Christian Europe...

Accept Secularization, but in a Different Way

It would be false and dangerous to see only the negative aspects
of secularization, to denounce them and to dream of a "new"
Christianity. In the secularized world, which will certainly en-
dure, even if only as a rampart against the assault of fanaticism,
one can certainly find traces of its Greek and biblical origins.
Respect for the "other," freedom of the spirit, the best in a pluralistic democracy (and new and different forms of democracy
can be created, different from the sometimes compromised
forms in western societies)—all of this, says Bartholomew, is
rooted in the biblical revelation of the person and the distinction made by Christ between the Kingdom of God and the
kingdom of Caesar.

A secularized society is therefore not alien to us Christians,
and we must seek to *re-orient* it from within. We must take the
word *re-orient* at its full meaning: If Eastern Europe must, in one
sense or another, serve its apprenticeship as a secularized society,
so Western Europe must, thanks in part to the witness of Orthodoxy, rediscover its interior "Orient." Indeed, it is not possible to
address problems only from an economic, social, or political perspective; their moral and religious aspects must also be considered. God is not the enemy or competitor of mankind. In Christ,
we discover that God alone is human. And where this God is not
understood, the human being in his or her fullness also cannot
properly be understood.

Secularization is therefore a transition necessary to achieve
awareness and freedom. Secularization leads man both to anguish
and to amazement, to an ultimate choice between the image of
God, "a microcosm and *microtheos*," said one Father of the
Church, and the derisive efflorescence of nothingness. Yes, if we
reach the end of the modern reductions, we find either emptiness—the "death of humanity" resulting from the "death of

God"—or the enigma of the irreducible person, open to the infinite.

How, then, can Christian faith remain present in a secularized society?

First, it seems, by promoting that which is free and which cannot be assimilated. In a world where everything is for sale, can be bought or exchanged, nothing is really important. It is the realm of the whim, of satiety, ultimately of a sort of self-satisfied indifference.

An authentic Christianity places humanity before that which appears to be useless, but which explains everything, a secret reality whose very manifestation is hidden, a reality which cannot be explained, cannot be bought, but can only be admired and contemplated. Then existence is given to us as celebration, as feast. Then a word, or images, or gestures touch a person, not in vain reasonings or in the exasperation of sexuality, but in the depths of the heart, which is awakened by them.

We Orthodox, the patriarch insists, wish to say a word to Western Man—even though the insane history of this century seems constantly to stifle us, to fill our mouths with dirt and blood. We wish to provide testimony about that spirituality which comes to us through the Fathers of the Church, through the Fathers of the Desert, through our liturgy, through the peaceful and luminous beauty of our hymns and icons, and also through that particular *ethos* by which we consider existence as such.

Christians must place themselves at the level of ultimate realities. The Church does not have the answer for everything. It is not defined by a code of laws, by a multiplication of recipes. But it must make society think. It must, through example, remind the world of the meaning of love (first, of the very possibility of love) and of the mystery of the child. It must warn the world about the fatal flaw of technocracy, which leads to barbarity because it considers that everything which is technologically possible must be realized. The Church must deepen the contemporary desire for human solidarity, so strong among some young people, by reminding society that men are not just "similar," but one single being, one single life in the resurrected Christ, in whom failure is never final. Filled with such confidence and power, the man of faith and compassion battles without discouragement against all forms of death in both culture and society. He develops a renewed approach to the "rights of man," together with all those who perceive the enigma of personhood. He dares to proclaim that this world, apparently closed in on itself, has been torn apart, opened up, on Easter morning, and that a life untouched by death and a love unmixed with hate emerge in that surge of light. *Faith then becomes the great blessing of life.*

On the Origin of Evil

But first, we need a theology that will answer the atheist position about evil, about that process imputed to God since Jean Paul Richter, Nietzsche, and Dostoevsky (think, for example, of the arguments presented by Ivan in *The Brothers Karamazov*). We must abolish once and for all that image of a "diabolical God" who, from all eternity, controls everything and thus appears as the only source of evil. Our God is the *Theos pathôn*, the crucified God about whom the Fathers spoke long before Moltmann! The creation of other freedoms—that of man, and also of angels—implies an incredible omnipotence and, simultaneously, an extreme weakness. God, in a certain manner, must remove himself to allow space for these other freedoms. He enters into a tragic love story. Deep inside man is the memory of "paradise," but also of a break, of a departure along the paths of freedom, like that of the prodigal son in the parable. And this freedom is strengthened through opposition—through forgetfulness. The prodigal son moves away from his Father, and this separation brings death. Though the Father does not desire this separation, because he has no conception of evil, he accepts the son like so many blows in the face. Just think of the images of Christ being attacked, bound, and struck on the face, both in eastern art: the icon of a totally humiliated Christ over the prothesis table in Greek churches of the 16th-18th centuries—and in western: that Christ painted by Fra Angelico in the convent of St Mark in Florence standing blindfolded as hands emerge out of the abyss, out of nothingness, to strike him.

For man, fascinated by the death which he conceals within himself, bears as well the agony of crime: against the "other" or against the self. How many murders we commit in spirit! This is why the Fathers of the Desert used to say that slander, contempt of the "other," is the greatest of sins! Thus humanity –which is composed of infinitely intertwined relations—allows the world to slide toward the nothingness out of which it was drawn, in the aptly worded remark of St Athanasius of Alexandria. Chaos returns, a chaos which the powers of darkness—which are at once within and outside us—pervert: the suffering of children, absurd wars, monstrous cosmic catastrophes. God—having become a king with no kingdom, in the words of Nicholas Cabasilas—supports the world from beyond, until the "yes" of a woman allows him to return to the heart of his creation to restore it sacramentally, to tear humanity away from nothingness and to restore to each of us our vocation of "created creator."

But the incarnate, crucified, and resurrected God can act, can bring light and peace, only through hearts that freely open to him. He is not the God of "holy wars," or even of supposedly "just wars." He is not the God of the Crusades, but of the life-giving Cross.

The experience of evil ultimately proves to humanity its meaningless. Through suffering—and the worst is to discover how much we make others suffer—man reaches repentance. And

Christ—who is freedom itself—resurrects his freedom from within, without the least amount of restraint. Then man accedes not only to the good—for the good judges and condemns those who are "evil"—but to a kind of supra-good which allows the transforming power of God to shine, bringing pardon and opening up the future. "Woman, where are they?" Jesus asks the woman caught in adultery. "Has no one condemned you?" "No One, Lord," she answers. "Neither do I condemn you; go, and do not sin again."[1]

Church and State?

Christianity should not attempt to use the powers of the state. The categories of power, the patriarch reminds us once more, are not Christian categories! The function of the state, said Vladimir Soloviev, is not to transform society into a paradise, but to prevent it from becoming a hell. The state finds both its meaning and its limits in reducing violence to the greatest possible extent and in supporting a vigorous civil society: this requires both true freedom of association and real freedom of conscience.

Christians can support only an authentic secularism, one not hostile to the churches, but one that is open, capable of accepting them as recognized and, of course, respected partners. In a truly secular culture, one will hear about the Bible in schools, about the Fathers of the Church in classes on the history of thought, and young people will be familiarized with the immense cultural and cultic heritage of Christianity. If not, then our youth will become a youth with no memory, and with no ethic as well, thus falling prey to all kinds of folly, to all kinds of sectarian proselytism! And what we say concerning the Bible—which should apply, of course, to Christian minorities in Moslem countries—applies also to the Koran with respect to Moslem minorities in predominantly Christian countries.

1   Jn 8:10-11.

The "new evangelization" of Europe cannot have as its goal to reconstitute a "Christianity" in which the state, for example, would impose the precepts of Christian morality on everyone. This would be to turn Christianity into an "ideology." Evangelization must have as its goal to deepen pluralism until "tolerance without skepticism" is achieved, in the words of Paul Ricoeur, a great contemporary French philosopher. This is accomplished through example and with discretion—that is, in silence.

In this fashion, a secularized society, while marking the end of clericalism, can become for the churches a neutral ground, both fertile and fraught with peril, because the partnership, in order to be prophetic, may at times become confrontational.

Let Christians renounce power and constraint. Let them become poor and peaceful servants of the crucified God who creates human freedom. Let them be the guarantors of the faith of others, the guarantors also of those who have no faith, or who are unable to express it—but by whose fault?—and who simply try to be human. Let them be the guardians of the *open* man in an *open* culture!

Towards a Europe Without Limits

The roots of Europe do not, from a strictly geographical perspective, lie in Europe. It is on the shoreline of Phoenicia that Zeus kidnapped the nymph Europa to bring her to the continent to which she gave her name! Does Europe end at the Bosphorus, in Istanbul? Some historians speak of an "intermediate area" stretching from the Balkans to the Fertile Crescent... The principal patristic and liturgical texts were composed in Cappadocia and in the area around Antioch. With respect to Hinduism, Islam is western! In the most important scene of *The Brothers Karamazov*—the dialogue between the one who conceived and the one who carried out the parricide—the "Spiritual Works of Our Father Among the Saints, Isaac of Syria," are placed on the table as a symbol of the fall and the salvation of humanity. St Isaac, an Arab from the shores of the Persian Gulf, came to Iraq and belonged to the Church of the East, which was at that time engaged in a centuries-long process of evangelizing, at least partially, Tibet, India, Mongolia, and China. Today, says the patriarch, the increasingly close relations between Chalcedonian and non-Chalcedonian Orthodox open up great opportunities for our Church in Africa and Asia.

How can we forget the modern explosion of Europe, which inextricably combines a missionary surge, the thirst for profit, and dreams of adventure? From 1492 to 1520, Europe left its indelible mark on the Americas. In the same period, Russian missionaries and merchants implanted Europe in upper Asia, as far as the northern shores of the Pacific: Irkutsk and Vladivostok are, after all, European cities!

Western Europe today is in a painful process of unification; there is much resignation and worry. There appears no great vision of the future, no great ideal, other than, it appears, to protect its riches from the "menace" and "invasion" of peoples from the South. And to protect it as well, it seems, from the turbulence in Eastern Europe, because, despite the cultural affinity, despite Dostoevsky and Solzhenitsyn, European money is very prudent!

The task of Christians—and the Orthodox, when they move beyond their suspicion and stereotypes, feel this very strongly—is to infuse a new breath into this European process, in the perspective of divinized humanity. Christian societies have often considered God as opposing humanity, opposing human freedom; while modern secularism often considers humanity as opposing God, opposing the spiritual depth of man. Yes, the time for a divinized humanity is arriving, in which God reveals himself in man, and man reveals himself in God. It is this divinized humanity that could provide meaning to the explorations of humanism, when depth psychology and micro-physics sense the spiritual dimension. It could give meaning also to explorations into the Oriental mystical traditions which, through their contact with the West, are obliged to account for a cosmic and historical future, as well as for the reality of the "other."

We must introduce three fundamental attitudes into the secularized society of contemporary Europe: repentance, which is particularly necessary after so many wars and persecutions among the nations; self-limitation, in order to share with the poorer nations of our planet; and, finally, respect for and the spiritualization of the earth.

The implacable rise in unemployment requires from us a strong critique of the absolute dominance of economic principles. We are trapped by the tyrannical pressure constantly to increase production, and therefore constantly to create new needs. Means of production are ever being perfected as the need for human labor decreases. Simultaneously, perceived needs are necessarily increasing. The economy functions with no regard for the person. Thus unemployment and exclusion increase.

For this reason, we must now place at the heart of our society an emphasis on creativity and personal sympathy in human relations. Even beyond the political realm, Christians must instigate a revolution in sensibilities and styles of living. This revolution would lead to the free and joyful abandonment of frenetic consumption, a rejection of the demands of productivity, in order to rediscover real life in the communion of persons.

Max Weber, Werner Sombart, and R.H. Towney have shown that a certain Christian theology, linked to an entire world view, expressing and possibly creating it, was at the basis of the contemporary notions of work and the economy. Perhaps a deep theological revision, linked with an encounter with the Christian East, could imbue work and the economy with new meaning.

The task is to turn Europe into a peculiar laboratory, beyond a secularized modernity. Here, according to the intuition of Christos Yannaras in one of his early works, the absence of God would be transformed into his "unknowability," and the negations of atheism into those of an apophatic theology that opens us to Revelation.

PART IV

And Others?

10

On Ecumenism and Fanaticism

The Memory and Example of the Undivided Church

For Bartholomew, ecumenism is not a luxury, but a duty. He likes to call to mind the undivided Church, the spiritual matrix of Europe, where East and West were united and worked together. The uniting factors—which remain our common roots—certainly consisted of Scripture, but also of the writings of the Fathers and the early monks. Today, we increasingly see the profound unity of thought among the Greek and Latin Fathers, a unity which a contemporary Greek theologian has called "Romanity," as long as we ignore something of a later hardening in the writings of St Augustine. The best example is the work of Irenaeus of Lyons, a Greek from Asia Minor who settled in Gaul. He began to write in Greek, but continued in Latin. Monasticism, born in the East, was implanted in the West by St John Cassian, who limited the excesses of Augustinian thought. Down to the present, Benedictine monasticism remains as a witness of the undivided Church. A monastery of Benedictines from Amalfi, moreover, existed on Mt Athos until the 13th century. It is no accident that, in 1926, a Benedictine, Dom Lambert Beauduin, published a daring and prophetic article, "The West at the School of the East. The Paschal Mystery."[1] This article rediscovered all the importance of Orthodoxy, which was at that time ignored or despised.

The Fathers and monks have developed a "spiritual theology" that is inseparable from the liturgy and from contemplation, a theology which is essentially identical in both East and West, at

1   In the first issue of the journal *Irénikon*.

least until the great Cistercian mystics of the 12th century. And it was the same for art. Despite difficulties at the time of Charlemagne in the "reception" of the teaching of the Seventh Ecumenical Council within Latin Christianity—due chiefly to a poor translation—Carolingian, Ottonian, Romanesque, and Italian art all manifest the same spiritual sensibilities as the Byzantine art of the period. The affirmation of the human element, still inseparable from the divine, begins even earlier in the Byzantine world. This resulted, on the one hand, in the first Italian Renaissance, strongly tinged by Franciscan influence, and, on the other, in the masterpieces of iconography at Nerezi, Mistra, and Chora (in Constantinople).

The undivided Church by instinct organized itself according to an ecclesiology of communion, based on the Pentarchy, with Rome and Constantinople as universal centers of agreement. The canons of the Council of Sardica concerning appeals to Rome and the Roman right to hear them were accepted in the East. East and West certainly did not interpret primacy in the same way, but the miracle of communion always prevailed—that communion which, said St Ambrose, must unite the churches, that *fidelium universitas*, wrote Pope St Leo.

✴ ✴ ✴

Excursus II

On the Relation Between Pope and Council in the First Millennium

Both Rome and the councils tended to affirm that their judgment was decisive.

But the popes were far from ignoring the conciliar principle, just as the councils did not lose sight of primacy.

1) Pope Celestine, in his letter to the Council of Ephesus, composed a true hymn to conciliarity: "The assembly of bishops

witnesses to the presence of the Holy Spirit... The Holy Spirit has established bishops to shepherd the Church of God."[2] After the conclusion of this tumultuous council, Celestine wrote to the clergy and the people of Constantinople that "Nestorius [who refused to call Mary the 'Mother of God,' *Theotokos*] was driven back by the universal Church and by our own sentence." For, at the council, "the Holy Spirit, who always lives in his priests, has decreed what was in the interest of all."

At the Council of Chalcedon, Leo the Great congratulated himself that his "Tome" had been "confirmed by the incontestable agreement of the entire college of brothers."[3]

During the Second Council of Constantinople, Pope Vigilius arrived at the capital city and refused to take part in the council because he disapproved of some of its tendencies. The council excommunicated him. Then, six months later, after reconciliation had been achieved, the pope recognized the council, as did his successors.

The Sixth Ecumenical Council (II Constantinople), with the agreement of Rome, condemned Pope Honorius for heresy (he had adopted a highly dubious position on the question of monotheletism[4]), and this condemnation remained in the profession of faith of the bishop of Rome for nearly four centuries.

2) On their side, the councils "received" the judgment issued by Rome with much attention and respect, but *in freedom*. The councils presupposed the participation of the pope, or at least of his legates. Texts prepared by the pope played an important part in the common reflection of the council and were often inserted into the conciliar degrees, though often with modifications! At Ephesus, after the reading of Celestine's letter, acclamations followed: "Celestine is one with the council! One Celestine, one Cy-

---

2   ACO VII, 22-24.
3   *Ep.* 120 (*PL* 54:1407).
4   According to which there is in Christ only "one single will," a divine will.

ril [of Alexandria, great defender of the *Theotokos*], one faith of
the *oikoumene!*"[5]

The conflict between the monarchical and collegial principles
became evident at Chalcedon, but the issue was resolved through
compromise. The East emphasized conciliarity, without rejecting
the primacy of the pope, but with a different understanding of
primacy than that maintained by St Leo. Rome affirmed its primacy but was unable to impose its pretension that it alone defined the truth, that it was the absolute criterion of communion:
the council's awareness of its own authority was simply too great.
But this in no way prevented the acclamations that followed the
reception of the "Tome" of Leo: "Peter has spoken through the
mouth of Leo!"[6]

In the same way, Pope Agatho's letter to the Sixth Ecumenical
Council was received with shouts that "Peter has spoken through
Agatho!" And the council asked the pope to ratify its decisions
(the term used was *kanonizein*).

In their struggle against iconoclasm, the monks strongly emphasized papal authority as a Petrine function. Empress Irene, a
strong defender of icons, wrote that the pope "is the very holy
head of the Church," that "he is the one who presides on the
throne of St Peter."[7] The Acts of the Seventh Ecumenical Council, whose assembly she reluctantly allowed, contain a message—thoroughly reworked, by the way—in which the pope
exhorts the emperors to venerate "the vicar of Peter," and in which
Rome is called "the head of all the churches of God."[8]

Yet the easterners who were most favorably inclined toward
Rome did not think that the ministry of the pope could function
ex sese: he could exercise it only in communion with the council,

5   ACO I/1, 3, 5-6.
6   ACO II/1, 2, 81.
7   Mansi XII, 984-986.
8   *Ibid.*, 1058.

in the communion of the Church, in its service. Only *the faith of Peter*, the common faith, can justify the ministry of his successor. The pope is able to receive appeals, to render judgment in such cases, but the canons protect the autonomy of local churches. In the seventh century, Martin I, who died a martyr like Maximus the Confessor, and for the same reason, in defense of the free human will in Christ and in us, wrote: "We are unable to abrogate the canons of the Church. We are rather their defender and their guardian, and not their transgressor."[9] The councils, respectfully hearing the words of the pope but discussing them freely, articulated the foundations of the faith and the discipline of the Church.

Finally, the truth imposed itself, and led to the resolution of apparent contradictions.

Thus the Church had at its disposal several antennae to hear what the Holy Spirit wished to tell it: the council was the expression of the "catholic" communion among the bishops; the pope was the servant of this communion; but also, particularly at moments of great uncertainty, the witness—the martyrdom—of several prophets, such as St Maximus the Confessor, St Theodore the Studite, and even a pope such as Martin I.

The East did not know and could not accept Roman primacy under the form it took after the Gregorian reform and the Council of Trent. But primacy in its earlier form was recognized and practiced in the East at the time of the ecumenical councils. Theories opposing this arose, but the life of the Church always overcame them. Ultimately, no one had the ultimate authority. Everyone pretended to have the last word, but no one had it, except the Holy Spirit. Moving beyond polemics, we need today to reflect on a period of ecclesial life in which tensions were resolved neither against the pope, nor against councils, but *in a different way.*

✳ ✳ ✳

9 *Letter to Pantaleon*, ARP, 551.

During his visit to Norway on June 4, 1995, for the millennium of its christianization under the leadership of King Olaf Trygvanson, Bartholomew recalled how much the unity of the Church was then alive in Europe. Certainly, Rome and Constantinople, the two great ecclesiastical centers, did not always agree. But they were conscious of being part of one, undivided Church. Otto III, the western Emperor, was, through his mother Theophano, the nephew of Basil II, the eastern Emperor, as was Prince Vladimir of Russia, who had just been converted. This was a period in which a multitude of nations entered the Church, the one Church of Christ: the Poles in 966; the Russians in 988; the Norwegians in 995; the Hungarians in 1000. It is significant that Olaf Trygvanson was baptized in England, that he conducted negotiations in Constantinople concerning the baptism of Vladimir of Russia, and that he organized the Church of Norway with the assistance of the Archbishopric of Hamburg and Bremen.

The Schism and Its Consequences

The schism, whose specific theological causes we discussed in the introductory chapters, appeared in history as the gradual alienation of two cultures, later brutally brought into conflict by the crusades. And we know very well how popular religion ascribes an almost magical importance to details! At the end of the 11th century, military and economic superiority shifted to the West. The Byzantine East became the first target of the "colonial" expansion of the West: recall, for example, the role of the Italian merchant republics.

In the West, the Gregorian reform strengthened papal monarchy—certainly in order to liberate the papacy from feudalism and imperial tutelage, but the momentum thus provided did not abate until the dogma of 1870. Soon the West which, in its theology, to some extent sacrifices mystery to rationality in its desire to *grasp*, entered into a kind of *Quest*: literary and deeply poetic in its quest for the Holy Grail, but also increasingly scientific, technical, and highly dynamic.

The East entered into contemplative reflection on deification, on grace, on the "light of Tabor." The ascendancy of the West was contrasted in the East, as a result of historical tragedies, by a gradual retreat into monastic and liturgical prayer. The East divorced itself from history, which appeared to it as hostile and malignant—a sentiment confirmed in our own century by the victory of communism and later of the "American way of life." The Eastern Roman Empire disappeared at a time when Portuguese and Spanish explorers were traversing the oceans, thirty or forty years before the discovery of America! It was at this time as well that pre-Reformation and nationalistic movements splintered the West.

The schism of the 11th and 13th centuries seems indeed to have led to that of the 16th. Not only did the centralization of the Church around Rome cause opposition from diverse local churches, but western Christianity—cut off from eastern pneumatology—was no longer able to absorb tensions, which were therefore transformed into oppositions: between Tradition and Scripture, between prophecy and sacrament, between freedom and authority, between ordained and universal priesthood.

The schism was a factor in turning the western *Quest* into an increasingly Promethean and secularized conquest. After the fall of Constantinople, many Byzantine humanists emigrated to the West, but the theology and spirituality of the divine "energies," which give to Christianity a cosmic scope, became the secret of eastern monasticism, with little impact on culture, except perhaps in art. Western developments in science and technology, therefore, occurred within a purely secular perspective. "Nature" was isolated from "super-nature" by an increasingly pietistic and moralizing religion.

This lessening of the sense of mystery and of the ecclesial *ethos* favored individualism, positivism, legalism—and very quickly, in reaction, led to revolt—all of which have contributed to the development of our modern anxiety. The Church, responding to threats with the Inquisition and the Counter-Reformation, created the first models of totalitarianism.

Within the Orthodox Church after the fall of Constantinople, the schism soon led to missionary aggressiveness and the rise of Uniatism, which produced a defensive attitude, accumulated grudges, and created a certain defiance.

Western Europe, the child of Rome and of the Reformation, has dominated the history of the world in the modern era. Its development has been racked by divisions: Reformers versus Rome, anti-clericalism versus clericalism, the rights of man versus the rights of God! A heterogeneous, open culture gradually developed, but it was long marked by a "Eurocentrism" (in the sense of Western Europe) that despised or ignored other cultures. And the "death of God," a God often caricatured by Christians themselves, risks today the result of the "death of man."

Eastern Europe, the child of Greek Hellenism, has long been the victim of history. Often, it has entered history only by deforming or compromising its own soul, i.e., by absolutizing western concepts in a non-denominational context. Hence the idolatrous rise of nationalism and socialism, both deformed by a messianism which secularizes the old "symphonic" and eschatological ideal of the Byzantine Empire. The 1917 Revolution in Russia and the communist take-over in southeastern Europe after World War II came at a time when these nations were just beginning to learn about freedom of the spirit, when modernity was just being absorbed and surpassed *from within*, and when a cultural and spiritual renewal was just taking hold.

Now it appears that everything needs to be started anew, and under even worse conditions. All reference points have disappeared, and there remains the almost animal sentiment of belonging to a group. And religion, stripped of its properly spiritual content, is merely an external sign of this belonging. When an "Orthodox" smashes a crucifix, and a "Catholic" destroys an icon of the Holy Face, it is evident that neither one of them knows any longer who Christ is! If Europe, in both West and East under different forms, is menaced by a culture of emptiness, by the violation of individual rights, if the number of psychopaths and social deviants keeps increasing—we Christians, or rather, so-called Christians, bear the responsibility, for we have reduced the Gospel to an infantile religiosity, a formalistic and nearly always hate-filled religiosity.

The confrontation between the two Europes is most clearly evident in the drama of the Uniate churches. They were formed in opposition to Orthodoxy—in 1596 in Poland-Lithuania, in 1700 in Transylvania—as a result of the superiority of western culture and through the power of the state. They were eradicated on the morrow of World War II, this time in opposition to Catholicism and with an even greater use of violence by the state. And their present reemergence often brings painful conflicts.

The Persistence of a Christian Europe

Nevertheless, despite divisions and conflicts, a Europe with Christian roots has never ceased to exist. We often forget that the Orthodox countries have served as its bulwark. The Byzantine Empire stopped the Arab advance more surely than did Charles Martel at Poitiers, as did Romania under Michael the Brave. And the Russians halted the Mongols. The Patriarchate of Constantinople, meanwhile, contributed to saving Christianity in the Greek and Balkan nations during the Ottoman era.

The patriarch recalls an example of truly Christian attitudes maintained under the worst of conditions, an example he raised in November 1994, in Belgium, when he visited Chèvetogne, a Catholic monastery dedicated to dialogue with Orthodoxy. Only a few years after 1204, the second Latin Emperor of Constantino-

ple, Henry, Count of Flanders and Hainaut, vigorously opposed
the papal legate, Cardinal Pelagius, and saved the Orthodox
clergy from persecution. Henry also preserved the monasteries of
Mt Athos. After his death, many Orthodox mourned him, and
the monks of the Great Lavra[10] long preserved his memory as a
benefactor. It is therefore possible to "proclaim peace" when others preach war, to call brothers those whom others see only as
enemies.

Uniatism has certainly been traumatic for the East; it has been
a wound in the body of Orthodoxy, similar to the trauma of
1204. Yet it seems that God has used it as a means to bring the
West into a living contact with Orthodoxy and to a discovery of
its treasures. After 1204, (stolen!) relics and the cult of many eastern saints spread to the West, which also underwent a veritable
conquest by Byzantine art. Bartholomew points, for example, to
the beautiful 13th century mosaics in the apse of St Mary Major
in Rome, or in the Baptistery in Florence. Knowledge of the
Greek Fathers also increased in the West and, toward the end of
the 13th century, to the four Latin doctors of the Church (Ambrose, Jerome, Augustine, and Gregory the Great) were added
four easterners (Athanasius, Basil, Gregory of Nazianzus, and
John Chrysostom).

Uniatism even led to a transfusion of eastern blood into the
Church of the West, which thus began to escape its Latin isolation. The existence of the Uniate churches and the efforts to consolidate and expand them often served as the primary motivation
for western theologians to study the Greek—and also Armenian
and Syriac—Fathers. Even the search for arguments against Orthodoxy has led to discoveries!

During the 17th century, one can see a much wider and sur-
prising influence of the Greek Fathers, first on Anglican theology
and spirituality—it suffices to name Lancelot Andrewes (see the

10   The first and one of the principal monasteries on Mt Athos, founded in 963.

magisterial study by Nicolas Lossky)—and second on French theology and spirituality. Basic texts are translated, notably by Arnaud d'Andilly (in the first half of the century, the works of Dorotheus of Gaza were translated twice into Russian, five times into French!). Finally a return to an original monastic spirituality led to the formation of the Trappists.

Confessionalism and the Ecumenism of the Camps

In the last three decades, there has been enormous progress in the rapprochement between churches. Thanks to Patriarch Athenagoras and Pope Paul VI, the anathemas of 1054 have been lifted and the dialogue of love has begun. Today, relations between Rome and Constantinople are better than they were before the schism, so great were the problems in mutual understanding caused by geographic separation and differences in language.

Our Churches, the patriarch insists, must overcome the problem of Uniatism. Then we can resume the normal agenda of our dialogue. An intermediate solution is already apparent, though it has not been accepted by all the Orthodox churches (intermediate, because when unity of faith approaches, there will no longer be Uniate churches!). When the Catholic-Orthodox Joint Commission met in 1993 at Balamand, in northern Lebanon, the Catholic side condemned Uniatism as a means to restore unity. And it had already done the same earlier at Freising. The Catholic Church has undergone a change of heart and now considers as unacceptable the methods it employed for centuries. The Orthodox, on their side, have agreed to tolerate an abnormal ecclesial situation, until the Uniate churches themselves finally come to understand their own situation.

For several years, it is true, we have also witnessed the massive return of confessionalism, notably, though certainly not uniquely, within the Orthodox Church. Sincere believers everywhere, upset by modern developments, react by violently affirming their identity, often in the most simplistic way, through opposition. Some Orthodox have a strictly exclusive view of the One Church and, against all evidence that real Christian life exists in other confessions, completely reject their ecclesial status. They take literally the fifth- and sixth-century canons forbidding praying with heretics, without realizing that historical conditions have radically changed. During those centuries, with the rise of the so-called "Monophysite" communities, the issue was the formation, in places where Orthodoxy was established, of parallel churches, altar versus altar, with each side having to affirm its identity. Today, if one puts aside Uniate proselytism in certain border areas or the activities of expansionist sects, the "heterodox," particularly in lands far from the traditionally Orthodox world, simply seek to be Christians and manifest not the slightest trace of hostility toward the Orthodox Church, about which they know very little.

But during the worst moments of our century, there was also an exorcism of such ignorance, suspicion, and hatred. This was the development, inside concentration camps, of an *ecumenism of the persecuted*. In Russia, an Ogorodnikov received communion from the hands of a Lithuanian Catholic priest, and together they prepared communion wine by placing dried raisins in water. Ogorodnikov, at those times when mail could get through, also received material and spiritual assistance from western Christians, and he thus spoke of the unity of "the great Christian family." In Romania, Nicholas Steinhardt, a remarkable writer and art critic, was converted in a terrible prison, where he was helped and catechized by an Orthodox hieromonk and two Greek-Catholic priests, who had all three become friends. The Orthodox priest baptized him with a few drops of filthy water in the presence of the two Catholic priests, to whom Steinhardt promised that, if God gave him life and freedom, he would consecrate himself to the cause of ecumenism. After regaining his freedom, he became a monk and offered a glowing witness in a book entitled, both ironically and seriously, *Journal of Happiness*.

Toward an Experiential Realism of Salvation

Contemporary ecumenism, it seems, needs to abandon verbal arguments in order to base itself on an experiential realism of salvation.
Systems and concepts, which are after all only markers, must be immersed in the total life of the Church, in the best of its experience.
We must enter into the perspective of the "other" to discover an aspect, for us unexpected or neglected, of the face of Christ. The disfigured face of the Crucified One, endlessly scrutinized by the
West, and the transfigured face of the Resurrected One, endlessly
glorified by the East, are one and the same face; and even their difference reveals the immensity of God's love for us.

The patriarch likes to cite examples of the richness of such an
experiential ecumenism. Between Chalcedonian Orthodoxy and
non-Chalcedonian Orthodoxy (that of the Armenians, Jacobites,
Copts, Ethiopians, and certain parts of the Church of India), we
have come to realize that the faith is the same. And this after so
many centuries of mutual condemnation and persecution! This
one faith is expressed in two conceptual systems which were long
mutually opposed. For the Chalcedonians, the word *physis*, nature, represents either the divinity or the humanity, both united
in the person of Christ. For the non-Chalcedonians, the same
word represents the unity of Christ, his living, personal reality in
which the divine and the human are united.

The issue of the *Filioque*, which divides the Christians of East
and West, is another example. In the patristic era (for the *Filioque*
was already formulated by St Ambrose, and perhaps by St Hilary
of Poitiers), there were two distinct, but both legitimate, approaches to the mystery of the Trinity. The West contemplated
the surging and, as it were, the overflowing, of divine love from
the Father to the Son, and from the Father and the Son to the
Spirit, and through the Spirit to us. With greater rigor, the East
(when the West tried to be rigorous, as with St Augustine, it got

confused!) saw the properly personal character of the Spirit in this procession (*ekporeusis*): The Spirit is the breath of the Father, who carries his Word, who dwells in the Word, who manifests himself through the Word. In the seventh century, St Maximus the Confessor explains (and accepts) the *Filioque* not in the perspective of the Spirit's ultimate origin—for the Father is the only principle in the Trinity—but of his manifestation and his "economy."

In the Middle Ages and subsequently, the West has identified the Latin *processio* with the Greek *ekporeusis*. This, from the patristic perspective, is not very exact. Scholasticism has sought to explain the Tri-unity by relating it—just as our own spirit functions—to two dualities: Father-Son, and (Father-Son) "as one single principle"—the Spirit. But is it possible, within the Trinity, to isolate a principle that is not Trinitarian?

We must admit also that the East, when the polemics became more acute, was tempted to reduce the Trinity to two dualities (Father-Son on the one hand, and Father-Spirit on the other). It had little to say about the relation between Son and Spirit, at least until Gregory of Cyprus who, toward the end of the 13th century, spoke of the eternal manifestation of the Spirit by the Son (thus, by the way, rediscovering the ancient Alexandrian theology).

Today, we humbly discover that relations within the Trinity are always Trinitarian, or rather, "tri-unitarian," which is indispensable also for the human spirit. If we say that the Spirit proceeds from the Father, we must specify: *from the Father of the Son.* If we say that he proceeds from the Father and the Son, rather than speaking of "one single principle" which is necessarily common to all Three (and which the Father cannot give his Son because it is the very essence of his personal uniqueness), we should specify that he proceeds *principaliter* from the Father, as St Augustine awkwardly said, or, better yet, that he proceeds *from the Father in the Son*, as Pope Dionysius of Rome wrote in the third century to his namesake in Alexandria.

When the patriarch visited Zurich in June 1995, he spoke of the publication in 1905 of *The Special Theory of Relativity*, by Albert Einstein, a graduate of the city's "Polytechnicum." This work shows that space, time, and mass are not absolute, but relative values, because they depend on the kinetic state of bodies. An astronaut traveling through space at nearly the speed of light and returning several years later would discover that others had aged more quickly than he. His time would have moved more slowly than the equivalent time on earth. Yet the two spans of time are both real, and we could not say that one was longer than the other.

Spiritual realities, of course, cannot be squeezed into an equation, and it would not be acceptable to apply the laws of relativity to them. Bartholomew simply points out that, in numerous conflicts, both adversaries have ultimately been proved correct. He claims to be not at all a "relativist" in what concerns the faith. He rejects whatever impoverishes or restrains our openness to the mystery. But our most profound theology is "apophatic," i.e., both negative and antinomic. It does not allow for concepts to be closed in on themselves, to imprison God—or the neighbor. And there is something blasphemous, or simply ridiculous, in pretending to investigate the secrets of divinity when one is driven by hatred of one's brother!

The Encounter with Rome

Yes, the patriarch has several times spoken of "our elder brother, Pope John Paul II," "Bishop of the First Rome, with whom we share a communion of love." But he always specified that we can progress toward unity only in the fear of God, with sincerity and prudence.

In Rome, he was the personal gust of the pope in the St John Tower, high up in the Vatican gardens. At the liturgy in St Peter's on June 29, in his homily, the patriarch openly raised the question of primacy, of its modes of expression. We must reflect together, in order finally to be made worthy of the grace of a common chalice. We must reflect together on the true meaning of Peter's confession of faith in Caesarea Philippi, a text which has provoked, and continues to provoke, so much controversy. Today, Bartholomew said, after much affliction and humiliation, we have reached the maturity of a truly apostolic awareness: we understand that primacy is less a question of persons than of ministries of service. These ministries are indeed urgent if we seek not to be admired by men, but to please God. The chief Christian virtue is humility, which is inseparable from repentance. It is not possible to confess, with the Byzantine liturgy, that "One is holy, one is Lord, Jesus Christ, to the glory of God the Father" and, simultaneously, to seek within the Church a power and glory other than an attitude of *kenosis* and service. The patriarch stressed the need for self-criticism and continuous repentance, adding that to denounce the one who erred first is not the issue, or whether he erred more or less. Even the ancient philosophers held that this was an unworthy preoccupation for persons of quality. For us, he affirmed, the fundamental question is the salvation of the world. How are we to save our neighbor, our innumerable neighbors, and, uniquely through the neighbor, save ourselves? To cite the golden rule formulated by St Paul: "Bear one another's burdens, and so fulfill the law of Christ."[11] When a kenotic *ethos* finally prevails, then we will easily restore the unity of faith.

The pope responded that his authority indeed has meaning only as service. He evoked Peter, but also Paul and Andrew. He cited the passage from Luke in which Christ sent the apostles out "two by two,"[12] adding:

> Perhaps this means that Christ also sends us out two by two to preach his Gospel in the West and in the East. Christ sends us together so that we may bear witness to him. Thus

11 Gal 6:2.
12 Lk 10:1.

we can no more remain separated, but we must walk together, because this is the will of the Lord.

The faithful applauded the two men long and hard, cheering them as they stood over the tomb of St Peter. Together they came to the central loggia of the basilica to recite the *Angelus* and to bless the crowds. And when the crowd began to disperse, the patriarch shouted out: "Courage! Let us love one another!"

Several times recently, and notably in Zurich on December 14, 1995, the patriarch has stated that there is no biblical foundation for the notion that the ministry of the pope involves governance over the entire Church. The command addressed by Christ to Simon Peter applies to each bishop, and to all the bishops together according to the conciliar principle. Certainly the Church of Rome, a church founded by the Apostles Peter and Paul, was given the responsibility of solicitude, of "presiding in love" among the local churches, but certainly not of governing over these churches. Before the schism, the Bishop of Rome was *primus inter pares*, in full interdependence with all bishops who were, collegially, the successors of the apostles.

In an interview given at the end of June, 1996, to the Polish weekly, *Tygodnik Powszechny*, the patriarch again criticized the developments in the papacy after the schism, to the point that it claimed a "direct and truly episcopal," worldwide jurisdiction over all the faithful and all bishops—this jurisdiction is "a theological error," Bartholomew affirmed.

And the Protestants?

The rapprochement between Rome and Constantinople must not ignore the Protestant churches, but should rather include them as well. For us, western Christianity consists of both Rome and its Reformation. Rome was unable to accept the Reform, but perhaps the Orthodox presence will enable Rome more readily to accept some of its demands. Relations between Protestants and the Orthodox are ancient, dating to the early days of the Reformation. A group of Hussites sought to enter into relation with the East. In the 16th century, there were at one time close ties between the theologians of Tübingen and Augsburg and those of Constantinople, but political circumstances, as well as difficulties in finding a common language, prevented this dialogue from developing further. During the following century, Orthodox and Protestants together battled the Counter-Reformation in Poland-Lithuania. The interest in Calvinist thought manifested by Cyril Loukaris, a patriarch of Constantinople, led to deep reflection on the nature of the Church among all the Orthodox. In the 18th century, Anglican and Lutheran mysticism penetrated into Russia and fed the spirituality of St Tikhon of Zadonsk; while Orthodox, particularly Macarian,[13] spirituality influenced Wesley, the founder of Methodism. During the 19th century, the English Bible Society promoted diffusion of the Gospel in the Russian language, and links between Orthodoxy and Anglicanism became very close. And in our own century, of course, we know of the role of the patriarchate of Constantinople in the rise of the ecumenical movement—its 1920 encyclical is one of the movement's founding documents—and in maintaining an Orthodox presence at the heart of the World Council of Churches, despite considerable opposition.

It has often been said that if the schism between East and West had not taken place, then the upheaval of the 16th century would have been avoided. Perhaps the understanding of the Church as *koinonia*—that "communion" about which we hear so much today—would have counterbalanced the role of Rome. Perhaps an

---

13 The corpus of fifty homilies dating to the early 5th century and attributed, falsely, it seems, to St Macarius of Egypt, is one of the basic sources on Orthodox spirituality. It places particular stress on the "heart."

appreciation for the sacramental character of prophecy, of the freedom of the Spirit, could have prevented the dissociation and reification that occurred in lower Scholasticism. Who can say?

The patriarch is not ignorant of the fact that a certain Orthodox intransigence causes problems for many Protestants. But this immobility—let them understand—can be explained as a result of historical trauma. Nearly all the Orthodox Churches in our century were for a long time churches "bearing the cross," as was said of the French Protestant communities after the revocation of the Edict of Nantes. This Orthodox immobility—liturgical, by the way, but not theological—signifies, during a long winter of history, a stubborn fidelity to that which is essential. Today, the large Protestant communities can help us greatly in awakening the pneumatological, prophetic dimension of Orthodoxy. They can help us overcome the temptation of ritualism by reminding us of the priority of the Gospel, of its revolutionary character! And the Orthodox, on their side, may well have something to say about the sacramental aspect of the Church and about prophecy, about the hermeneutics of the Fathers, about the true vocation of the ecumenical council.

As for the sects, which are today engaged in a frenzy of proselytism in Orthodox countries left helpless after the collapse of Communism, they should not be confused with the large communions issuing from the Reformation. The sects worry our faithful and arouse confessionalistic reflexes. But perhaps the sects also force us to question our practices, and sometimes our liturgical languages, or the presence of a real, living community in our parishes...

On Fanaticism

The 20th century ends with a great victory for the Christian faith. This victory is certainly unexpected since, after the Russian Revolution and the spread of Marxist regimes throughout the world, an aggressive, destructive atheism seemed irresistibly to gain ground.

But our joy in this victory must not conceal a new danger developing in the "religious" sphere, of which it is a perversion. This danger consists in fanaticism, which already disfigures the face of the great eastern religions and now rears its head within Christianity as well. The confessionalism about which we spoke earlier is one manifestation. Fed by grave psychological and social uneasiness, by national conflicts, religious fanaticism is propagated by cynical and bloodthirsty men who conceal their ambitions or personal folly under the banner of God. Might we be on the eve of a new age of religious wars, the patriarch asks himself.

Fanaticism, as a perverse psychic phenomenon, is a threat to every person, for it does not limit itself to the religious sphere, though it always combines the desire for power with a psychologically "religious" absolutism. It can manifest itself among both atheists and believers, progressives and conservatives. It roots itself in anguish and in pride: the anguish of feeling that the historical forms, to which one is accustomed and which provide one's identity, are threatened; the pride that comes from belonging to a small group of the elect, who therefore have the right to reject and to punish those considered responsible for these upheavals. The fanatic psychosis often sees plots everywhere! Yes, a kind of exasperated pride can lead anyone to convince himself that he alone has the truth, a truth that he absolutizes, that he *possesses*. Whoever disagrees is the instrument of demonic powers. If you are different from me, it is because you seek my death! The fanatic is often insecure, worried. Lacking structure, he seeks stability, for good or bad, in a quasi-incestuous attachment to his own truth. He desires to see only negative differences, a neurosis of "small differences," said Freud. He considers that anyone who disagrees with him, even on a minor point, is totally in error in every respect. He is incapable of entering into the "otherness" of the "other," to understand it ever so little, to accept that the "other" might be correct, even if only partially. Certain expressions, whose true meaning he ignores, send him into a rage. Say them and you are disqualified, labeled, pigeonholed—thrown into the garbage bin of history, Trotsky would have said—as a heretic, a deviant, a modernist, or a reactionary!

We know that the Holy Spirit is at work everywhere, that words cannot possess the truth because only things can be possessed, while God is the fullness of personal existence. This God who, as the Inaccessible One, is always beyond, but who, as the Crucified One, is always here, reveals himself to us in the free encounter of faith. The revelation is always personal and allows us to discover the "other" as a person whom we are called to respect and to love, even in his otherness. And if the difference seems too great to overcome, let it lead to prayer, not to war! We can certainly agree with this, but has the Church, in its long history, not continued to reject, to exclude, to excommunicate those it considered as deviant? Here, we must understand that we are building a house whose doors are open to all of humanity, the New Jerusalem, the Kingdom. If some workers refuse to abide by the building plan or compromise it, we must determine this and ask them to work with us no longer. But the house will, of course, be for them as well! In the meantime, the person who is truly faithful to Christ, who seeks to love even his enemies, seeks first that which is best in the "other," seeks elements which unite. This is the key, for both ecumenical and inter-faith dialogue.

Against religious hatred, which is in reality hatred of religion, against religious war, which is in reality war against religion, as the 1994 "Bosphorus Declaration" put it, the patriarch posits the love of Christ: "Do not be overcome by evil, but overcome evil with good."[14]

Toward Common Service

The more contemporary nihilism increases—drugs, pornography, teen-age suicide, terrorism, absurd, endless, bestial wars, fanaticism—the more we come to understand that the funda-

14 Rom 12:21.

mental alienation, from which stem all the others, is death: death in its total sense, the slide toward emptiness of a world cut off from the resurrection.

The prayers and service of a renewed ecumenism thus amount to witness about the victory of Christ over death and hell. It is a creative witness that, at the heart of reality, there is not emptiness but love, i.e., the Trinity. A decisive race begins between resurrection and the abyss, between divinized humanity and an alienated humanity, which becomes bestial in seeking to divinize itself. It is a race between Pentecost and the Tower of Babel.

At the conclusion of the *Synopsis* of the film he dedicated to Andrei Rublev, Tarkovsky writes:

> Here finally is the "Trinity," the meaning and summit of Andrei's life. The "Trinity," large, serene, totally penetrated by a quivering joy, which is the source of human brotherhood. The rhythm of the One in Three and Three in One offers a prodigious perspective to a future which is still dispersed in the centuries... But on the golden background of the Trinity one sees rare explosions of raindrops; they multiply, melt together, and flow in sparkling streams... And beyond this liquid wall appear meadows—and horses standing immobile in the rain.

The Trinity, source of all unity which respects difference. The only possible foundation for the undivided Church, of an undivided Europe, of an undivided world. The rain, sign of abundance. And the unfettered horses which, Tarkovsky notes elsewhere, represent freedom.

11

On Judaism

A Nation of Witnesses

Since 1972, the Orthodox Church has maintained a high-level academic dialogue with Judaism. The goal is simply to achieve better mutual understanding. Both Jews and Christians, says the patriarch, have the same roots and follow the same Ten Commandments. The revelation of the Law on Mt Sinai was a decisive event in human history. The Law can be reduced to two fundamental prohibitions: against idolatry and against murder. It humanizes man, protecting him against magic and violence. Certainly, the Law did not abolish death, but it prepared for the moment when God, through the resurrection, would transform man's "heart of stone" into a "heart of flesh."

During the trial of Jesus, all the actors, the judges as well as the accused, his mother and his disciples, were Jews. The Book of Acts repeatedly speaks of the conversion of thousands of Jews to Jesus. For this reason the Gospel of John, composed very late, and thus after the final break between Judaism and Christianity, uses the term "Jewish" not for the entire people, but only for those of its leaders who rejected Jesus. "A hardening has come upon part of Israel, until the full number of the Gentiles come in, and so all Israel will be saved... For the gifts and the call of God are irrevocable."[1]

One sometimes hears the Jews called a "God-killing people." But a large segment of this people, the patriarch repeats, has rallied behind Christ. Who, then, has killed Jesus? It is we who mas-

1 Rom 11:25-26, 29.

sacre love every day. But we are unable to bear this thought. It is easier to accuse others, to accuse the Jews. Thus a terrible reversal took place: so-called "Christian" societies, instead of revealing the face of Christ to the Jews, instead crucified them. And so the face of the Suffering Servant—present, certainly in our saints and martyrs—has also become the face of so many humiliated, beaten, and massacred Jews. This has been the case from the time of Heraclius, Emperor of Constantinople, who wanted to baptize them by force, to the era of the First Crusade, to the pogroms of the early 20th century, down to the Holocaust.

The Jewish nation has been a people of witnesses, a people of martyrs (in Greek, the two words are identical). If this people has, so often in the course of history, been the object of cruel persecution, to the point that Hitler sought to eliminate it, it may be that its very historical presence, its very survival, recalled the "vertical" relation between God and humanity, originally revealed in the call of Abraham. This reminder was and remains unbearable for societies dominated by issues of race, fanaticism, and power. We have recently celebrated the 50th anniversary of the end of World War II, the end of the *shoah*. This anniversary provoked our anger, indignation, as well as repentance. We Orthodox Christians must reject the errors of the past, we must repent and change our heart. We must seek a new relationship with the Jewish people, one based on justice, respect, love, and, ultimately, sanctity.

On Behalf of the Jews...

We should also remember several occasions on which clergy and lay persons intervened on behalf of the Jews, both in Russia during the pogroms, and during the Second World War. In Tomsk in 1905, a young monk addressed an angry crowd: "Why do you strike my brother?" In Kiev that same year, Bishop Platon organized a solemn procession and, falling to his knees, invited the angry mob to beat him. The Russian religious philosophers of this era were fed by Jewish spirituality. So-loviev learned Hebrew from a rabbi and stated that there is no "Jewish question," but only a "Christian question," because "Christians have not yet learned to act in a Christian manner toward the Jews."[2] In the second decade of this century, Sergius Bulgakov, in his *Unfading Light*, and Nicholas Berdiaev, in his *Meaning of Creativity*, constantly drew on the *Zohar* and explained the mystery of the two Adams through the notion of *Adam Kadmon*—the primordial and universal man. Russian Christian intellectuals have just reprinted these texts, and numerous others, in a collection entitled *The Orthodox Church and the Jews: 19th and 20th Centuries.*

During World War II, the Russian emigration in Paris counted among its members two significant personalities, both friends of Berdiaev: a nun, Maria Skobtsova, and a priest, Dimitri Klepinin. Both spared no effort in saving Jewish lives, and Mother Maria today has a tree planted in her honor in the Forest of the Just, in Jerusalem. Both were arrested and died in the camps. Father Dimitri, when the Gestapo questioned him about his interest in the Jews, simply pointed to his pectoral cross and said: "And what are you going to do with this Jew?" Orthodox Greeks and Serbs, themselves victims of the tempest that nearly swallowed the Jewish people, stood by the side of the Jews and offered their assistance. The Metropolitan of Zante in Greece, Metropolitan (then Archimandrite) Chrysostomos (Tsitos) in Vienna, as well as other Greek prelates, all provided much assistance to the Jews.

Convergence

The Orthodox tradition is in fact deeply semitic. It has taken up numerous biblical prescriptions. Its clergy constitutes a

2   *Le Judaisme et la Question chrétienne*, Oeuvres complètes, vol. 4, p. 135.

veritable Levitical caste with married priests and, for centuries in certain countries, actual priestly dynasties. The so-called "Byzantine" liturgy, in fact composed by linguistically hellen-ized Semites, expresses Israel's fear and trembling before the transcendent. The Orthodox tradition has an ontology similar to that of Judaism. The differences between the Jewish onto-logical perspective and that of the western Christian confes-sions is similar to the distinction between Orthodoxy and these same confessions. At the basis of both Jewish and Orthodox ontology, one finds the primacy of the person, rather than the intelligible essence. Man exists in the image of God, i.e., as a personal existence, to the measure that he is named and called by God.

In both traditions, the Divine Name bears the divine energy. There is an amazing convergence between the Jewish conceptions of *Sephiroth* and *Shekinah* and the Palamite theology of divine en-ergies. For both Jewish and Orthodox mystics, the divine attrib-utes appear as the effulgence of the very life of God. The patristic distinction between the divine essence, which is inaccessible, and the divine energies, in which we can participate, is also found in Jewish tradition.

> We must know, said Rabbi Levi Isaac, that in the Holy One (may he be blessed!) there are two aspects, so to speak: *far* and *near. Far*… for it is not possible for thought to embrace the One who is absolutely first, whom no angel or archangel can embrace, for he beyond any conception. *Near*, for we be-lieve that the Creator (may he be blessed!) fills every world…, and the world is full of his glory. And we, the sons of Israel, must believe in both of these aspects: *far* and *near*."[3]

---

3   *Quedushat Levi*, p. 101.

In both traditions, God is considered to be not only the cause of creation, but the Presence who, while always remaining beyond it—as the "hidden root," according to the Cabalists—sustains and penetrates creation. God is present in his energies, the Orthodox would say; according to the Jewish mystics, he is present in his *Sephiroth*. The *Sephiroth* are the principal divine names, arranged in two columns, one of severity and the other of clemency, but ultimately united in the *Sephiroth* of beauty and mercy. The *Sephiroth* are the tree of life, the universal man, the celestial man. And one thinks of Christ, the true universal man in whom, according to Maximus the Confessor, the world becomes a "burning bush."

Another notion common to the two traditions is the concept of Wisdom. Wisdom is *Shekinah*, the divine presence that has been exiled in the fallen world, torn away by human evil from its transcendent Source. According to Sergius Bulgakov, if we understand him correctly, there is an actual "sophianic character" of creation. Man must allow the reunion between God and his Wisdom in order for the universe to be transfigured.

Hence the notion of Wisdom is connected to the Christian theme of mediation. In Judaism, mediation takes place when Israel liberates the *Shekinah* and manifests the *Adam Kadmon*, who is a "corporate" personality (as Metropolitan John of Pergamum would say) representing all of humanity. There is a near-perfect identity, it seems, between this celestial Man and the tree of *Sephiroth*. The patriarch points out that, in the synoptic Gospels, Jesus calls himself by no other name than that of the "Son of Man," an expression that hearkens back to the celestial Man of the Book of Daniel.

For Jewish spirituality, the task of humanity is therefore to liberate the sparks of the *Shekinah*, to "raise the holy remnant," and thus to sanctify all existence. The Orthodox tradition, more cosmic than the Christian traditions of the West, speaks of the need to reveal and to offer up the *logoi* of creation, its spiritual essence. Both traditions also share a sense of the holiness of matter, and the mission to bless life. Is this common perception not significant today, when ecological catastrophes require more than ever that we become allies with nature?

Finally, the moment of creation implies, in both Jewish and Orthodox theology, a kind of divine retreat, a *tsimtsum* (to use the beautiful concept developed by Galilean Cabalists in the 16th century). When someone truly loves, he does not impose himself, but steps back to allow the other to have full freedom of choice. At the same time, he offers his life. Here we see the Orthodox notion of *kenosis*, of the suffering of God. "Our prayers must be not only for our own needs, but first for the sufferings of God," said Rabbi Jehuda Leib of Polna.[4]

A Partially Common Hope

We share a convergence in daily life and in thought, but also a partially common hope. Eschatological expectation has always been a dominant strain in Orthodox sensibility and thought. For this reason, we must stress the providential nature of the hope kept by Israel. "Israel" means "he who struggles with God." The Jews fight bitterly for justice—just think of the sublime bargaining of Abraham. The Jews always battle against idols; they seek human justice in history itself. They prevent Christianity from becoming frozen, closed in on itself, either through static sacralization or through escape into the celestial or liturgical realms. On a wider scale, they prevent history from closing in on itself. They have always been present when history moved towards totalitarianism. They succeeded in bursting the bonds of history by the means of the very persecution which history inflicted upon them. They were influential in

4   *Horod.* I, p. 137.

bringing about needed cultural changes. Open to the transcendent, they have remained a thorn in the side of history, a thorn of hope.

This Jewish aspiration certainly differs from the Christian inosfar as it is a *not yet*. For Christians, there is a tension between a hidden *already* and a *not yet*, in which the *already* will be openly revealed. The Jews prevent us from celebrating with songs of triumph and love, when justice has not yet been achieved. But for us, it is true, all justice is fulfilled on the Cross. Justice can only come from God and consists of love. It leads only to the resurrection. But didn't Rabbi Elimelek say that "the *tsaddikim* [the saints] transform the virtue of justice into the virtue of mercy"?[5]

A Mysterious Exchange of Destinies

We must note, finally, a mysterious exchange of destinies between Judaism and Orthodoxy. I am referring to the simultaneity, and perhaps the connection, between the renaissance of hesychasm and that of Hassidism between 1750 and 1850. This double renaissance took place in the Subcarpathian region, including southern Poland, northern Romania, and western Russia. Both revivals were centered on charismatic witnesses, the Orthodox *starets* and the Jewish *tsaddik*. The chief figures, the pioneers, we might say, were Baal Shem Tov, the "master of the [divine] Name," and Paisii Velichkovskii, the master of the prayer of the divine-human Name, the Jesus Prayer. Paisii himself was of Jewish origin; his maternal grandmother was a Jew from Poltava. It is possible that the two masters carried on a secret communication. The Romanian and Ukrainian populations sincerely venerated the *tsaddikim*, despite the fact that, for economic reasons, they were generally hostile toward the Jewish *compradors*, who served as intermedi-

5 *Noam Elimelekh*, p. 59.

aries between the landowners, who were usually Polish, and the Orthodox peasantry. Neo-hesychasm and neo-Hassidism were similar spiritual movements, whose goal was to adapt the tradition to the new age of reason and technology. On both sides, spiritual knowledge and methods that had heretofore remained more or less secret, available only to a few, were now communicated to the simple people in a language they could understand. On both sides, the themes of light and the heart dominated. The heart "catches on fire," the hesychasts would say; and the *tsaddikim* compared it to the chariot of Elijah before the fiery throne of the Lord. On both sides, the separation between the sacred and the profane was breached: the aim was to sanctify the most mundane gestures, the simplest things—sometimes to the point of absurdity. In Germany between the two world wars, on the eve of the tragic events, Gustav Landauer said that everything must be done *with* religion and not *by* religion. And Martin Buber, himself an heir to the Hassidic movement, from which he drew many sayings and parables, elaborated the philosophy, so familiar to us today, of the *I* and the *Thou*.

A State Facing the Test of History

Franz Rosenzweig described the Jews as the elder sons of the Father and the Christians as the younger sons, charged with spreading biblical values to all the peoples of the world. He considered—and he died in 1932!—that the Jews were an ahistorical people.[6] And, indeed, history nearly swallowed them in the holocaust. But then, with the creation of the state of Israel, they made a dramatic return to the historical scene. In our modern civilization, which so often seems to lack reference

---

6   In *Der Stern des Erlösung* (The Star of Redemption) (Frankfurt on Main, 1921).

points, the state of Israel is alone in having its institutions and functions based on a moral and religious tradition, while successfully assimilating the major achievements of our age. Today, however, with the Palestinian problem, history is putting Israel to the test. The alliance between God, humanity, and the earth can be based only on peace and justice. Respect of the ethical conditions of this alliance brings blessing. Their compromise or rejection entails real dangers, which place Israel's spiritual vocation in doubt. We can only thank God that he has allowed some brave and wise persons to emerge from among the Israelis and the Palestinians, persons who, despite the bloody folly of the extremists, have chosen life and peace and seek to lay the groundwork for coexistence in reconciliation and justice.

As Christians and Jews, we join each other in anticipation, in the common obligation of an active, creative eschatology. They await a coming Messiah. We await the return of our "Messiah in reverse": but he rises again and authenticates the Word of Israel by giving it the power to vanquish death! Each moment therefore becomes decisive. "Each second," wrote Rosenzweig, "is the narrow door through which the Messiah could enter." He comes, or returns, like a thief in the night, the Gospel says.

On Islam and On the Mediterranean

The Same God

The patriarchate of Constantinople has opened a high-level academic dialogue with Islam, just as it has with Judaism. Reopening the school on Halki would be very helpful for this dialogue. Relations between Orthodoxy and Islam have been highly complex and difficult, at times tragic, and this remains the case today. The patriarch has said that in Bosnia religion is most often nothing more than the folklore of an idolatrous nationalism. And Patriarch Pavle, Primate of the Serbian Orthodox Church, has written:

> Any baptized person who kills or mistreats noncombatants, who blockades towns and cities, who prevents the distribution of food, medicines, or other necessities, who commits violent acts against civilians or prisoners of war, or who expels populations of other nationalities from their homes, violates the commandments of Christ, is excommunicated, and can be restored into communion only after his sincere repentance has been accepted.

> …If this war continues, the only victors will be the Devil and evil, and not the peoples or the nations involved. For our peoples live under the same sun, drink the same water from the Sava River, and pray to the same God.

The same God—this is what Alexis, Patriarch of Moscow, also said to the Grand Mufti of Chechnia in a message calling for peace and negotiation. This what Bartholomew constantly and solemnly repeated in the "Bosphorus Declaration" of February

1994, at the conclusion of a colloquium in which Christians, Moslems, and Jews all participated.

In the Middle East, millions of Arabic-speaking Christians live among Moslems. A majority of these Christians are Orthodox. During the war in Lebanon, they refused to take up weapons. They have supported and continue to support the Palestinian cause. They have no ties to western churches, and therefore they emigrate less frequently than members of other Christian communities. Among them, men of knowledge and peace have dedicated themselves to conducting a profound dialogue with Islam. Bartholomew thinks in particular of Patriarch Ignatius of Antioch and of Georges Khodr, Metropolitan of Mount-Lebanon.

According to Metropolitan Khodr, Christians must seek traces of Christ throughout human reality, they must "awaken Christ who sleeps in the night of the different religions." And Islam is certainly the only "religion" in which Christ is definitely present. This is a point worth pondering.

Jesus in the Koran and in Islamic Spirituality

The Koran calls Jesus the "Messiah" and the "Spirit of God": "Yes, the Messiah Jesus, the son of Mary, is the prophet of God, his Word which he projected on Mary, and the Spirit emanates from him."[1] The Koran proclaims the virginal conception and birth of Jesus and emphasizes the role he will play "on the day of the resurrection."

In Islamic mysticism, Jesus appears as the prototype of the way of love. He fully expresses the divine Names of Mercy and Beauty. According to Muhyi al-Din Arabi, if Mohammed is the "seal of the prophecy," Jesus is the "seal of holiness," not as the great mystics can achieve, but in a way that is "universal" and "absolute."[2]

1   Koran 4:17.
2   *Futuhat* II, 56.

We know, of course, that in the Koran Jesus was not crucified, that a double was substituted for him. This is based on an immense respect for God: it would be impossible and unworthy for God to allow his Messiah, his Servant, to be killed. This is the difference between two apophatic approaches. For Islam, all theology is negative; beyond the ninety-nine divine names (symbolic of their infinite number), the hundredth is silence. "He is *Huwa*," cry the mystics, and it is indeed a cry of silence. Christian apophaticism, on the other hand, is beyond all negation and all affirmation, maintaining an indispensable antinomy. God is so transcendent that he transcends his own transcendence to come to us in the tragedy of death, and, already now, to raise us up. Today, it is history itself, the suffering of the Palestinian and Iraqi people, the crisis in Algeria, which allows some Moslems to sense the mystery of the Cross. In the Middle East, the theme of the Passion often appears in the great Arab poets.

There is more. Around 900, the Cross appeared both at the heart and on the periphery of Islam. One of its great spiritual men, Hossein Mansur Hallaj, wished to die like Jesus "in the supreme confession of the Cross."[3] He apparently knew of Jesus only through the Koran. For Ibn Arabi, "the form of the world and the divine form, which are the two hands of God," are united in Jesus.[4] It is also well-known that the Koran vigorously denies the Trinity. But which Trinity? During the seventh century, the margins of the Byzantine Empire were a refuge for numerous sectarians, as well as numerous Arab Christians, whose faith was mingled with various pagan beliefs. In these areas, the authentic teaching about the unity of the Trinity was little known. Thus it may have been necessary to oppose the temptations of naturalism or tritheism. The Koran, however, speaks of the Word of God and of his Spirit. Discussions between Christians and Moslems should therefore focus on the theme of the *Logos*.

3   *Muquatta'at* LVII.
4   *Fusus el Hikam*, p. 66.

An eighth-century recluse from Bassorah, Rabi'a, was in some ways similar to St Mary of Egypt. She celebrated the One who pours, the Cup which is filled, and the Wine which overflows.[5] She would run through the streets carrying a pail full of water in one hand, a lighted torch in the other. The water, she explained, was to extinguish the flames of hell, and the torch to burn the delights of paradise, so that God might be loved for himself.[6]

Islam for Eastern Christians

There is no point in recalling the long and empty controversy which, for many centuries, has pitted Christian and Moslem theologians against each other. But we should remember that the Syriac-speaking churches, and particularly the remarkable "Church of the East," very early came to appreciate the spiritual depths of Islam. Around 800, Patriarch Timothy I recognized that Mohammed had indeed "followed the way of the prophets" when he turned numerous pagans away from "the adoration of idols" and taught not only about the one God, but about "the Word of God and his Spirit."[7] Not until the beginning of our century did a Palestinian Orthodox, Bendali Jaouzi, in a thesis presented at the Theological Academy of Kazan, also discern an authentic prophecy in the proclamations of the Meccan period. Metropolitan Georges Khodr similarly sees a "mysterious, providential path... in the Abrahamic line extending from the father of believers to the Arabic prophet."[8] For Khodr, the "divine economies"—about which he speaks in the plural just as did St Irenaeus of Lyons and St Maximus the Confessor—do not succeed one another in linear fashion. They

5   Reported by Ibn Ganim al-Maydisi. Translation from Caterina Valdré, *I detti di Rabi'a* (Milan, 1979).
6   Reported by Aflaki, in *ibid.*
7   Cited by I. Moubarac, *Pentologie islamo-chrétienne*, vol. 3 (Beirut, 1972-1973), pp. 261-2.
8   "Contacts," #110, 2nd trim. 1980, p. 97.

can be understood only when considered from the perspective of Christ who is coming again. Mohammed, therefore, is not simply a prophet who leads entire nations to an Old Testament perspective, but an announcer of the ultimate reality, of the imminent Judgment: through him, God takes Christians to task for "the hostility and the hatred" which divide them.[9]

Radical Islam as a False Response to Modernity

Even more so than in Orthodox lands, modernity came to Islamic territory from the outside. The ravages of this cultural mutation, in which vast human resources have been developed in this age of science and technology, have been immense. The environment, customs, and mental attitudes have all been affected.

The fundamentalist reaction in its own way makes it clear that this development has reached its limits—not temporally, of course, but in the human soul. At the very heart of Western civilization, humanity is acquainted with the agony of the "descent into hell," and it pays the price for its self-divinization. We can sense a new awareness, a vertical tendency that seeks to move beyond the simple historical future and the perils of technology. It is one that is based on the desire for the survival of humanity and of the earth.

But modernity is a powerful force which devours those who would challenge it "from the outside." Radical Islam, in seeking a brutal shortcut to overcome modernity, finds only the reality it seeks to oppose. The same type of socio-political discourse crystallizes into an ideological system! Radical Islam "ideologizes" Islam and is swallowed up in anti-Westernism, in a violence which is nothing but a sign of powerlessness, and ultimately leads only to cultural regression. It compromises the highest values of Islam: its sense of justice, and its notion of an "egalitarian, secular theoc-

9   Koran 5:14.

racy," which it seeks, not without reason, to oppose the develop-
mental model imposed by the West. In the words of Parsifal,
however, "only the weapon that inflicted the wound can heal it."

Christians—and Orthodox Christians in particular, who
know similar temptations, but perhaps less than others—must
ally themselves with an authentic Islam to overcome modernity
"from the inside," through a new cultural transformation. Together, they will remind the world of the irreducible nature of the
person, the "image of God" for Christians, the *khalifa* (meaning
God's vicar) for Moslems. This does not, for either side, imply
blind domination. For the earth, according to the Koran, is man's
"place of dwelling and joy"—as long as he rejects *irraf,* i.e., passionate possessiveness. As for the Orthodox, they see the world in
a eucharistic perspective, from the perspective of transfiguration.

A new form of secularism, rooted in Islam, would place the accent both on the rights of God and the rights of man. It would
not neglect the connection made by primitive Islam between the
spiritual world and the profane, and it would rediscover the open,
"pluralistic" character of the Umayyad period, which was so creative in art, thought, and science. Suffice it to recall the discoveries
of that era in the fields of optics, algebra, astronomy, as well as developments in Greek thought. Moslems, Christians, agnostics,
and Neoplatonists worked together without difficulty. Similar cooperation occurred repeatedly in the Ottoman Empire, in the art
of the 16th and 17th centuries, as well as in the evolution toward
true federalism in the 19th. Contemporary Turkey seeks to find
its place between God and man. It does so with difficulty and
pain, but it provides a model for both the Islamic world and for
Europe. The statue erected in Ankara in honor of Kemal Ataturk
exalts the courage, the strength, and the greatness of humanity.
But one also sees minarets everywhere, proclaiming the presence
of the transcendent. How can the human and the divine be placed
in their proper perspective? Fundamentalist Islam would crush

the former. The western approach would be to separate them totally. This is the challenge that my country must face today, the
patriarch affirms. And the Christian minorities, he believes, must
be part of the solution.

Peace in the Holy Land, Peace in the Mediterranean

Islam can be freed of its fundamentalist tendencies by eliminating its fear of modernity, by creating a new modernity which,
among European intellectuals, is now open to Islamic mysticism and particularly Suffism. The immediate task is to restore
peace between the Israelis and the Palestinians, because the
Arab defeat in June, 1967, and the subsequent occupation of
vast Arab territories, have contributed greatly to the birth and
emergence of fundamentalist Islam. When he made a pilgrim-
age to Jerusalem, Bartholomew wrote to Yasser Arafat:

The compassion you have expressed toward the victims of the
Jewish genocide entitles you to receive in return the same compassionate witness from Israel for the sufferings of the Palestinian
people. This witness must be translated into deeds and in the
daily life of your people.

We must all remember that Jerusalem is, par excellence, the
site of the three Abrahamic traditions, and we cannot resolve the
conflict if we forget this.

The second, more long term task is the rediscovery and revival
of the Mediterranean genius. The people living around this sea
must be invited, freely and voluntarily, to build peace in the
Mediterranean through the rediscovery of the principles and values which flourished for many centuries in this region of the
world: faith in one single God, who created heaven and earth, and
who is our common Father; the sacred character of the human
person; a love which, through compassion, forgiveness, justice,
and peace, transcends all boundaries and does not discriminate. A
relatively unified Mediterranean culture was established during

the Middle Ages, a culture based, among both Christians and
Moslems, on a rationale that remained close to the Greek *logos*
and biblical Wisdom.

Such reasoning, based on modesty and a sense of limitations, was
invoked in our own century by Albert Camus. Facing the monster of
totalitarianism, he spoke of "the admitted ignorance [in this way he
opened up for others the possibility of faith, and perhaps ultimately
for himself as well], a refusal of fanaticism... the beloved face, and finally beauty... The philosophy of darkness will once again be dissi-
pated above the sparkling sea." Because, according to another writer,
this time a Greek, Costis Palamas,

> All is laid bare...
> day bursts forth from all directions...
> Fill yourselves with light...
> This land is an unmixed wine.

The revelations of monotheism and, already in ancient Greece,
the awakening of the individual, freed the Mediterranean man from
being absorbed into a sacred nature and liberated him from the
world of myth. But this was not in order to violate and destroy the
cosmos, or to consider it merely as an inexhaustible reservoir of energy to be exploited by technology. The Mediterranean man is neither an embryo asleep in the belly of Mother-Earth, nor an abstract
dominator. His relation to the earth should rather be expressed in
terms of friendship. He prefers a good, solid object to a manufac-
tured trinket. Consistent with a Byzantine esthetic, he believes that
the purpose of *techne* is to reveal the secret beauty of *physis*: for example, by cutting open a block of marble to manifest the lines and colors which lie dormant within it. Myth has become poetry, which
allows humanity to assume the world by seeing it as an epiphany.
Nothing illustrates the esthetics of a Heidegger—the celebration of
being—better than the landscape of the Greek archipelago, where
white churches unite earth with heaven. However—and in this re-

gard the Mediterranean approach differs from Heidegger's more
Germanic view—being is here "relational," as Christos Yannaras
and John Zizioulas affirm. Being is interior to the communion of
men among themselves and with the living God.

Mediterranean people live intensely. Some, on certain summer
days, abandon themselves to the sweetness of the world:

> Who is the one who dwells, stretched on his back, upon the sand,
> smoking olive leaves of burnished silver.
> Grasshoppers warm themselves in his ears...
> Lizards slide through the grass of his armpit,
> And a wave washes over the algae of his feet, lightly.[10]

Others tear themselves away from the world so as to rediscover
it as a "burning bush." They seek transcendence: if they are Christians, they enter voluntarily into death in order to rise again; if
Moslems, they obliterate themselves in bearing witness to the
Unique One. Such today are the monks of Mt Athos, for whom
modern culture is a culture of death, but who celebrate the cosmic
liturgy on the altar of the heart.

"For me," wrote Sikelianos, "the ground was taut like a skin
stretched upon the drum."

Probably as a result of such attitudes, scientific and industrial
progress fled to northwestern Europe, then to America and Japan.
But if such attitudes are rediscovered, if they enter again into our
consciousness, then they can restore the harmony between post-
modern man and nature, without his being absorbed by the latter.
He would be protected from greed; he would become more accepting, for a world that is loved encourages sharing. Let us not allow our Mediterranean sea to die from physical and moral pollution,
the patriarch insists, from our inability to regulate its northern shore,
where people eat their fill, or its southern shore, over-populated,
poorly developed, where there grows today a fanaticism born of de-

10 Odysseus Elitis, *Chair d'été* (The Flesh of Summer).

spair. Achieving such an equilibrium, which to many may seem utopian, requires visionary planning. The religious, cultural, and political leaders of the Mediterranean countries must cooperate if they want this blessed sea, which seems to recapitulate the history of the world, to avoid the fate of the Dead Sea, which lies so close...

Two Closing Quotes

The first citation comes from the great Turkish mystical poet, Younous Emre, who lived between the 13th and 14th centuries, in the reign of Osman, founder of the Ottoman Dynasty:

> Day and night, the great nocturnal bear, commandments inscribed on the Tables of the Law, everything is in the being. Sinai... the Bible and the Gospel, the Koran, the Talmud, the words of light, everything is in the being...

But what is the meaning of "the being"? Younous answers:

> I go, and every step draws me closer to him.
> I go, I run toward him, the Beloved...
> I am immolated in the city of love.
> Younous offers your soul as a holocaust to the Friend,
> and may you, in secret, make that offering known.[11]

Metropolitan Georges Khodr says much the same:

> Christ is not an institution. He is ultimate value, action, the transformation of hearts into gentleness, simplicity, humility, into a Jihad[12] for those who suffer.[13]

---

11 *Diwan* #19: *The Gospel and the Koran.*
12 The word means effort, interior combat. It stands for war only in a derived sense.
13 *Op. cit.*

13

About the New Age, About India, and Especially About Buddhism

The Search and the Challenge of the "New Age"

A "New Age" mentality little by little penetrates our era. One no longer speaks of religion, but of spirituality. Religion, it is said, breeds intolerance and hatred. We no longer speak of prayer, but of meditation. We no longer speak of faith, but of experience, which we achieve through "methods" whose success is guaranteed. A "New Age" dawns, indicated astrologically by the passage from the Age of Pisces to the Age of Aquarius! This represents a "paradigm shift," a new consciousness, a new civilization. This anticipated and already perceived "paradigm" rejects positivism, which restricts reality to a measurable "exterior" (the "rule of quantity"). But it also rejects the biblical and Christian tradition, which it knows chiefly through its most questionable western expressions: the absurd notion of a Father requiring the passion and death of his Son to reconcile himself with humanity. Jesus is presented as one of many manifestations of a cosmic Christ, who is ultimately only a symbol of the Self.

We witness also the reemergence of an archaic, diffuse sacredness, in which the divine is seen as the profundity of the world. This view enters into an alliance with certain forms of scientific research in the realms of physics and psychology, or parapsychology. Particularly in California, where Far-West meets Far-East, one studies ultimate experiences, referred to as "peak experiences."

In this complex search, which combines the best with the worst, we must seek to "discern the spirits." In the words of St Paul: "Test everything and retain what is good."

✹ ✹ ✹

In the "New Age" perspective, the divine is not "an individual in the sky." It is Spirit, Conscience, Energy, "the Silence from which come all sounds." Or again, according to those who have entered the confines of death—as Leo Tolstoy also said—it is a gentle, warm light, a brilliant shining forth of peace and love. The divine is approached in two ways which, ultimately, reveal themselves to be identical: the interior path and the cosmic path. The divine is revealed in man's deepest being, according to the famous Hindu equations: "You are it"; "the *Atman* [the self] = the *Brahman* [the divine]." The experience that is sought is cosmic, in which man identifies himself with the absolute through the mediation of the universe. By *channeling*, one is able to "plug into" cosmic Consciousness. This "plugging in" is not individual, but "pan-human." Thus one rediscovers MacLuhan's "planetary village," which must be pacified and united through a respect for customs and cultures. The more archaic and magical the approach, the more attractive it is...

The same Spirit animates both the stars and men, and it is he who renders fertile Mother-Earth, *Gaia*. It is therefore important, as part of the ecological effort, to "re-enchant the world," to re-sacralize nature, to venerate the Great Mother, who has been demonized by the exclusively male God of the Judeo-Christian tradition. Followers in one "New Age" center in Scotland, supposedly made an ungrateful earth fertile by considering it to be sacred and by venerating the "spirits" of plants!

Some Orthodox Remarks

Let us not too quickly cry "neo-paganism," though the temptation is certainly strong. The "New Age" search sends us back to the high theology of the Orthodox Church, which is by definition mystical. This theology, apophatic and antinomic, does not refer to God as a "supreme being," as "an individual in the sky." It is from the resurrected Christ, who is the Face of the Father, that the Spirit shines forth—the Spirit who is the Consciousness and the Energy that animate the cosmos. Everything exists in the Word, who creates and re-creates the world. The horizon, the goal, and the future of the cosmos is the incarnation, i.e., the divinization of a world called to become the Body of the Word, the Body of God. St Maximus the Confessor speaks of several "incarnations" of the Word: first of all in the cosmos itself, in which each creature is borne and attracted by a *logos* of the *Logos*, by a word of the divine Word. Man, who is priest and king of the world, must disclose and offer these *logoi* (the spiritual essences of things) to God, must reintegrate them into the *Logos*. As a 20th century poet has said, man must "feverishly gather the honey from the visible world into the great, golden bee-hive of the invisible."

In discovering this cosmic presence of God, however, the "New Age" ignores man in his irreducible personal reality, just as—and precisely because—it sees the divine only as an impersonal energy.

For this reason, says Maximus, the second "incarnation" of the Word takes place in history, in the revelation of the Law. The Law, in order to individualize man (and the individual is the necessary seed of the person), tears him away from the immense, cosmic matrix, from the deadly impulses of a nature which is both innocent and fallen.

The revelation of the Law, however, is unable totally to change the heart and to bring about a real union between the human and the divine. "God is in heaven, and man is on earth."

Hence the third "incarnation" of the Word, the incarnation and resurrection. This last incarnation recapitulates the first two, which are actually based on it, as there is no difference at all between the cosmic and meta-cosmic Christ. In him, the divine and the human, and through the human, all creation, are united without separation or confusion. In him is offered and takes place the true "channeling" between heaven and earth! The eucharist fulfills (and reveals) the sacramental potentiality of matter. Christian ascesis, "the acquisition of the Holy Spirit," permits the "contemplation of the glory of God hidden in creatures and in objects." Out of this vision of Christ, in the Holy Spirit and in the great Breath of a Life freed from death, flow the divine "energies." This vision assumes the hopes of the "New Age," but integrates them into the irreducible mystery of the person, which exists as a *Self* only because it is a *particular* self. Man is not saved simply by reaching an awareness of the cosmos; he saves the cosmos by discerning its silent celebration. The Wisdom described in the last books of the Old Testament is a feminine figure expressing the maternal tenderness of God. It is his mercy, which the Bible designates by the word *rahanim*, the emphatic plural of *rehem*, the womb. The concept of Gaia is both exorcised and assumed by that of Wisdom. The old myths can therefore be reclaimed as the poetics of communion. Sergius Bulgakov, a great Russian "sophiologist," whose thought was sometimes unclear, but who had a brilliant intuition, wrote:

> Wisdom reveals herself in the world as beauty, and this beauty is the sensible "sophianic nature" of the world... Spring flowers surge from the dark bed of Demeter... Why are the tiger and the leopard so beautiful in their formidable grace, and the lion in his majesty? Why the beauty of young women...? Is it not the light of Wisdom which, from within, illumines the inert flesh and "matter"?[1]

1 *La Lumière sans déclin* (*The Unfading Light*), French trans. (Lausanne, 1990), p. 223.

The Greek Fathers insisted on human unity in the most realistic sense. It is a unity which hatred and killing constantly destroy, but which the incarnate Word ever restores. In him, therefore, we are able constantly to recreate that unity. According to Gregory of Nyssa, the statement "Let us make man in our image" refers to humanity in its ontological unity.

> To say that there are "several men" is to abuse the language... Certainly there are many who share the same human nature... but, through them all, man is one.[2]

Hence the fundamental importance of the resurrection of Christ, which tears all humanity out of the grasp of nothingness. And through humanity, the universe itself becomes theophany. Eternally, and in communion, it affirms all the ancient theophanies. For, as our Fathers in the faith have declared, man is at the same time a "little world," a *microcosm*, and a *macrocosm*, who transcends the universe in order to transform it into Eucharist.

On India and Buddhism

Behind the "New Age" one can also discern a rediscovery of India, and particularly of Buddhism.

Many westerners today report that they find true serenity in Buddhism. They learn that there exist a *dharma* (to use the Sanskrit word), a path of salvation, a world order; one could even call it Wisdom, almost in the Biblical sense of the word. And this *dharma*, not unlike the Decalogue, asks them not to kill, steal, or lie, to be chaste, and (very useful for our societies) to abstain from alcohol and drugs! They seem to distance themselves somewhat from their emotions and to view others, and themselves, with greater tolerance and peace.

2   *That There Are Not Three Gods* (PG 45:117).

Curiously, the popularity of Buddhism today replaces that of Hinduism, which seemed greater during the period following World War II. This may be the result of the spread of Tibetan Buddhism, which is today building monasteries throughout Western Europe and North America. Or it may be due to the remarkable personality of the Dalai Lama, who is able to interpret Buddhism to the West. But there is also more to it: India represents something luxurious, superabundant, a kind of robust cheerfulness; whereas Buddhism speaks essentially of suffering and of deliverance from pain. Buddhism therefore seems particularly attractive to many persons from western societies who are tired, who are "stressed out," and who seek a little peace and quiet...

For Buddhism, indeed, everything is painful: to be born, inexorably to decline, to suffer so much torment, to be subjected to what one hates, to be separated from what one loves. And what is the reason for this suffering? It is because one never ceases to desire, to be "thirsty," to "burn." Desire is born out of ignorance. It believes in the reality, in the importance, of beings and of things. Thus it produces error, lust, and hatred, which are "the three roots of evil." The "way of deliverance" corrects our behavior (the moral requirements are extreme—something that the West usually forgets), and, through the practice of meditation, allows us to discern the process of growth and finally to awaken ourselves. To awaken to the unique, ineffable reality is to put out the flames of passion, error, and illusion. It is to become passionless, i.e., to triumph over the passions which constantly and actively toy with us.

This type of asceticism, which is monastic, is similar to our own monastic ascesis. Hesychastic spirituality, "the art of arts and science of sciences," also speaks of ignorance and of the passions, which begin with pride and avidity, with self-centeredness—*philautia*—which are all born from our hidden anguish when we are faced with the transitory nature of this world. And the methods to achieve this liberation from the "passions" are similar: cleanse the mind of "thoughts," achieve *apatheia* (passionlessness) and "wakefulness." This last word is as important in hesychasm as it is in Buddhism, because the word *buddha* means "awake." Indeed, the great witnesses of hesychasm are called the "neptic" Fathers, an adjective derived from the Greek *nepsis*, meaning wakefulness!

The tern *Nirvana*, often so poorly understood, means *extinction*—of desire, of thirst, of fire. It designates a state of completion about which one can speak only in negations. This reminds us of the hesychastic "prayer beyond prayer," when man is rendered infinitely small as he comes to see the divine light.

Was Buddhism, in the depths of Asia, not a kind of pre-Christian anticipation? It would itself, of course, be ignorant of this fact. We can discern two aspects in its doctrine: the first is a partial truth; the second remains enclosed in this partiality.

Nirvana is a negative symbol of an entry into the divine at the center of one's very being. That a liberating love is revealed in this "emptiness" which is fullness, a love which restores both the other and the world—all this is unknown to Buddhism. Or not yet known? The question remains. Within the hesychastic tradition, the heart and the spirit must die to themselves in order to rediscover the "otherness" of God in unity, a unity which is transformed into communion.

We agree with the Buddhists that "this world," as the Gospel says, lies in evil. But for Buddhists, the world is nothing more than that. It consists of transitory aggregates of matter, which are constantly being transformed and disappear, only to give birth to new aggregates, which are no less transitory. Ignorance consists in considering as substantial that which is merely apparent. For us Orthodox, under the veil of illusion which we are indeed called to remove, God's creation has substance. It is good, good precisely because of its diversity. *This world* does not exhaust the reality of *God's world*.

For Buddhism, similarly, man is simply a nonessential "combination," which can, for example, be compared to a cart. Man is a simple process, a continuity with no identity. There is certainly reincarnation, but it occurs through the simple causality of actions producing effects. There is actually no transmigration, because there is no soul that can pass from one habitation to another. To be delivered is to reject the notion of the "self"—as well, of course, as any notion of the "other." Reincarnation, the "wheel of existence," is an infernal cycle, but there exist no condemned individuals! Buddha never ceased to denounce the "ignorant multitude" which nourished itself on absurd "theories of the soul" and believed in "personal" reincarnations. This "non-Self," whether mitigated or not, is in fact no different from the Self of the *Vedanta*—that Hindu school which succeeded in chasing Buddhism from India! One can speak of the Self only in negative terms, in order to identify it with the divine—and it is only this divine aspect which is transmigrated!

This, we can see, is a far cry from western "reincarnationism," that invention of western tourists. We also totally misunderstand yoga (and its metaphysical goals are nearly always misunderstood in the West). Yoga gives its western practitioner the illusion of discovering his true Self, whereas it usually leads him only to expand and show off his ego!

Everything, the patriarch adds, centers on the concept of the "person." According to Buddhism, the person does not exist. The Christian, however, affirms the existence of the person. But Orthodoxy does not identify the person with the individual, with the "individual substance of a rational nature," as Boethius awkwardly stated in the Latin world. This would mean that the person is nothing more than a mask, which is indeed the original meaning of the Latin word *persona*, or the Greek *prosopon*. The person is revealed only at the conclusion of a negative anthropology, and the efforts of Hinduism and Buddhism can be helpful for us. The absolute is not beyond the person (for then, in effect, there would be no one!). Rather, the absolute is the very depth, the "bottomless depth," of the person, or rather, of communion. And if the person, and therefore the possibility of encounter, do exist, then history exists. Yet neither Hinduism nor Buddhism is interested in history, because for them time, with its endless cycles, consists of nothing but terror. If the person, and therefore communion, exists, then man's attraction toward God transfigures desire: *eros* is transformed into *agape*. It is particularly the miracle of grace and forgiveness that destroys the fatality of *karma*—that automatic link between the act and its consequences—and the fear "that we will need to repay everything," as say some Christians who fail to comprehend the infinite grace of the cross and the resurrection.

From Buddha to Gandhi

We must, however, be aware that Hinduism and Buddhism have never ceased to develop. This is certainly true in our own era, when values of Christian origin have been spread throughout the world. But it has also been the case for centuries, either because of a Christian impulse we can only guess at, or through the influence of the long "Nestorian" evangelization in the heart of Asia.

Within Chinese and Japanese Buddhism, for example, there has been an evolution, on the one hand, toward ascesis and an esthetic of cosmic beauty, and, on the other, toward a religion of mercy. In the *Zen* movement—*Ch'an* in China—the keen ascetic, during and after a moment of illumination, sharply experiences the birth of a tree, of a flower, of light. He knows things as they are. He hears "the ah! of things." This is not far from the Christian "contemplation of nature," which is a necessary stage of hesychasm. In Amidism, monotheism asserts itself. Amida (Omito in Chinese), the mediator, was a monk who voluntarily halted his ascent on the path of illumination, putting the achievement of perfection on hold, until all humanity and all creation down to the last blade of grass are saved through his intercession. The faithful practice the *nembutsu*, the humble invocation of the formula, "Buddha Amida, save me." One group that came from Amidism has even called itself the *Yuzu Nembutsu*, "invocation in communion"! All this makes any Christian pause who is familiar with the Jesus Prayer.

A monotheism of love has gradually spread throughout Hinduism. Even yoga, a methodical human exercise, has come to focus more and more on attraction to the divinity. The Vishnic *Vedanta* confesses and adores a personal God who was present at creation as the soul is present in the body—an image that St Gregory of Nyssa liked to use! The Vishnic God, out of his free will, has created a real world which expresses his beauty and which therefore merits positive consideration by man. He has provided each person with an identity, thus making possible not fusion, but communion. As one mystic from this school has said, "If I love sugar, that does not mean that I wish to become sugar!" The Shakti movement celebrates the divine energy, which it perceives as a feminine presence: here again, we are reminded of Wisdom! And this religion has promoted respect toward woman, toward the wife.

In our own century, an encounter between this kind of Hinduism and the Gospel has already begun, particularly in the person, deeds, and martyrdom of Gandhi and his followers. Disciples of Gandhi remain in the United States and in South Africa.

We Christians have a great deal to do to prepare for this encounter. And it is far more interesting than arguing among ourselves.

To Conclude and to Begin

14

The Newness of the Spirit

Let Us Be Open to the Spirit

There is no end, and there will be none until the death of death has been revealed to every one, and until the world has been openly transfigured. And this transfiguration, which sometimes breaks through into the present, will itself be infinitely dynamic, passing "from beginning to beginning, through beginnings which shall have no end."[1] To love a person is to need eternity, for the person is unknown as much as it is known. And what can we say about the living God, who makes us enter into that infinite reciprocity of love of which he consists?

So we must not conclude, but open ourselves to the Breath of resurrected life, to the Spirit who is impetus, fire, and inspiration. The Spirit really has no name, because God in his entirety is Spirit. But though he has no name, he is the one who names everything. He is the one who makes our faces to shine in the immense glow of the communion of the saints, i.e., of sinners who accept forgiveness.

"If God has put on flesh," say the Fathers, "it is so that man might become a bearer of the Spirit [*pneumatophoros*]."[2] Christ, from all eternity as in the incarnation, is the anointed of the Spirit. And in Christ, despite all the vicissitudes of history and despite our own sins, the Church is "the Church of the Holy Spirit," not for its own sake, but, as St Basil says, "for the life of the world."

1 *Homily on the Song of Songs* (*PG* 44:941A).
2 St Athansius, *On the Incarnation* (*PG* 26:996).

The Spirit is the hidden God who enters into the innermost depth of our inner life, as he unites with our outer life through communion. He reveals God in the incarnate Christ, and in the neighbor he reveals the person called to become God, i.e., for all eternity and fully *alive*. The Spirit is the beauty of the world and, at times, reveals the transparency of the human face. He evokes the cry of Job in history (yes, he evokes even the atheistic revolt against so many false images of God). He answers this cry through the Resurrection, and by setting humanity on the path to the universal resurrection. He directs Israel toward its Messiah, whose name the Jews will then recognize. He directs Moslems toward the *Mahdi*, who will stand upon the highest minaret in Damascus. He directs Hindus and Buddhists toward the full discovery of the antinomy which unites unity and otherness without confusion. The Spirit is the silence at the heart of the Word. The Spirit is the silence which allows a word to emerge out of the babble of the "information superhighway." The Spirit is the silence which transforms the presence of an unknown saint into a source of blessing. The Spirit is the great blessing of life.

Spiritual life is both "life in Christ" and "life in the Spirit," because the Spirit leads us "to the depths of God."[3] Deep within ourselves, the Spirit transforms the agony of death into the joy of the resurrection. Now, guided by the monks, we learn to live not in death but in the Spirit. We "breathe the Spirit"—in him we love, we know, we create. In him the partial deaths which mark our existence become the necessary breakthroughs to a higher level, and physical death is transformed into a path of light. This light is simultaneously terrible and gentle, terrible precisely because it is gentle: it dissolves all our masks and illusions, but it also makes the Cross shine brightly as "the judgment of judgment."

In the Spirit, we are able to break the endless cycle of violence by "loving our enemies," by bringing them as well along the paths of creation and life.

3   1 Cor 2:10.

In the Spirit, Christianity is neither moralism nor ritualism, but calling, power, and light. Christianity is no longer ideological constraint, that heresy of the "Christian era." Nor is it simply one aspect of culture, alongside so many others, the heresy of modern times. Rather, Christianity is exorcism, it is substance, the profundity of all existence, available to everyone who desires it in love and freedom. It exists for the sake of love and freedom.

Let Us Discern Between the Living and the Dead

Today, many historical forms of Christianity are dead or dying. Trying to preserve them through blind conservatism can lead only to the creation of malicious and distrustful ghettos which idolize formalism, or to "fascist" adventures that lead nowhere. On the contrary, we must trust in the "newness of the Spirit," who will transform this death into resurrection. New approaches are already developing, approaches which rediscover and develop the deepest intuitions of thinkers such as Gregory of Nyssa, Maximus the Confessor, or Isaac of Syria. The sadism of expiatory conceptions of salvation is being replaced with paschal joy. The notion of hell as an eternal concentration camp is being replaced by prayer for universal salvation. The obsession with individual salvation (for which only a few, in any case, are destined) is being replaced by a sense of limitless communion. Fear of the flesh is being replaced by the call to transfigure it, whether through monastic ascesis, the love between a man and a woman, or the struggle of the creative act. Escapism into the heavenly realm is being replaced by a union between heaven and earth, by "fidelity to the earth" and all its creatures, so as to transfigure them. The list could go on and on.

The sacred is dying, as the Gospel has predicted. The Sabbath is for man, and not man for the Sabbath. It is not that which enters into the mouth that defiles man, but that which comes from his heart. Regulations concerning purity and impurity are being rejected. And particularly regulations concerning woman, who is no longer seen as the necessarily inferior "complement" of man, but as a person of infinite importance, called to be human in a feminine mode, destined for the free and reciprocal encounter with the male.

The Gospel, therefore, reveals the ultimate value of the person and of the communion of persons. The Decalogue—which is revelation and not "natural law"—forbids murder and idolatry. And in the light of the resurrection, the Gospel introduces an ethic of creative love. In the Holy Spirit, man discovers his vocation as "created creator." To the frozen opposition between sacred and profane, between pure and impure, the Spirit substitutes the power of sanctification. Israel has transformed the cosmos into history. The Spirit assumes *both* the cosmos *and* history into the Body of Christ: Gaia becomes the prefiguration of the Virgin-Mother, and the ancient myths are transformed into a poetry of communion. Holiness can therefore reinvent the sacred, which is the poetry of creation and of faces, a trembling before the immensity of love.

The Role of Orthodoxy

In this transition, Orthodoxy could play a major role. But in order to become the critical and prophetic conscience of the peoples entrusted to it, Orthodoxy must free itself of the idolatry of nationalism. It must provide an unbiased witness to all humanity. And it must free itself also from a cold ritualism, not so as to lose the ability to communicate with God, as has happened in the West, but in order to understand that the liturgy and ritual are nothing else than the symbols of an encounter, a music of faith, a music which unites itself to the music of creation and sets it free.

We must also recover a dialectic of unity and diversity within a Church that has finally been freed from the power of the state, a

Church that has become a source of light, life, and transfiguration. Its indispensable structures include the episcopate, which serves as a guarantee of the apostolic continuity of the Gospel message and of the eucharist, but also the different degrees of primacy, and particularly a universal primacy "presiding in love." All the primacies must be in the service of the People of God, a People of kings, priests, and prophets, who all together concelebrate at the eucharistic liturgy (the bishop and the priest represent the people and pronounce the common prayer of the people). Then the centers of primacy will appear not as centralizing powers, but as places of encounter, of conciliar reflection, of communion. The simultaneous rediscovery of the universality of the Church and of a eucharistic ecclesiology will little by little break down the boundaries of the "autocephalies." The diaconal function of the universal primate to watch over the unity and universality of the Church can then be fully expressed. What an example this could be for Rome, which faces the opposite temptation! What an example for Europe as it seeks to achieve unity! What an example for our entire planet, which aspires to unity but fears uniformity!

Beyond the typical controversies, the Gospel antinomy between the Inaccessible One and the Crucified One, which has been elaborated by the Fathers, is the basis for a theology that cannot be separated from the liturgical and ascetical experience of death and resurrection: of death to death and of deification through the Spirit (or, if you prefer, adoption, filiation, revival—it makes no difference!). The only absolute sin, said St Isaac of Syria, is "insensibility to the resurrection." It is in this perspective that we must approach divergences among Christians, and not simply on the basis of words. After all, for more than a thousand years the undivided Church accepted a great diversity of interpretations! But it has always maintained the two inseparable mysteries which, through confession of faith and the eucharist, keep open the way to life. The first is that God has become man so that our separation might be overcome and that we might be fully made alive—we Orthodox dare to use the term "deified." The second is the mystery of the unity of the Trinity, in whose light we each become, and must become, a unique person in communion with all other persons. This means our participation in the infinite love (St Maximus the Confessor uses the expression "mad love") of a God who is liberating paternity and indivisible communion.

The time is coming for Orthodoxy unselfishly to share its riches so as to hasten the emergence of the undivided Church. Let it humbly offer its experiential theology—the paschal joy celebrated in its liturgy and reflected in its icons, which everyone can attain through life-giving ascesis.

If the separation between Christian East and West led to the disintegration of the Christian world, their encounter could lead to its reintegration. An Orthodox witness stripped to its bare essentials could assist in overcoming "modernism" and "fundamentalism" by a return to the original Tradition, the life of the Spirit in the Body of Christ, a life which needs no constraints to remain coherent and faithful.

Scientific Knowledge and Wisdom

The possibilities of human intelligence, in which the image of God is, in a certain way, concentrated, or rather reflected, are limitless. They are limitless in both a "horizontal" sense and in the sense that they will not end. For the image of God, which is a call, can be rejected. The Orthodox, together with all other Christians, can engage in scientific research with the Name of Christ inscribed in their hearts and can enter into dialogue and collaboration with men of science. They have the duty to witness to the irreducible and inexhaustible character of humanity, as well as to the prodigious intelligence which fills the universe—*another* intelligence, which inscribes numbers and symbols of transcendence on all of creation. The presence of this inexhaustible dimension and of this Wisdom makes the scientific quest possible and can correct its mistakes. Against a science closed in on itself, spiritual men call for a science that remains open, capable of refining and directing its aims, capable also of self-limitation out of respect for humanity and the earth. For the first time in history, employing the forces of creation without any sense of limits, we have achieved the capacity to destroy human life on the planet. The earth itself is menaced by the threat of nuclear destruction and environmental pollution. In this context, scientists and religious believers should recognize that they need each other. The former can explain what is happening to our earth. The latter can inspire a love of God's creation, for which humanity is increasingly responsible. The "contemplation of the glory of God hidden in creatures and things," about which our ascetics speak, must move beyond monastic cells and hermitages to inspire the efforts of science and culture. It must teach scientific research and technology not to disintegrate matter and destroy nature, but to reintegrate all in Wisdom.

The Great "Spiritual Battles" Ahead

If God is love, then humanity also, or at least a few persons, must become truly compassionate. This can be accomplished through the bitter but necessary experience of individualization, which faith and the Spirit can little by little transform into communion. Here the affirmation of the self becomes inseparable from the affirmation of the "other" and opens itself to mystery. We must, once more, quote from Isaac of Syria:

> When God sees that you have, in all purity of heart, placed your trust in him more than in yourself, then a power unknown to you will make its dwelling within you. And you will perceive in all your senses the power of the One who is with you.

The time will come when the Christian world will rebuild itself in unity and, with courage and all humility, will wage the great "spiritual battles." It will fight for peace among men. It will fight for a self-limitation that will liberate our desire for the frenzy of consumption and for a sexuality devoid of meaning. It will challenge the forces of emptiness, a perverse emptiness that seeks to decompose the soul, to deliver it to vulgarity, to derision, to the violence of despair, to pseudo-religions that destroy the person... These battles will force us to shift constantly from kenosis and martyrdom to the beginnings of a divinely-inspired humanism for which there no precise definition, for "the Lord is the Spirit, and where the Spirit of the Lord is, there is freedom."[4]

Is there no end, no fulfillment? The Apocalypse, which is not history but the revelation of its meaning, assures us that there will indeed be an end, and that this end is already here, within the heart of the Church. The Apocalypse—which simply means "Revelation"—tells us that real history is not programmed by earthly powers, but is in the hands of God. Whatever the apparent strength of evil and injustice in the world, the last word belongs to God. His Son has come to destroy death—in secret, in sacrament, out of respect for our freedom. And now his Spirit helps us to spread this victory everywhere. We do this in his presence and in expectation, for

> The Spirit and the Bride say, "Come." And let him who hears say, "Come." And let him who is thirsty come, let him who desires take the water of life without price... "Surely I am coming soon." Amen. Come, Lord Jesus![5]

4   2 Cor 3:17.
5   Rev 22: 17, 20.

Appendices

Patriarchal Texts

I

By Faith Alone…

(London, May 31, 1994)

Extracts from the patriarch's speech at the University of London, as it conferred upon him a doctorate honoris causa.

The ancient Greeks used to say that man, in order to develop, needs the city.

But in our cities today, we also see children who are poorly dressed, malnourished, lacking shelter. We see the unemployed. We witness violence. We count broken families, broken lives, broken dreams. Why is this? And what are we to do?

The answer can only be faith. Not knowledge, not wealth, not political action – but only faith.

Knowledge develops the mind, but faith can open the heart.

Wealth builds houses, but faith can move mountains.

Politics accomplishes the possible, but faith can do the impossible.

Western civilization has made possible the greatest human achievements: from true medical miracles to landing a man on the moon; from stable democracies to high standards of living. But we have only to look at the streets of our cities to see the price we have paid.

Politicians and professors alone cannot solve the problems of western society – pornography, pollution, drug addiction, misery, crime, wars, and so many homeless people. Religious leaders have a central role to play in providing inspiration.

Our task today is to apply the power of the Holy Spirit, the power that heals, to persons who are all children of God. This task is more essential than ever.

The spirituality of the Church provides a different form of accomplishment than is promised by the secularism of modern life. But it is not opposed to modernity.

The failure of anthropocentric ideologies has left a void. The frenetic pursuit of the future has sacrificed what interior peace existed in the past.

The Church's teaching about man and the world elevates the search for the temporal by taking into account the eternal. It places the two in harmony.

The misery of some concerns us all. To the question, "Who is my neighbor?" Christ responds with the parable of the Good Samaritan. He changes the question: it is no more "Who is my neighbor?" but: Who proves to be the neighbor to the wounded man who needs medical care and shelter?

There is today no more important question than this one. In Bosnia, are we neighbors to the victims, or do we pass by at a distance, our eyes averted, like the priest in the parable?

In Los Angeles, London, or St Petersburg, are we neighbors to abandoned children?

In South Africa, by contrast, nearly all proved themselves to be each other's neighbors.

"Go, ye, and do likewise." Every *human being is our neighbor.*

II

Via Crucis[1]

Prayer and meditation on the Way of the Cross read on Holy Friday 1994 (by, and then in the presence of John Paul II, in Rome).

1

The Gospel of Jesus Christ according to St Mark (14:32-36)

> *They came to a plot of land*
> *called Gethsemane.*
> *Then Jesus took Peter, James and John with him.*
> *And he said to them:*
> *"My soul is sorrowful to the point of death.*
> *Wait here and stay awake."*
> *And going on a little further*
> *he threw himself on the ground and prayed:*
> *"Abba, Father! For you everything is possible.*
> *Take this cup away from me.*
> *But let it be as you, not I, would have it."*

Meditation

> The garden of age-old olive trees.
> The olives must be crushed
> so that the oil of fire, the Holy Spirit
> may be poured over the wounds of the world.
>
> The passion of Jesus, alone,
> his closest friends have fallen asleep.
> Lord, deliver us from this sleep,
> while the passion of Christ continues in that of man.

---

1 Translator's note: English text adapted from the English translation published by The Pontifical Council for Promoting Christian Unity in its *Information Service* No. 86 (1994/II-III). By permission.

Passion of Jesus, silence of the Father.
I and the Father are one,
only one will, only one love,
but the human will of Jesus cries out in anguish,
as if his deepest being, divine-human,
were being torn apart.

Human will of Jesus,
in solidarity with all our loneliness,
with our sorrows and our rejections,
with us who were driven from the garden.

In Christ, God experiences in a human way
all our agonies,
the immense agonies of history,
the immense Job-like cry of our destinies,
sweating blood.

Yet, for all that,
trust is coming through the darkness,
a trembling voice, still stumbling,
not what I will,
but what you...
Holding on.
In Jesus, humanity holds on
to the Father's will.

O let this will overwhelm us
through the darkness.
The olives are being crushed.
In each tree the victorious Cross is awakening.
Garden of old:
Today you will be with me in Paradise.

Prayer
Bloodied face
yet face of the Father,
this face which in the darkness gushes with blood,
and which we ignore.

You, who are infinitely close,
replace in our hearts
anguish with thankfulness.

May the passion of human beings
become resurrection in you.

Glory and praise to you, O Christ,
who becomes more completely one of us
than we ourselves could ever be.
Fill with yourself, and with your love,
all our agonies, all our deaths.

2

The Gospel of Jesus Christ according to St Mark (14:43-46)

*And at once Judas, one of the Twelve, came up
and with him a number of men
armed with swords and clubs,
sent by the chief priests and the scribes and the elders.
He went up to Jesus at once and said,
"Rabbi!"
and kissed him.
The others seized Jesus and arrested him.*

Meditation

Some of them sleep,
but the one who stays awake
betrays.
Torpor, treason,
is this all our history is to be?

The kiss which speaks of love
becomes the sign of hatred.
All of Jesus' passion
is already friendship betrayed,
love turned into hatred.

The swords glitter in the darkness
but God does not defend himself.
He gives himself up into the hands of murderers
out of infinite respect for mankind.

He delivers himself into the hands of murderers
as he will allow himself to be killed by them

so that—by his death—he can offer them his very life.

Those who believe they possess God,
the High Priests, Scribes and elders,
prefer him at a distance,
harshly supreme.
And when God made man comes to them,
meek and humble of heart, they cast him into prison.

Prayer

Lord, I will not give you the kiss of Judas,
but like the thief I confess you:
Remember me when you come
into your Kingdom.

Of Judas we know nothing
beyond his despair.
God's mercy is boundless.
But save us, Lord,
from the Judas we carry within ourselves
when the desire for money or power
takes hold of us.

Remind us, Lord,
that the swords which pierce,
and the cudgels which crush
may cause death but cannot overcome it.

Too often our Churches
have persecuted their enemies.
So give Christians now
the power of humble love.

3

The Gospel of Jesus Christ according to St Mark (14:55, 60-61, 62, 64)

The chief priest and the whole Sanhedrin
were looking for evidence against Jesus
in order to have him executed.
But they could not find any.
The high priest then rose before the whole assembly

and put this question to Jesus:
"Are you the Christ, the Son of the Blessed One?"
"I am he," said Jesus.
Their verdict was unanimous:
he deserved to die.

Meditation

For a long time now the wise and important
have been condemning him.
He never existed, some say.
Maybe he did, but we know nothing about him,
say others.
Or even: he was a charismatic leader,
a great prophet,
but a man, nothing more than a man.

As for us, we hardly think of him.
We live as if he never existed.
But one day we find the question is burning within us:
Are you the Christ
in whom God who is holy gives himself to us?

Then, in the sound of church bells,
through the beauty of icons,
in the depths of our hearts,
Jesus ends his silence
and says: "I am he,"
and says: "I am,"
which means: I am God.

We can do nothing but put him to death
or throw ourselves at his feet,
repeating what he once said:
"I thank you, Father, that you have hidden these things
from the wise and understanding
and revealed them to little children.
Yes, Father, for such was your gracious will."

Prayer

Jesus, the Innocent One who came from elsewhere,
we have such a thirst for innocence,
we, who murder love daily.

Give us the fellowship of the innocent,
of the foolish in Christ,
of those who knew nothing—
except perhaps you—
when they were being thrown into the gas chambers,
or into a freezing hell,
when they are thrown into torture chambers,
in this torture chamber that life so often is.

For you came not to condemn but to save,
you came not to imprison but to set free.
Put your innocence into our struggles.
The great struggles of the spirit,
so that they may be free of violence and hatred.
Put your innocence into our love,
and into our families.
Put your innocence into our gaze,
so that we may see in you the Father's face,
so that we may discover in you the flame of things,
the icon of human faces.

4

The Gospel of Jesus Christ according to St Mark (14:72)

And at once the cock crowed for the second time,
and Peter recalled
what Jesus had said to him:
"Before the cock crows thrice,
you will have disowned me three times."
And he burst into deep tears.

Meditation

The cock announces the day,
the everlasting day of the Kingdom.
Yet this is when Peter takes fright
because the Kingdom does not come
with battalions of angels
or men with swords and bombs,
but with the death of the self
and first with that of the Master.

"No, this will never happen to you,"
he had said to Jesus
when he had foretold his passion.
But now it is happening.

Jesus has sensed beforehand
the hidden weakness of the strongest one,
the hasty ardor that suddenly falls away:
"Before the cock has crowed twice,
you will have denied me three times."

Judas went away and hanged himself,
despairing of being saved
on the day of universal salvation.
But Peter breaks down weeping.
The tears of Peter
in which his pride is burnt away.
The tears of Peter:
he will be first, but only as a pardoned sinner,
so as to preside not in glory but in love.

Prayer

Lord, give us tears like Peter's
when we do not wish to know
that the Passion is the price of Pascha,
that you conquer death, but by your death.
When we do not wish to know
that the Cross is the only tree of life.
We are so proud of our faith,
eager to drink it in, but remaining on the threshold
and falling away
if something frightening occurs;
give us the tears of Peter,
that is, your unlimited forgiveness.

5

The Gospel of Jesus Christ according to St Mark (15:14-15)

But they shouted all the louder, "Crucify him!"
So Pilate, anxious to placate the crowd,
released Barabbas for them.

After having Jesus scourged,
he handed him over to be crucified.

Meditation
> The crowds had acclaimed Jesus
> when he entered Jerusalem.
> Now they cry "Kill him!"
> They are no longer persons;
> all of them have together degenerated
> into a collective wild beast,
> thirsting for torture and blood.
> What evil there is in humanity,
> what a hold darkness has,
> that this ritual of cruelty
> targets the Innocent One.
>
> Jesus is king.
> He entered Jerusalem as a King.
> Now he is a king without a city.
> Such indeed is our God,
> whom we exclude from his creation
> and who, having become flesh in that creation,
> takes every exclusion on himself.
>
> Cruel history, mesmerized by destruction,
> killing in order to forget that we must die.
> Cruel history and how ironic,
> for the name Barabbas means "son of the Father."
>
> And the man who governs, Pilate,
> taking only his power for truth,
> flatters the crowd so as to channel its madness
> and preserve order for Caesar:
> the terrible wisdom of those who dominate,
> who throw scapegoats to the masses.
>
> But all will be reversed:
> because the suffering servant
> offers his life in a sacrifice of atonement,
> he will see the light and will be fulfilled.
> And through him all the excluded,
> all the faceless ones
> —as slaves were called—
> shall see the light and shall be fulfilled.

Prayer

> Lord, Jesus, king without a kingdom,
> open the door of our hearts
> so that your light so gentle,
> yet strong as a life that will not die,
> may shine in the world of the Barabbases and Pilates.
>
> Lord Jesus, scourged by our sins,
> you who never had even a thought of evil
> and accepted those blows in silence,
> take away from us the dark part,
> the vertigo of our nothingness,
> so that we may need no more scapegoats
> and may recognize in every person
> "bar-abbas," the son of the Father,
> the murderer so unexpectedly set free.

6

The Gospel of Jesus Christ according to St Mark and St John (Mk 15:17-19 and Jn 19:5)

> *They dressed him up in purple,*
> *twisted some thorns into a crown*
> *and put it on him.*
> *And they began saluting him,*
> *"Hail, king of the Jews!"*
> *They struck his head with a reed*
> *and spat upon him.*
> *Jesus then came out*
> *wearing the crown of thorns and the purple robe.*
> *Pilate said,*
> *"Here is the man."*

Meditation

> When the garden of Eden was closed,
> God said that the earth was to bear thorns,
> the ground be cursed, and mankind be stricken by death.
> With the thorns of our sufferings and hatreds
> the executioners crown you.
> The Father "lets fall upon you

all our faults.
Ill-treated, you do not open your mouth,
and like a lamb you are led to the slaughter."

All the members of your holy body
have suffered foul abuse on our behalf.
Your head the thorns,
your face the blows and spittle,
your back the scourges,
your hand the reed.

In spite of this you are king,
you are the king of life.
The executioners crown you,
they clothe you in the royal purple of your blood.
In your hand a scepter of derision,
but a scepter nonetheless—
they prophesy without knowing it.

In spite of this you are a priest:
with quiet majesty
you carry the sorrow of the world
to consume it in the fire of your love.

You took part in the wedding feast of Cana,
now you are at the wedding feast of blood.

Prayer

Here is the man.
In the face of everyone who is tortured,
show us the man.

Here is the man.
In the face of everyone who hungers,
show us the man.

Here is the man.
In the face of the well-fed brute
who stumbles backward towards death
show us the face,
your face,
God's image in the man.

7

The Gospel of Jesus Christ according to St Mark (15:20)

And when they had finished making fun of him,
they took off the purple
and dressed him in his own clothes.
They led him out
to crucify him.

Meditation

After the purple robe
the white one again;
after the king comes the priest,
and here is the altar of sacrifice:
the Cross.

They have led him out,
out of the holy city,
out of the well-protected sacred place
from which the unholy was excluded.
For he will from now on be the source of holiness,
he does away with all exclusion:
there is nothing which cannot be made holy.

They have led him out
far from the temple where the lambs were slaughtered.
He is the Lamb who bears the sin of the world.
There is no more temple
but his body:
the eucharist, our refuge.

They have led him out
far from people and from God,
at least from the God they claimed to know,
because "cursed is anyone hanged upon the wood."
But in him the true God is revealed.

They have led him out
with the Cross.

Prayer

O Jesus cast out,
may I never again cast you out.
Join my heart together again
that it may be your dwelling.

O Jesus cast out,
may it not be out of our Churches
from which we drive you out when they oppose each other.

O Jesus cast out,
so that nothing may be excluded any more,
so that no one may be excluded from the banquet
you offer us from age to age.

O Jesus cast out of this world
now you will give it light.

8

The Gospel of Jesus Christ according to St Mark (15:21)

They enlisted a passer-by,
Simon of Cyrene,
who was coming in from the country,
to carry his cross.

Meditation

Simon is a Jewish name,
but Cyrene was a Greek city
somewhere in Africa.
Back in the land of his fathers,
he cultivated it.
A strong peasant, soiled by the nourishing earth,
perhaps rejoicing that the fruit trees had blossomed.

Now he is at the gates of the city,
he makes his way, unaware of what is happening.
The officer of the occupying forces
spots him—a poor and vigorous man—
and recruits him
to carry with haste the cross of Jesus.

He is not a disciple, he is not a friend,
the apostles have scattered.
But he does not flee and carries the cross
which was intended not for him.

Many are obliged by life to carry the cross,
without knowing it is the cross of Christ.
They carry it every time they reach out beyond themselves
to feed, clothe or welcome the stranger.
"We did not know it was you,"
they say to Christ.
But he answers them:
"Indeed you did it to me."

Simon still had before his eyes the tree in blossom,
but through the caked blood, perhaps he glimpsed
a face of light
and realized that he was carrying something better
than a tree that would soon wither,
that he was carrying the new Tree of Life.

Prayer

Lord, destiny forces us to carry your cross.
Reveal to us that it is yours,
and that it is really you who carry ours.

Lord, we carry our passions like crosses,
they are not without love,
they are not without lies.
By your passion free us from illusions
and transform our passions
–they are not without love—
into compassion.

Lord, we carry the cross of our death,
of the death of our loved ones.
Reveal to us that in this difficult journey
you yourself await us.
It is you who make my cross
into your own,
the cross of resurrection.

9

The Gospel of Jesus Christ according to St Luke (23:27-28, 31)

Large numbers of people followed him,
and women too, who mourned and lamented for him.
But Jesus turned to them and said,
"Daughters of Jerusalem, do not weep for me;
weep rather for yourselves and for your children.
For if this is what is done to green wood,
what will be done when the wood is dry."

Meditation

The men have condemned Jesus,
but the women follow him weeping.
There are no women among the enemies of Jesus.
Expressing mocked motherhood,
they beat their breasts.

But Jesus says to them: "Do not weep.
Do not weep, Mother,
in three days I will rise again."
There is no need to weep for the priest
who celebrates the sacrifice
of universal sanctity.

We must weep over the destiny of man,
over what man has made of his destiny.
Lazarus is dead, he stinks already;
already the enemies besiege the city,
the forces of nothingness besiege man
and drag him toward the empty abyss.

Jesus takes on this destiny to defeat it.
He raised Lazarus
and prepares to take on the Divider
who has no hold over him.
So that one day he may say to us at last:
"I wipe away every tear from your eyes;
death, weeping and sorrow are no more,
because the old world has disappeared."

Prayer

The tower of Siloam still falls,
armies still set fire to cities.
It is not that you would punish us,
it is because we have become as dry wood.

You, the green wood, give us your sap,
so that we might know how to dry the tears
of the women of Jerusalem.

Make each of us a Veronica
who wipes the sweat off your face
so that your features on our icons
–and every human person is your icon–
may be for us the door to eternity.

10

The Gospel of Jesus Christ according to St Mark (15:24)

*Then they crucified him and shared out his clothing,
casting lots to decide what each should get.*

Meditation

On this day they hang from the gibbet the one who
suspended the world in the infinity of space.
He is pinned there by nails,
the Spouse of the Church.
He is pierced by a lance,
the Son of the Virgin.
We venerate your sufferings, O Christ,
may your resurrection come.

On this day, Jesus knows at once
the horror of the body which is stretched out,
the distress of the soul,
and the scorn of men.
From now on he is the brother of those who are tortured,
those who despair, those who are despised.

On this day he, the only living one
—"I am the resurrection and the life"—

who was born without tearing the Virgin
knows a tearing beyond all measure.
Folly for those who esteem wisdom,
but for us the power of God and the wisdom of God.

O Jesus, with arms forever open,
from your pierced side gushes the water of baptism
and the blood of the eucharist.
A few drops of blood renew the whole universe,
the early dawn of the Spirit rises from the tortured body.

We needed God to take flesh and die
so that we might live again.
The tree of shame becomes the Tree of Life,
the axis of the world which gathers up all our sorrows
to offer them in the fire of the Spirit.

This tree rises from earth to heaven.
Jacob's ladder, the pathway of angels.
Its fruit contains the whole of life,
we eat it, and eating of it die no more.

Prayer

O Cross of Christ,
you alone can pass judgment
over the judgment which condemns us,
you alone can reveal to us God's foolish love.

O Cross of Christ,
the only reply to Job,
to the countless Jobs of history,
may the sight of you quench all rebellion in us,
and make all hatred seem ridiculous.

O Cross of Christ,
in the most difficult moments grant
that we fall not into despair,
but at your feet,
so that He who is lifted up on you
may draw us to Himself
in his paradoxical glory.

11

The Gospel of Jesus Christ according to St Luke (23:39-43)

One of the criminals hanging there abused Jesus:
"Are you not the Christ? Save yourself and us as well."
But the other spoke up and rebuked him.
"Have you no fear of God at all?" he said.
"In our case, we deserved it: we are paying for what we did.
But this man has done nothing wrong."
Then he said, "Jesus, remember me
when you come into your kingdom."
Jesus answered him: "In truth I tell you,
today you will be with me in paradise."

Meditation

All our destiny is summed up
in that of these two thieves.
They are not strangers to us,
they are ourselves.
Our only choice is
between the one on the right and the one on the left.

The thief on the left offers
the final temptation to Jesus:
"If you are the Messiah, save yourself."
The priests and soldiers had already said:
"Let him save himself and we will believe in him."

But while Jesus remains silent,
the second thief says to the first:
"We men, we kill and are killed in turn,
death is deeply written into us.
But in Jesus, in whom there is no evil,
there is not this inevitability of death,
but only death out of love."

And the thief who is immobilized by the nails
preserves the ultimate freedom, that of faith,
and cries out, "Jesus, remember me,
when you come into your kingdom."

Did he sense that the kingdom was no longer in the future?
It is here, it is Jesus in his sacrifice of love.

It is here, it is Jesus, one Breath with the Father.
In him the world of sorrows becomes paradise.

And now, turning his eyes towards the thief, he says:
"Today you will be with me in paradise."

Prayer

Jesus, each of us is both the thief who blasphemes
and the one who believes.
I believe, Lord, help my unbelief.
I am nailed to death, there is nothing I can do
but cry out: "Jesus, remember me
when you come with your kingdom."

Jesus, I know nothing, I understand nothing
in this horrific world.
But you, you come to me, with open arms,
with open heart,
and your presence alone is my paradise.
Ah, remember me
when you come with your kingdom.

Glory and praise to you,
you who welcome not the healthy, but the sick,
you whose unexpected friend is a thief
cut off by the justice of men.
Already you descend to hell to set free
those who thought that they were damned.
They cry out to you: "Remember us, Lord,
when you come with your kingdom."

12

The Gospel of Jesus Christ according to St John (19:26-27)

Seeing his mother
and the disciple whom he loved standing near her,
Jesus said to his mother:
"Woman, this is your son."
Then to the disciple he said:
"This is your mother."
And from that hour the disciple took her into his home.

Meditation

> At the foot of the Cross, Mary and John,
> the Mother and the beloved disciple.
> Mary, Mother of God: she has said yes to the angel,
> undoing in a supreme way the tragedy of our freedom.
> She gave birth in the serene transparency of her body.
> Now a sword pierces her heart,
>
> John, the only disciple faithful to the end.
> At the Last Supper,
> his head rested on the Master's heart,
> on the heart of the world.
> He has retained the final words,
> the unity of Jesus and the Father,
> the promise of the Holy Spirit.
>
> Woman, says Jesus.
> Woman: in her all womanliness,
> all tenderness, all beauty.
> Woman strong and grave,
> you keep all these things in your heart,
> your resurrected Son will disappear
> from the eyes of men,
> but here is a son who is also in your Son.
> The guardian of adoption,
> Mother of all men,
> Hail, full of grace, the Lord is with you.
>
> And John welcomes her into his home,
> into his love,
> and from now on a silent presence.
> The great silence of adoration.
> May she also be in our homes,
> Mother of all faithfulness, of all tenderness.
> May she be also in the dwelling that is the world,
> the earth of boundless fertility.
>
> See here then the first Church
> born from the wood of the Cross.
> It is like a first Pentecost
> when Jesus, bowing down his head,
> gives up the Spirit.

Prayer

> Jesus, son of heaven by your Father,
> son of the earth by your mother,
> make us sons of earth and heaven,
> through the prayers of the Mother of God.
>
> Jesus, a lance has pierced your side,
> perhaps your heart.
> And you, Mary, a sword pierces your heart.
> Lord, may we become part of this terrible exchange
> through the prayers of the Mother of God.
>
> Jesus, son of the Virgin,
> may we, like the disciple whom you loved,
> be witnesses to the light and to the life,
> to the light of life,
> through the prayers of the Mother of God.

13

The Gospel of Jesus Christ according to St Mark (15:34, 36-37)

> *And at the ninth hour*
> *Jesus cried out in a loud voice,*
> *"Eloi, eloi, lama sabach-thani?"*
> *which means,*
> *My God, my God, why have you forsaken me?*
> *Someone ran and soaked a sponge in vinegar*
> *and, putting it on a reed, gave it to him to drink.*
> *But Jesus gave a loud cry and breathed his last.*

Meditation

> Jesus, the Word made flesh,
> has gone the farthest distance
> that lost humanity is able to go.
> My God, my God, why have you forsaken me?
> Endless distance, limitless separation,
> wonder of love.
>
> Between God and God,
> between the Father and his incarnate Son,
> our despair intervenes

with which Jesus wishes to remain in solidarity
to the bitter end.

The absence of God indeed constitutes hell.
"I am thirsty," says Jesus again, echoing the psalm:
"My mouth is dry as earthenware,
my tongue sticks to my jaw.
You lay me down in the dust of death."

God thirsts for man and man flees from him,
raising up a "wall of separation."
Jesus, nailed to this wall, says: "I thirst"
and is answered with vinegar.

The eternal embrace of the Father and the Son
becomes the distance between heaven and hell.
"Eloi, eloi, lama sabach-thani?"
It is as if the crucified God, for a moment,
finds himself an atheist.

Now, all is turned upside down.
In Jesus, the human will,
as in Gethsemane,
holds on.
"Father, into your hands I commit my spirit."
The abyss of despair vanishes
like a negligible drop of hatred
in the infinite abyss of love.
The distance between the Father and the Son
is no more the space of hell, but of the Spirit.

Prayer

Jesus, you emptied yourself
by taking on the form of a slave
even to accepting death, death on a cross.
Teach us to say,
on the day of distress, or perhaps agony,
"Father, into you hands I commit my Spirit."

Henceforth heaven, earth and hell shall be full of light.
Nothing will be able to separate us from you.
Where shall I go to escape your spirit?
Even if I hide in hell, you are there.

O sacrificed Shepherd,
take us on you shoulders
and carry us toward your Father.
May the most troubled atheist
eventually find his answer in you.

Praise to you, Jesus our God,
because from the cross of despair
you have made the Paschal cross.

14

The Gospel of Jesus Christ according to St Mark (15:46)

*Joseph of Arimathea brought a shroud,
took Jesus down from the cross,
wrapped him in the shroud
and laid him in a tomb
which had been hewn from the rock.*

Meditation

One Joseph protected you as a little child,
another Joseph gently unnails you from the cross.
In his hands you are more helpless
than a little one in the hands of its mother.
He places the remains of your immaculate body
into the bosom of the rock.

The stone is rolled across, all is silence.
It is the mysterious Sabbath.
Everything is silent, creation holds its breath.
Into the total emptiness of love Christ descends.
But as a Victor.

He blazes with the fire of the Spirit.
At his touch, humanity's bonds are burned away.
O life, how could you die?
It is to destroy the power of death
and to raise the dead from hell.

All is silent. But the great battle is won.
The Divider is vanquished.

Beneath the earth, in the depth of our souls,
a spark of fire is lighted.

Pascha eve. Everything is silent, but in hope.
The last Adam extends his hand to the first Adam.
The Mother of God dries the tears of Eve.
Around the rock of death the garden blooms.

Prayer

O my Liberator,
I have fled far from you
into the deadly depths of the rock.
But you break down every barrier,
you lead out all who are imprisoned,
prisoners of themselves and of the devil.
You lead them forth towards the early dawn of Pascha,
for love is strong as death.

I keep my soul in peace and silence
like a little child in its mother's arms.
I know that you will find me.

Royal Jesus, let your light shine in the darkness,
lamp of life.
May the silence thrill at your presence,
that the world may no longer be like an empty tomb!
The two Adams recognize each other in the light,
and there are no more dead in the tombs.

Christ is risen from the dead,
trampling down death by death,
and upon those in the tombs,
bestowing life.